FAULKNER *and* WHITENESS

FAULKNER
—— *and* ——
WHITENESS

Edited by
Jay Watson

University Press of Mississippi / Jackson

www.upress.state.ms.us

The University Press of Mississippi is a member of
the Association of American University Presses.

The editor wishes to thank *The Faulkner Journal* of the
University of Central Florida for permission to reprint
essays from "Faulkner and Whiteness" (22.1/2), a special
issue published in 2007. These previously published essays
have been revised for this volume.

Copyright © 2011 by University Press of Mississippi
All rights reserved
Manufactured in the United States of America

First printing 2011

∞

Library of Congress Cataloging-in-Publication Data

Faulkner and whiteness / edited by Jay Watson.
p. cm.
Includes bibliographical references and index.
ISBN 978-1-61703-020-8 (cloth : alk. paper)—ISBN 978-1-
61703-021-5 1. Faulkner, William, 1897–1962—Criticism and
interpretation. 2. Whites in literature. 3. Race in literature.
4. Whites—Race identity—United States. I. Watson, Jay.
PS3511.A86Z78321117 2011
813'.52—dc22   2010049420

British Library Cataloging-in-Publication Data available

CONTENTS

vii INTRODUCTION
Situating Whiteness in Faulkner Studies, Situating Faulkner in Whiteness Studies
—JAY WATSON

3 NEGOTIATING THE MARBLE BONDS OF WHITENESS
Hybridity and Imperial Impulse in Faulkner
—TAYLOR HAGOOD

19 GENEALOGIES OF WHITE DEVIANCE
The Eugenic Family Studies, *Buck v. Bell*, and William Faulkner, 1926–1931
—JAY WATSON

56 QUEERING WHITENESS, QUEERING FAULKNER
Hightower's "Wild Bulges"
—ALFRED J. LÓPEZ

75 PASSING AS MISCEGENATION
Whiteness and Homoeroticism in Faulkner's *Absalom, Absalom!*
—BETINA ENTZMINGER

92 "A STRANGE NIGGER"
Faulkner and the Minstrel Performance of Whiteness
—JOHN N. DUVALL

107 MOONSHINE AND MAGNOLIAS
The Story of Temple Drake and *The Birth of a Nation*
—DEBORAH E. BARKER

147 INSIDE AND OUTSIDE SOUTHERN WHITENESS
Film Viewing, the Frame, and the Racing of Space in Yoknapatawpha
—PETER LURIE

170 WHITE DISAVOWAL, BLACK ENFRANCHISEMENT, AND THE HOMOEROTIC IN WILLIAM FAULKNER'S *LIGHT IN AUGUST*
—ALIYYAH I. ABDUR-RAHMAN

189 AMERICAN EMERGENCIES
Whiteness, the National Guard, and *Light in August*
—CHUCK JACKSON

207 NOTES

231 WORKS CITED

247 NOTES ON CONTRIBUTORS

251 INDEX

INTRODUCTION
Situating Whiteness in Faulkner Studies,
Situating Faulkner in Whiteness Studies

—JAY WATSON

Why whiteness? The emergence of critical whiteness studies over the last decade and a half has engendered its share of skepticism. After all, in a society whose central legal, social, and political institutions are still controlled largely by whites, and whose resources and privileges still fall disproportionately to them, what do we accomplish by—once again—putting whites in the proverbial spotlight? Richard Dyer, one of the most influential voices in whiteness studies, has labeled this "the green light problem": "Writing about whiteness gives white people the go-ahead to write and talk about what in any case we have always talked about: ourselves" (*White* 10). Other observers such as Robyn Wiegman have worried aloud that the increasing attention to whiteness in the academy may reflect—or at least inadvertently contribute to—a rearguard effort to take the identity politics and empowerment strategies developed over the past half-century by civil rights activists, critical race theorists, feminists, and postcolonial movements, and to reappropriate them for a dominant group alert to the political and rhetorical advantage to be gained by retrofitting itself as a minoritized racial or ethnic identity.[1] Seen in this light, whiteness studies simply drains away critical and political energies better devoted to other subjects, worthier and more embattled causes.

    Yet a chorus of voices has countered that we ignore whiteness at our peril. They argue that the key to its dominance as identity and/or ideology lies precisely in its ability to go uncommented on, to pass beneath critical inspection as an unremarkable, neutral standard against which other identities can be measured and known. "The unexamined," Ross Chambers has called it, adding that "whiteness is perhaps the primary unmarked and so unexamined—let's say 'blank'—category.... Whiteness is not itself compared with anything, but other things are compared unfavorably with it, and their own comparability with one another derives from their distance from that touchstone" (189). This blank quality allows whiteness to fly beneath the radar of race, as if it were not a racial category at all, and this helps account for the phenomenon noted by Toni Morrison in *Playing in the Dark*, in which readers of American literature can instantly and unthinkingly recognize that a character is white "because nobody says so" (72). The whiteness of such characters is never specified yet is indisputable—all the more indisputable, in fact, *because* never specified. In this silence, the silence of what goes without saying, lies the extraordinary power, persistence, and adaptability of whiteness.

Or, shifting the metaphor to the visual register, we might say that whiteness is at its most effective when it not only evades the "spotlight" I alluded to above but *becomes* that spotlight, an invisible source and transparent field of racial illumination "situated outside the paradigm it defines" (Chambers 189): the frame in and against which other figures acquire racial definition.[2] "As long as race is something only applied to non-white people," writes Dyer, "as long as white people are not racially seen and named, they/we function as a human norm. Other people are raced, we are just people" (*White* 1), and "[t]here is no more powerful position than that of being 'just' human. The claim to power is the claim to speak for the commonality of humanity. Raced people can't do that—they can only speak for their race. But non-raced people can, for they do not represent the interests of a race" (2). And this, insists Dyer, is precisely why whiteness must be attended to, must be made visible: to demystify and dismantle the inconspicuous workings of its privilege. "[T]he point of looking at whiteness is to *dislodge* it from its centrality and authority, not to reinstate it" (10). Annalee Newitz and Matt Wray put the matter even more forcefully: "Making whiteness visible to whites—exposing the discourses, the social and cultural practices, and the material conditions that cloak whiteness and hide its dominating effects—is a necessary part of any anti-racist project" (Introduction 3–4). The practice they describe is not a bad-faith effort to distract attention from other, increasingly clamorous social groups emerging from the long historical shadow of white domination to articulate their own experiences, their own needs—and not incidentally their own critiques of whiteness. Nor is it simply a roundabout neonativist way of claiming victim status for whites forced to compete for economic and political resources on a (relatively) more level playing field. It is instead a *critical* effort to lure whiteness out of hiding (it hides in plain sight) and to place it in crisis.

Why take this practice to Faulkner? Don't we thereby risk minimizing the multiracial complexities of his world, and the volatile collision of those complexities with the reductive polarities of Jim Crow? Or discounting the impact of African American identity and culture in particular as a spur and stumbling block to his imagination? I cannot improve on the words of Thadious M. Davis in responding to such questions. Acknowledging "the construction of race" to be "central" to Faulkner's work (208), Davis goes on to locate whiteness at the very heart of the Faulknerian project:

> Most impressive about his achievement is not that he created black characters and positioned them within his fictional world of Yoknapatawpha, but rather that he envisioned what Melville represented as "the whiteness of whiteness." Faulkner constructed characters who are consciously white, racialized as white, and depicted the construction of whiteness within Southern and American society. As a result, he allowed outsiders to know in ways not otherwise available to them one ongoing narrative of white people in psychological nudity. His treatment of white people, within the normalizing, universalizing elision of racial identity, but with the complexity of the burden of racial subjectivity is an extraordinary achievement, unequaled in the first half of the century and unparalleled in the second. (254)

This leads Davis to the perhaps surprising judgment that *As I Lay Dying*, *The Hamlet*, *The Town*, and *The Mansion* are "the most racialized" of all Faulkner's novels: "those with no visible black presence at all."[3] "This particular aspect of his achievement," she continues, "is not usually acknowledged primarily because most attention has been devoted to his construction of racial Others" (208). But it is a "particularly salient" aspect, opening up "possibilities for fresh conversations about Faulkner's particular achievement and the potential for future scholarship." This collection is an attempt to develop such conversations and carry them forward.

It is not enough to attribute Faulkner's insights into the construction and contestation of whiteness to the fact that he was (i.e., considered himself to be) white, or that he was southern. For he also came of age and wrote his major novels and stories during a period characterized by paradigm shifts in the theorization of race generally and the conceptualization of the white race in particular. According to sociologists Michael Omi and Howard Winant, the decade of the 1920s, during which Faulkner published his first four novels, marks a turning point in the orientation of American racial projects, when "biologistic" accounts of race rooted in nineteenth-century science began to give way to new models grounded in ethnicity (14). Race, in other words, began to "soften" conceptually, from a natural absolute to a more culturally contingent phenomenon, a matter of affiliation and practice. (A similar reorganization of "race into culture" is a central theme of Walter Benn Michaels's work on American nativism and modernism in *Our America*, a study that opens with an analysis of *The Sound and the Fury* [1–12].) This transition roughly coincides with a crucial shift in the configuration and meaning of American whiteness, as charted by historian Matthew Frye Jacobson. During the early national period, observes Jacobson, whiteness as a racial basis for U.S. citizenship was a broadly inclusive category defined against the otherness of Native Americans and African Americans. Its contours were "unconflicted" and "unambiguous" (7): a citizen was above all someone who could help the young nation defend itself against Indian incursions or slave insurrections (25). If you weren't black or red, you were white. This racial consensus reigned until the 1840s, when changing immigration patterns and the rise of biological and anthropological racism prompted a "fracturing of whiteness into a hierarchy of plural and scientifically determined white races" (7), with the "Anglo-Saxon" population at the top of the heap. According to Jacobson, 1924, the year of the Johnson-Reed Act, marks the historical moment when this multiracial order and its "probationary white groups" began to yield to a "reconsolidated" form of whiteness "granted the scientific stamp of authenticity as the unitary Caucasian race" (8), as the "earlier era's Celts, Slavs, Hebrews, Iberics, and Saracens, among others," were rechristened "the Caucasians so familiar to our own visual economy and racial lexicon." In Faulkner's South, the fundamental biracialism of this new phase of U.S. whiteness (in which to be "Caucasian" was necessarily not to be black and vice versa) was powerfully reinforced by the culture of segregation, which, as Grace Elizabeth Hale usefully reminds us, was always as much about "making whiteness," forging a post-Confederate cross-class regional (and eventually national) sensibility, as it was about fixing and stigmatizing blackness. Faulkner thus launched his career from atop a seismic fault line between U.S. racial regimes. He wrote at what a latter-day Allen Tate, liberated from his Confederate graveyard to contemplate instead the Verso Books back catalog, might call a crossing of the ways of whiteness. His unusual sensitivity to the processes and pressures of white racialization, in other words, arguably resulted from the "peculiarly historical consciousness" that Tate ascribed to writers situated at such cultural conjunctures (533).

At this point it might be useful to briefly summarize some of the more influential methodological positions within critical whiteness studies, and to link these positions provisionally with examples from the modest body of existing Faulkner scholarship on whiteness. Drawing on feminist precedent, Mike Hill has described distinct "waves" of whiteness scholarship: an initial phase devoted to making white privilege culturally visible, and a second wave responding to the "awkwardness of distance," "epistemological stickiness[,] and ontological wiggling" that befalls scholars who find themselves claiming whiteness (for critique) and disclaiming it (as power, as lie) at the same time (Introduction 3). I will refer instead to three main "branches" within whiteness scholarship, loose confederations whose boundaries are porous enough to allow for overlap and collaboration. These branches approach whiteness (1) in terms of subject formation, (2) in terms of performance, or (3) in historicist and materialist terms (which is to say in terms of ideology).[4]

SUBJECT FORMATION

Richard Dyer's work is the most fully developed and influential example of this approach. In the construction of the racialized self, becoming white—acquiring whiteness—above all means aspiring to the condition of what

Dyer, borrowing from the philosopher David Lloyd, calls the "subject without properties" (*White* 38). "[R]acial theories as such," Dyer writes, "are less crucial to the development of white identity than the attainment of a position of disinterest—abstraction, distance, separation, objectivity—which creates a public sphere that is the mark of civilization" (38–39). Like whiteness, itself a product of the Enlightenment, the subject without properties "provides the philosophical underpinnings of the conception of white people as everything and nothing" (39). But as the phrase "everything and nothing" suggests, this notion of white identity is caught in a double bind, since a being without properties "may be thought of as pure spirit, but it also hints at non-existence, or death." Dyer has traced this double bind through centuries of Western visual representations (paintings, photographs, films) that link whiteness with a "culture of light" that underscores its abstract spiritual qualities (84) and enhances its authority in the public sphere.[5]

Toni Morrison's focus on the role of literary representation in the construction of American whiteness nicely complements Dyer's emphasis on visual culture. In Morrison's well-known account, the formation of the American national subject, Crevecoeur's "new man"—an implicitly white figure inasmuch as nobody has to say so—would have been unthinkable without the assistance of "a dark, abiding, signing Africanist presence" onto which the more unsavory properties of Anglo-American settler, pioneer, and entrepreneurial identities could be projected and alternatively disavowed and grappled with (5). In the U.S., at least, Morrison emphasizes, white subject formation has never been a matter of identification alone. It has always been oppositional as well, "organiz[ed] . . . through a distancing Africanism" (8), and classic American literature has played an indispensable role in this cultural project. bell hooks's essay "Representations of Whiteness in the Black Imagination" additionally complicates Dyer's account of the white subject position. For African Americans, hooks argues, white people can hardly be considered subjects without properties. Rather, black observers attribute quite specific properties to whiteness, above all the properties of mystery, strangeness, and terror (166). The insights of Morrison and hooks into white subjectivity should remind us that scholars of color have been responsible for some of the earliest and most incisive efforts to subject whiteness to critical scrutiny.[6]

In Faulkner studies, the work of Philip M. Weinstein exhibits a comparable attention to whiteness as an element in the drama of what Weinstein prefers to call "identity formation." That drama is the organizing principle of *What Else But Love?*, one of the germinal works of Faulkner scholarship of the 1990s. "Identity formation," writes Weinstein, "is inseparable from the absorption, refusal, and reaccenting of the subject roles that make up our culture's repertoire for ways of being" (xxii), roles we treat "as mirrors in which to recognize ourselves, as we go about the never-innocent business of negotiating identity, becoming white and black, men and women." The direct and refracted insights into Faulknernian subjectivity that Weinstein gleans from examining Faulkner's texts in tandem with Morrison's lead him to locate the Faulknerian master narrative in constantly recirculating stories of "failed white-male becomings" (171), "drama[s] of interior dispossession" (92) whose protagonists (including multiracial figures such as Joe Christmas and Charles Bon) are not so much subjects without properties as subjects without *property*, the most valuable property of all: Lockean self-ownership.[7]

Weinstein's account of subject formation is more indebted to Freudian and Lacanian psychoanalysis than Dyer's. He works closely with the Oedipal model throughout his study, which in turn becomes the basis of another striking insight, the recognition that in Faulkner's South the Oedipal paradigm works to racialize the emergent subjectivity it activates. In Yoknapatawpha, that is, Oedipus does not produce universal human subjects, as Freud seemed to think, or late-Victorian bourgeois subjects, as feminist and Marxist critiques of Freud have stressed, so much as *white* bourgeois subjects, operating through family relations to instantiate specifically white social norms (99). So that when the Oedipal dynamic stalls or fails, as it so often does in Faulkner's narratives, the result is lapsed whiteness and pervasive racial anxiety and suspicion. Though Weinstein's study makes little direct use of contemporary scholarship on whiteness (with the exception of *Playing in the Dark*), his insights into the racial dimension of white subject construction make his work an important forerunner of this collection of essays.

Unlike Weinstein, Patricia McKee in *Producing American Races* draws liberally on whiteness studies scholarship by Dyer, hooks, Morrison, and others. McKee, however, maps out a methodological agenda that goes beyond Dyer's emphasis on making whiteness visible. Noting the connections between "the kind of symbolic construction that produces whiteness [and] the sort that produces twentieth-century visual culture" (4), she argues that white hegemony has less to do with questions of "visibility" than with the issue of "visuality," by which McKee means "the capacity to produce images" (210), hold "views," and take "positions" in a public sphere increasingly configured as spatial and open rather than verbal and bounded (13–14, 104–5). McKee is less concerned with representations *of* whiteness than with representations *that whiten* those with the ability to produce them. Such representations may be the work of conventional media or of more personal modes of reproduction such as memory, imagination, and role-playing (100). Faulkner's novels (and Henry James's), according to McKee, produce racial identities along this axis of visual image circulation: white males are able to "occupy positions interchangeably" (105), contain "multiple points of view within their psyche," entertain the views of other white male subjects, and "shift their identity into symbolic dimensions" (20); nonwhites are depicted as lacking these abilities; and white females like Caddy Compson and Lena Grove occupy a fluctuating position in between. Despite her differences with Dyer over the deep structures of white cultural normativity, McKee's account of how white subjects en-vision identity and occupy public space can sound remarkably like Dyer's reflections on the subject without properties. Also drawing on Morrison, Theresa M. Towner in *Faulkner on the Color Line* makes a case for the post-1948 novels, so often read as evidence of a shift in Faulkner's imagination from racial issues to class conflict, as "ongoing investigation[s]" of "how racial identity is formed and maintained" (8). Morrison's concept of the Africanist presence in American writing gives Towner a way to address the role played by the many minor and unnamed African American characters of the late novels in "the racialization of the white subject's imagination" (11).

PERFORMANCE

Whiteness, according to Dyer, must not only be made visible. It must be made strange (4), its pretense to coherence and neutrality defamiliarized and discredited. One way to do this is to focus, as Weinstein has, on breakdowns in white subject formation. Another way is to turn from the formation to the performance (or more precisely the *mis*performance) of social subjects and groups that don't seem to get their whiteness right. Such performances, whether inadvertent or deliberately subversive, have the potential to expose and disrupt the operation of normative whiteness. This has led Newitz and Wray, a pair of scholars who come to whiteness studies from a research collaborative called, appropriately enough, the Bad Subjects Collective, to zero in on economically marginal whites, or "white trash," as a group whose often excessive, socially conspicuous forms of cultural expression and practice help foreground the ways in which U.S. whiteness has always been different from itself. "Unlike hegemonic forms of whiteness," they argue,

> the category of white trash is marked from the start. But in addition to being racially marked, it is simultaneously marked as trash, as something that must be discarded, expelled, and disposed of in order for whiteness to achieve and maintain social dominance. Thus white trash must be understood as both an external and an internal threat to whiteness. It is externalized by class difference but made the same through racial identification. White trash lies simultaneously inside and outside whiteness, becoming the difference within, the white Other that inhabits the core of whiteness. ("What is 'White Trash'?" 169–70)

White-trash scholars like the ones collected in Newitz and Wray's lively volume *White Trash: Race and Class in America* study the ways nonnormative or "deviant" patterns of speech, clothing, body modification, sexual behavior, kinship, recreation, social affiliation, consumption, and so on, when adopted by white-skin or otherwise white-identified subjects, work to dismantle the monolithic façade of U.S. whiteness. On a related note, the growing body of scholarship on blackface minstrelsy in nineteenth- and twentieth-century America has shed valuable light on how exaggerated performances of African American racial identity by white subjects—and the enthusiastic white consumption of such performances—have been constitutive of collective white identity in the U.S., contributing to the formation of a white working class (Lott; Roediger 115–31), the emergence of explicitly white forms of U.S. nationalism (Saxton 165–82), and the assimilation of Irish Americans, Jewish Americans, and other European immigrant groups into "the white race" (Ignatiev 42; Jacobson 119–22; Rogin).

This performance-based approach to whiteness has been underrepresented in Faulkner scholarship, a deficiency this collection sets out in part to remedy. One important precursor might be found in John N. Duvall, whose *Faulkner's Marginal Couple* mines Faulkner's mature fiction for "counterhegemonic alliances" (xiv) between and among characters who interact in ways that challenge conventional models of community. Though Duvall is primarily interested in how these microcommunities, typically arranged in pairs or threesomes, subvert patriarchal norms of gender and sexuality, I would point out that his impressive inventory of untenable subject positions and "invisible, outlaw, and unspeakable communities" is dominated by characters who do whiteness wrong, sometimes flamboyantly, spectacularly wrong: Caddy Compson, Emily Grierson, Susan Reed of "Hair," Horace Benbow, Temple Drake, Lee Goodwin, Ruby Lamar, Joe Christmas, Joanna Burden, Laverne Shumann of *Pylon*, Thomas Sutpen, Wash Jones, Charlotte Rittenmeyer. In particular, white males who are weak and passive (or alternately "nurturing and caring" [130]) and white females who are sexually active before or outside marriage fall afoul of the gendered conceptions of honor that work in the timocratic social order of the South to confer white identity on elite and middle-class subjects. As such, the sexual misperformances of Duvall's white outliers place them not only on the margins of "community" but arguably on the margins of whiteness itself. Indeed, it would not be difficult to extend Duvall's paradigm of the alternative community to troubled white kinship groups like the Bundrens, the Snopeses, and even the Compsons, and to approach Faulkner's narratives of these clans as I do in my contribution to this volume: as on the one hand creative elaborations and on the other hand critical interrogations and outright deconstructions of the eugenic family studies excavated and analyzed by Nicole Hahn Rafter in her sociology of late-nineteenth- and early-twentieth-century discourses of white degeneracy (see *White Trash* 1–31). Seen in this light, the sagas of the Compsons and Bundrens in particular become key gateway documents between earlier eugenic studies typically set in rural areas of the North and Midwest and Depression-era classics like Caldwell's *Tobacco Road*, Agee and Evans's *Let Us Now Praise Famous Men*, and Steinbeck's *Grapes of Wrath*, which placed specifically southern versions of white family deviance on a national stage.

IDEOLOGY

But whiteness is not merely an element in identity construction or a style of cultural performance. It is also a concrete historical and social formation that emerged with modernity on the North American continent out of the English colonial encounter with indigenous and forcibly imported non-European peoples. As Marxist scholar Theodore Allen has carefully reconstructed, the ideology of whiteness was the product of deliberate ruling-class policy in the tobacco colonies of late-seventeenth- and early-eighteenth-century Anglo-America, a cynical gambit to divide the ranks of African and European bondservants by creating a "buffer group" (which Allen alternately refers to as an "intermediate social control stratum") out of the latter that would help insure a docile, orderly labor supply at minimal expense to the English tobacco lords (*Invention*, vol. 2). This ideology rested on, and was made tangible in, a set of material but nonmonetary privileges created by statutory fiat out of old English common-law rights that had formerly been extended to all citizens of the colonies but were reconfigured as white-skin entitlements available only to those of European descent: the right to move freely through public space without a pass; the presumption (for males) of legal "possession" over wife and children (the ancient principle of *coverture*); the right to vote in elections to colonial assemblies; the right to use force against an assailant in self-defense; the right to own a gun.[8] These privileges came to identify members of "the white race" in the colonies and later in the United States, which is to say that they simultaneously conferred whiteness upon their beneficiaries and served to illustrate, on an immediate material level, what that whiteness consisted in. They also served as the basis for what the legal scholar Cheryl I. Harris has described as a specific property interest in whiteness (1715–45), one that has been repeatedly upheld by U.S. policymakers and jurists even as it has expanded to include freedom from harassment by law enforcement and preferential treatment in hiring, housing, access to education, and the procurement of loans. As George Lipsitz argues, this "possessive investment in whiteness" silently entitles all European Americans whether or not they are overtly racist—and whether or not they would choose to receive such privileges.

Some of the most exciting scholarship in critical whiteness studies sets out to trace the historical evolution and excavate the material foundations of "the white race." As that work makes clear, the project of establishing, extending, and guarding the material grounds of whiteness has been a comprehensive ideological effort drawing on a huge array of cultural resources: immigration and naturalization law (Haney López; Jacobson 223–45), property law (Harris), government policy (Allen 2: 239–59; Lipsitz), public education and settlement work (Babb 138–58), science (Jacobson 31–38, 44–47, 78–90, 178–80, 226–37 passim; Wiegman, *American Anatomies* 21–78), cartography (Babb 48–58), history (Hale 43–84), newspapers (Hale 210–24; Saxton 96–108, 205–25), captivity, criminal, and immigrant narratives (Babb 68–87, 119–25), theater (Lott; Roediger 115–32; Saxton 113–26, 184–87), film (Hale 216–21, 282–83; Jacobson 117–22, 132–33; Rogin), religious discourse (Babb 62–68), advertising (Hale 151–68), mass amusement (Babb 126–37), story papers and dime novels (Saxton 322–41), etiquette manuals (Babb 158–66), and canonical literature (Babb 89–117; Hale 37–41, 54–60, 241–79; Jacobson 125–31, 187–98, 265–71; Morrison 18–28, 31–33, 54–59, 69–91; Saxton 187–201, 235–41, 341–44, 353–56). Interestingly, a number of these scholars pinpoint the antebellum decades of the 1830s and 1840s as an era of particular ferment for American whiteness, when that ideology went through fluctuating phases of external contestation, internal contradiction, and consolidation (Allen 1: 159–99; Ignatiev; Jacobson 37–44; Lott 136–211; Roediger 43–163; Saxton 77–209). This is the same period, of course, when north Mississippi was opened to European American settlement and to which Faulkner assigned the genesis of Jefferson and Yoknapatawpha County—a thoroughly racialized story of origins that can be pieced together from *Absalom, Absalom!*, *Go Down, Moses*, the Compson Appendix, and the prologues of *Requiem for a Nun*.

Among Faulkner scholars, two in particular have made valuable use of this historicist/materialist branch of whiteness studies. Kevin Railey's *Natural Aristocracy* draws directly on the work of Theodore Allen to cast the story of Thomas Sutpen as a historical allegory tracing the emergence of U.S. racial ideology (129–37). According to Railey, Faulkner's choice of Tidewater Virginia as the scene of young Sutpen's racial awakening and education is historically on target, since it was, a century before Sutpen's birth, the principal setting for Allen's "invention of the white race." Though Sutpen encounters the limits to his whiteness at the front door of the elite planter Pettibone, he also learns to recognize a set of compensatory privileges that go along with that whiteness, privileges that Faulkner presents in some of the same material forms described by Allen: the "freedom" of the Sutpen patriarch to beat up slaves and to exercise lordship over "his" womenfolk, and the freedom of mobility that young Sutpen exercises as "the right to leave the Tidewater" for Haiti (Railey 131). By the time he does so, he has internalized the lesson "that his whiteness means something" and that, for a poor-white migrant, that something "is all he has to offer." What is more, though Railey does not pursue the connection, the picture he draws of the social anxiety generated by Sutpen's arrival in Mississippi evokes another precedent from the prehistory of U.S. whiteness in Virginia. "[I]magine," writes Railey,

> the literal threat to Jefferson society—and specifically to the profit-making enterprises of [General] Compson, his ilk, and [Goodhue] Coldfield—that Sutpen and his 'tribe' [of black slaves] represented. They could burn fields, crops, stores, houses; they could steal goods, money; they could kill. And it would not be difficult to envision Sutpen engaging in these activities. In fact, Sutpen represents the ruling class's biggest nightmare. (135)

This nightmare scenario reads like a nineteenth-century version of the seventeenth-century social emergency known as Bacon's Rebellion (1676–77), another insurrection led by a frontier planter presiding over a volatile coalition of bondsmen. In Allen's analysis, Bacon's Rebellion was, more than any other single event, the historical catalyst that prompted the Virginia plantocracy to craft the legal entitlements that gave birth to the white race (2: 203–22). Small wonder, then, that the Yoknapatawpha elders are so quick to offer similar entitlement to the ex-Virginian in their midst, promoting him from a probationary whiteness to the genuine article. "By testifying for Sutpen," Railey argues, "Compson and Coldfield establish the identity Sutpen has in effect demanded they establish: unlike what the townspeople think, Sutpen, they say, is 'white'" (135). On a number of levels, then, Sutpen's Tidewater encounter with the ideology of whiteness and his subsequent role in exporting that ideology to the frontier reaches of the developing nation reenact the process by which "the ordeal of Virginia ... became the ordeal of America" (Railey 129).

Where Railey turns to Allen, Davis's previously cited *Games of Property* works closely with Haney López and especially Harris in order to probe "the crucial role of law in constructing whiteness" in the multiracial, multigenerational world of *Go Down, Moses* (198). For slaveholders such as Hubert Beauchamp and Buck and Buddy McCaslin, "white raciality" manifests itself above all "[i]n owning and bequeathing property" and "in legitimating matrimony through contracts and patrimony through wills" (69). But for postbellum figures like Lucas Beauchamp, Roth Edmonds, and Ike McCaslin, the legacy of whiteness grows more uncertain. Lucas's attempt to invoke such a legacy in tracing his courage and integrity in a moment of racial crisis to the white blood he has inherited from his slaveowning grandfather, L. Q. C. McCaslin, amounts in Davis's view to a tacit "property claim in old Carothers's whiteness" (132) that is severely qualified due to its "eras[ure]" of Lucas's "tie to the *black* part of his family and history" represented by a more proximate male ancestor, his father, the slave trickster Tomey's Turl (136). Roth's fall from the racial innocence of his youth into the lordly but lonely estate of the white planter, a drama played out in his increasingly strained relationship with his childhood playmate (and Lucas's son), Henry Beauchamp, becomes in Davis's analysis "one of the most powerful and race-conscious [scenes] of whiteness in Faulkner's canon" (205), as Roth "is made to feel his race as otherness" (206) and learns "there is a price to pay" in human intimacy "for his exercise of white privilege." Ike, meanwhile, flirts with the role of race-traitor in renouncing his plantation "patrimony of ownership and aggression" (206) yet finds it more difficult to repudiate a property interest in "white racial difference," as his self-righteous exchanges with his nephew's African American lover (and kinswoman) in "Delta Autumn" make clear (220). Faulkner's authorial stance toward whiteness in the novel is no less conflicted. Still, Davis credits him for his use throughout the text of the adjective "white" as "a designation of race" and "an insistent marker of identity" (208). In *Go Down,*

Moses, at least, we know some characters are white because *somebody*— "Faulkner," the narrator—says so. For Faulkner thus "[t]o own [his] color and [his] race ... in a time of pretended obliviousness to white as a racial designation is, on reflection, a quite remarkable way of comprehending the unmarked power of race and racial hierarchies" (255).⁹

This collection, which originated with a 2006–2007 special issue of *The Faulkner Journal*, brings together nine essays that experiment with, and occasionally even combine, these methodological approaches to whiteness. Taylor Hagood's "Negotiating the Marble Bonds of Whiteness: Hybridity and Imperial Impulse in Faulkner" opens the volume by revisiting a figure from early in Faulkner's career that was to prove central to his artistic vision: the marble faun. For Hagood, though, the faun is ultimately less significant as an image of Keatsian aesthetic stasis or of Prufrockian indecision and self-absorption than as an image of racial hybridity, "a white but creolized body whose amalgamated make-up is hidden but that nonetheless encodes the dynamics arising from the juxtaposition and interaction of groups of oppressors and oppressed who must negotiate the hegemony of imperial impulse" (4). Part Elgin marble, with its overtones of imperial power, and part Hawthornean goat-man, with its subtext of "dark" racial alterity— part cigar-store Indian, part Confederate statue—the faun's hybridization of imperial and subaltern sensibilities, of white and nonwhite histories and subject positions, emerged as one of Faulkner's most durable motifs, as Hagood demonstrates with economical yet lively readings of *Soldiers' Pay, Mosquitoes, As I Lay Dying, Light in August, Absalom, Absalom!, The Hamlet, A Fable*, and, perhaps most memorably, the 1934 short story "Black Music," where the narrative of the faun figure unfolds against the cultural and political backdrop of a global South.

My "Genealogies of White Deviance: The Eugenic Family Studies, *Buck v. Bell*, and William Faulkner, 1926–1931" picks up another motif from early Faulkner that rises to prominence with the advent of the Yoknapatawpha fiction: genealogy. Before he created the complexly miscegenated genealogies of *Absalom, Absalom!* and *Go Down, Moses*, Faulkner constructed lineages for the Snopes, Sartoris, Compson, Bundren, and Goodwin clans that were for the most part studies in aberrant forms of whiteness. This preoccupation with white deviance, dysfunction, and decline dovetails provocatively with that of the U.S. eugenics movement, which, along with its leading organ of knowledge production and defining interdisciplinary genre, the family study, was turning its attention to the rural uplands of the U.S. South at precisely the moment that Faulkner was shifting the focus of his fiction northward from New Orleans to rural and small-town north Mississippi—the move that catalyzed his discovery/invention of Yoknapatawpha County. In a series of fictions stretching from *Father Abraham* (1926) to *Sanctuary* (1931), Faulkner created individual characters and entire family lines that illustrated some of the leading diagnostic categories cited in (or fabricated by) eugenics literature, invented other characters who draw on the vocabulary of eugenics in their spoken remarks and unvoiced thoughts, and reproduced a number of the representational tools and strategies that defined the family studies genre and its quasi-Mendelian methods for explaining and containing socially undesirable white behavior. He also put these tools to critical use, in ways that challenged some of the guiding assumptions of the mainstream eugenics movement and some of the leading precepts of the ruling-class ideology of his native region. "Genealogies of White Deviance" proposes a new source and context for a trope that has long been recognized as vital to Faulkner's artistic vision.

Performance-based approaches to whiteness have the potential for fruitful dialogue with contemporary queer studies scholarship on the performance of sexuality. After all, the "trashing" of normative racial identity explored by Wray and Newitz is roughly analogous to the "queering" of normative sexual identity analyzed by Eve Kosofsky Sedgwick, Judith Butler, and many others. Alfred J. López seeks to capitalize on these connections in his essay, "Queering Whiteness, Queering Faulkner: Hightower's 'Wild Bulges.'" López reads the defrocked minister of *Light in August* as "the divided, repressed psyche of closeted gay whiteness in the Jim Crow South" (57–58), doubly marked by failed performances of normative whiteness and compulsory heterosexuality. López, however, also seeks "the pathogenic nucleus of Hightower's suffering" (61), which leads him into a more classically psychoanalytic emphasis on Hightower's subject formation—apparently following the lead of the minister himself, who pores over his own childhood memories in the novel's penultimate chapter. There López unearths a primal scene in young Gail's discovery and ecstatic/terrified contemplation of his father's Civil War frock coat. The coat's significance, in fact, is doubly primal. First, its dark patch of Union blue carries overtones of male-male physical intimacy that the boy immediately cathects with his own erotic desire for his father, in a visceral "moment of queer vertiginous pleasure and self-loathing" (63). But his glimpse of the dark scrap of cloth arguably queers whiteness as well, by exposing on the visual plane the proximity and implicit intermingling of the normative and nonnormative colorations of Confederate gray and Union blue. No wonder Hightower comes to displace this disturbing content onto the ghost of his grandfather, a Confederate cavalryman supposedly shot down on the streets of Jefferson. But as López explains, even this compensatory Lost Cause screen-image is queered twice over: first, by the boy's own suspicion that his glamorous ancestor may have died not as a hero in the saddle but as a fornicator in a countryman's bedroom or a thief in a chicken house—which is to say, as an egregious misperformer of martial whiteness—and second, by the lexical associations between the grandfather's rumored and feared identity as chicken thief and the transgressive sexual role of the "chicken hawk," a slang term for a male seducer of boys (71–72). At every stage of Hightower's life, then, and every level of his psyche, lapses in white racial normativity and lapses in heteronormativity go hand in hand.

This "mutually imbricative" relationship between sexual and racial normativity (76) is also the subject of Betina Entzminger's "Passing as Miscegenation: Whiteness and Homoeroticism in Faulkner's *Absalom, Absalom!*" But where in López's essay whiteness is itself queered by fault lines in compulsory heterosexuality, Entzminger concentrates on how that threat is ultimately averted in *Absalom, Absalom!*, a novel where queer energies arguably circulate even more freely than in *Light in August*. It is averted, Entzminger argues, by the strategic substitution of breaches in whiteness for breaches in heteronormativity in the homoerotically charged affairs of young men, so that anxieties about racial identity serve to screen anxieties about sexuality rather than being triggered by them. Sutpen's revelation to Henry that Bon is black, for instance, encourages the misrecognition (perhaps even by Henry himself) of Henry's phallic violence against Bon as the product of miscegenation fears rather than the "symbolic consummation of ... homosexual desire" or the "enactment of ... homosexual panic" (83), both plausible explanations given the unusually close relations between the two men. (*Sodomy threat: Credible Yes*, Bon's lawyer might have written.)

Introducing racial difference into the relationship, that is, helps deflect attention from its troubling, potentially transgressive intimacies, even as it whitens Henry by positioning him as the guardian of his sister's racial (and not just sexual) purity from contamination by a nonwhite (br)other. In a related way, Quentin and Shreve, themselves no strangers to homoerotic intensities and longings, manage to shore up their own whiteness by imposing blackness on Bon—after all, from a narrative perspective, the novel's climactic racial allegation is more properly understood as their work than as Sutpen's—and in so doing, they too misdirect readers (and no doubt each other as well) from the troubling inflection of their desires. "By discovering [i.e., fabricating] miscegenation as the 'truth'" of the Sutpen story, Entzminger observes, "Quentin and Shreve attempt to locate the Otherness of Charles and Henry in the antebellum past, thereby containing it. A homosexual Otherness might seem more frightening because it resonates more closely with Quentin and Shreve's present" (91), so the two construct a tale in which "what prevents heterosexuality [between Judith and Bon] is not homosexuality [between Henry and Bon] but blackness" (90). Thus the scandal of passing for white masks the even more unspeakable scandal of passing for straight (75). Ultimately, for Quentin and Shreve, the assurances of what we might call "same-race solidarity"—the extraordinary normative, suturing power of whiteness—conceal and defuse the anxieties of same-sex desire.

John N. Duvall's "'A Strange Nigger': Faulkner and the Minstrel Performance of Whiteness" brings us squarely within the realm of performance studies. According to Duvall, Faulkner's fictional explorations of racial performance were influenced not only by "American blackface minstrelsy" but also by the conventions of "an older European whiteface minstrelsy" that helped him underscore the fact "that not all Caucasians are fully white in a South that wishes to absolutize all racial difference" (92). Such "presumptively white" figures "instantiate blackness in ways that complicate the southern racial binarism," "where 'black' is not exactly race any longer, but (because it is the South), not exactly not race either" (93). These figures, Duvall argues, fall into two groups. On the one hand, Caucasian characters "who exhibit sexual or gender ambiguity," or who are strongly associated with art and aesthetics, often find themselves "exclude[d] ... from the metaphysical privilege of whiteness" (94). Such characters include Popeye,

Quentin, Ike McCaslin, Pierrot in the verse play *The Marionettes*, the sculptor Gordon of *Mosquitoes*, and even "Faulkner" himself as the "funny little black man" in the latter novel, who "present[s] a white face to the world" (95) that does not quite succeed in masking an underlying "black" identity linked with his excessive, confusing performance of sexual desire, which flusters a young female acquaintance. On the other hand, Faulkner's poor-white characters "experience identity in diasporic fashion as locationless, hybrid, and uncomfortably mixed" (98), which renders their whiteness "simultaneously knowable and unhinged by a figurative relation to blackness." Thomas Sutpen, for instance, learns at Pettibone's front door that "being Caucasian is a necessary but insufficient condition to enjoying the status of Southern whiteness" (99). His fall into class consciousness leaves him "white" yet "not-White," since "the primary marker of whiteness, which is an experience of the self as unmarked by race," is no longer available to him; and this intense self-consciousness carries forward into all his subsequent performances of whiteness, which are unfailingly awkward. Abner Snopes of "Barn Burning" is only too aware of his interchangeability as a white sharecropper with "exploited black labor" (103), and, as Duvall slyly suggests, he may even have embraced and appropriated his lowly role as "artificial nigger" by blacking up as the "strange nigger" who delivers Mr. Harris the message that wood and hay can burn (104). All in all, these "racechanging Caucasians" generate "multiple performative possibilities" that helped Faulkner "unhinge the southern binary that would oppose whiteness to 'the Negro'" (93).

Deborah E. Barker's "Moonshine and Magnolias: *The Story of Temple Drake* and *The Birth of a Nation*" explores the disfiguring yet illuminating impact of white-trash subject matter on narrative genre in Faulkner. Barker's genre is the southern rape narrative, which she traces from Thomas Dixon's 1905 novel *The Clansman* and its 1915 adaptation by D. W. Griffith as *The Birth of a Nation*—the "classic" examples of this narrative at the height of its cultural power—to Faulkner's *Sanctuary* (1931) and its film adaptation as *The Story of Temple Drake* (1933). As Barker demonstrates, the *Sanctuary* narratives recast both of the crucial figures of the southern rape story, the so-called black beast rapist and his virginal white victim, as racially marked or compromised whites: the working-class "ethnic" gangster and sociopath Popeye (Trigger in the film), and the sexually adventurous, morally ambiguous once-and-future belle, Temple. This (white) "trashing" of the southern rape narrative, Barker argues, reflects Depression-era anxieties about downward class mobility and new configurations of American ethnicity and American womanhood. In this essay we see the power and potential of white-trash figures not only to unsettle their fictional milieux but to "contaminate" conventional narrative forms as well.

Also employing a critical perspective informed by film studies, Peter Lurie's "Inside and Outside Southern Whiteness: Film Viewing, the Frame, and the Racing of Space in Yoknapatawpha" proceeds from an initial thought experiment—whether the Bundren family might have taken in a movie on their trip to Jefferson to bury Addie in *As I Lay Dying*—to consider how the act of cinema-going in the racially organized and coded space of the southern Jim Crow movie house worked to construct and consolidate a white racial identity for economically and/or spatially peripheral whites sampling the new goods, services, and pleasures available in modernizing, urbanizing environments like Faulkner's Jefferson. Drawing on recent scholarship on the social history of film viewership in the segregation-era South, Lurie traces provocative links between white film spectatorship and the equally visualist, equally collective, and equally racializing activity of "consuming" racial violence in the form of spectacle lynching—links that are already there in Faulkner fictions such as "Dry September" and *Light in August*, where the racial violence that erupts in the town's public spaces is accompanied by explicit scenes of moviegoing and moreover gathers to itself discursively a variety of cinematic tropes, allusions, and evocations. By foregrounding these connections, Faulkner makes them available for critical scrutiny, fashioning a space of viewership for his reader that is simultaneously inside and outside the operation of normative whiteness in Yoknapatawpha.

We close with a pair of essays that historicize whiteness as a racial formation in *Light in August*. For Aliyyah I. Abdur-Rahman in "White Disavowal, Black Enfranchisement, and the Homoerotic in William Faulkner's *Light in August*," the key historical context is the post-Reconstruction era in the South. Recognizing along with materialist historians of whiteness that "[w]hat determined white manhood in the nineteenth century was not simply white skin but access to the vote, to the bodies of women, the right to defend one's country in war, to hold arms or to hold property, the right to acquire capital, and, especially, the right and ability to dominate black people" (174), Abdur-Rahman observes that with the postbellum enfranchisement of African American men, "racial blackness in the U.S. itself underwent a cultural miscegenation: it became infused with some of the rights and properties of white manhood." The result was a crisis of confidence for white masculinity, which found itself in "an imperiled state" (171) mixing defeat, desire, and dread: the defeat of southern white men in the Civil War (174), and the "unspoken desires and hidden dread" that white men came to feel "for black men who were no longer their legal property" (179). In *Light in August*, these anxieties coalesce around Joe Christmas, who in Abdur-Rahman's words "represents Faulkner's meditation on the civic equality of black men in the post-Reconstruction era and its effect on the psyche of whites" (171). Noting that "the main focus of Faulkner's depiction of Joe Christmas is the awe and rage he inspires in white men" (177), Abdur-Rahman adds that "the threat that Christmas's white skin poses to white manhood" is "the threat that all black men posed to the racial order in the post-Reconstruction period after they had been given the vote and the legal position as head of their families" (175–76). This threat takes on a specifically homoerotic dimension in the case of Christmas's relationship with Joe Brown/Lucas Burch, which may or may not be sexually consummated but is certainly sexually suggestive enough to upset other white men in the community with the specter of Brown/Burch's "white racial subordination" to his cabinmate's phallic charisma (182). Indeed, Joe's brutal murder at the hands of Percy Grimm reveals how "Brown's desire for Joe Christmas, as well as its disavowal, is extended to . . . other white men in Jefferson" (185).

Grimm's atrocities also figure prominently in Chuck Jackson's "American Emergencies: Whiteness, the National Guard, and *Light in August*." Jackson traces "the historical development of new forms of military defense in the early twentieth century" such as Grimm's beloved National Guard, which "changed the look of the nation during times of civil unrest" by creating citizen-soldiers out of local or state militiamen (192). In the Jim Crow South, this process was explicitly racialized, the National Guard's "promise of militarized modernization" reserved almost exclusively for white men. In this way the National Guard "assisted in disciplining and federalizing a whiteness that belonged to the masses . . . and thus resignified local or regional whiteness as the official domain of the U.S. military." According to Jackson, Joanna Burden's violent death—or more precisely, Joe Brown's reconfiguration of that death as a race murder—launches a "national emergency narrative" (193), a distinct genre whose "peculiar temporal structure... builds with an alarmingly steady momentum and... speeds forward by moments of panic and violence." Under its auspices, Joanna is promoted from the nonnormative whiteness of a Yankee race-traitor to an exemplary white victim of black male sexual violence, Christmas is demoted from foreigner to "nigger," and the National Guard emerges in the figure of Grimm to police the borders of the body and the nation and thereby turn a "local southern region into a site of national pride" (203). As this project inevitably morphs into the violent policing of the color line, "a terrible touching of National Guard and National Other" (204), the National Guard collapses into its ostensible opposite, the lynch mob. In this way *Light in August* critically "reimagines whiteness as tied to the horror of state-based violence" in modern America (191). In the end, Jackson sees the novel as a Gothic fable of a militarized whiteness that reproduces the very violence, excess, and transgression it sets out to contain. Indeed, Gothic strategies and motifs arguably offered Faulkner a way to explore white racialization in moments of crisis or dysfunction.

So where do we go from here? I would like to close by sketching a few possible directions for future Faulkner scholarship on whiteness. The recent publication of López's edited collection of essays, *Postcolonial Whiteness*, suggests that exciting synergies may lie in wait between the study of whiteness in Faulkner and the growing body of criticism that approaches his work in comparative hemispheric and global contexts.[10] Homi K. Bhabha's theoretical account of the "almost the same but not quite/almost the same but not white" colonial subject engaged in a "bad" form of mimeticism that productively distorts the cultural style of the colonizers (85–92) should ring a bell with readers who have pondered the versions of racial mimicry performed, with varying degrees of success, by Faulknerian mixed-race and poor-white figures like Joe Christmas, Lucas Beauchamp, Charles Bon, Lena Grove, and Flem Snopes. Hagood's essay, which situates southern whiteness in transatlantic geographies of power, is a promising early foray in this postcolonial direction. There is also more to learn about the direct influence of film, photography, and other elements of visual culture on Faulkner's understanding and textual representations of whiteness, from scholars willing to follow Barker, Lurie, McKee, and Dyer to the vanishing point where their lines of inquiry converge. Also worthy of further study are Faulkner's own real-life performances and misperformances of white racial identity. James G. Watson is only the latest scholar to remind us that, in his life as well as his art, Faulkner was an inveterate role-player who understood personal as well as social identity in thoroughly performative terms.[11] Duvall's essay in this volume directs our attention to the "funny little black man" of *Mosquitoes*, but Faulkner just as often experimented with various public versions of whiteface, including a white-trash persona blending sartorial shabbiness with an air of fecklessness, a salty tongue, and a whiff of hard liquor. Moreover, as Noel Polk ("Man" 135–42) and Joel Williamson (*William Faulkner* 300–312) have shown, some of Faulkner's most disastrous and embarrassing public performances were attempts to improvise a politically moderate form of southern white identity at midcentury. All in all, performance-oriented studies of whiteness in Faulkner have much to gain from tapping biographical resources as well as textual ones.

A generation ago, Albert Murray gave us a miscegenated Faulkner as writer-in-residence for an incontestably mulatto nation (32–34). More recently, Edouard Glissant has given us a creolized Faulkner, from the vantage point of a Caribbean whose northern rim also goes by the name of the U.S. South (30–31, 83–88). The essays collected here don't so much contradict these accounts as complement them (and challenge us) with a Faulkner, and a Faulkner canon, that are white in ways we might not have suspected—differently, strangely so.

FAULKNER *and* WHITENESS

NEGOTIATING THE MARBLE BONDS OF WHITENESS

Hybridity and Imperial Impulse in Faulkner

—TAYLOR HAGOOD

Finding links between Faulkner the young romantic poet and Faulkner the adult modernist fiction writer has proven difficult; the exuberant but melancholy singer of nymphs and fauns seems, at most, perhaps reborn as a sardonic aspect of the mature writer's complex and multifaceted ego, a narrative persona adopted primarily to make fun of itself.[1] Judith L. Sensibar has shown how indispensable Faulkner's early work is in completing the composite picture of his career, and H. Edward Richardson and Gary Lee Stonum trace paths that lead from the Arcadian world of Faulkner's early imagination to the tortured modern landscape of his mature vision. Nevertheless, Faulkner scholarship often sees more *dis*sociation than *as*sociation between the poet and the novelist and short-story writer. A return to one of these early texts, however, reveals a figure that reappears throughout Faulkner's career, as the maturing writer returned to it continually, reexamining its many aesthetic, symbolic, and cultural implications. The text is *The Marble Faun* and the figure is the speaker itself: the half-goat and half-man image carved of marble and set in a formal garden. This figure is important because it is an image of whiteness that functions as a trope of hybridity: a hybrid body that at least partially if not completely subsumes the Other in its whiteness. As such, this figure informs the politics of a recurring body in Faulkner's work, a white but creolized body whose amalgamated makeup is hidden but that nonetheless encodes the dynamics arising from the juxtaposition and interaction of groups of oppressors and oppressed who must negotiate the hegemony of imperial impulse.

In the poem, a carved faun ruminates over his desire to escape his marble bonds and flee the garden in which he stands so he can roam about the surrounding glade. The faun would gladly relinquish his inherent rigidity as cold white marble and participate in the warm fluidity of the sylvan setting beyond the confines of the garden. Stonum reads the poem as a purely aesthetic complaint in which the faun attempts to negotiate a Nietzschean intersection of Apollonian and Dionysian artistic desires and experiences. Additionally, frozen as it is within its marble confines in a paradox of motion and stasis, the faun, as Sensibar notes, echoes the image on the urn in Keats's "Ode on a Grecian Urn." In light of recent discussion of hybridity and the liminal position and nature of the United States South, however, the body of the marble faun can be further complicated and understood in terms of the racial constructs and imperial impulses and counterimpulses it registers.[2]

Delineating the complexities of the marble faun figure requires a reconsideration of the cultural, economic, and imperial aspects of the poem's sources. In fact, Keats's urn signifies more than the sum of the parts of its external aesthetics; it contains and makes meaning as an object, as a signifier of empire. As in other Keats poems, such as "On Seeing the Elgin Marbles" or "On First Looking into Chapman's Homer," in this poem Keats's urn merits the imperial gaze that would apostrophize it because it is a possession of and participant in the iconography of not just Greek but also *British* imperialism. The power of the British Empire is implicit in the ownership of the Greek sculptures in "The Elgin Marbles"—Lord Elgin's removing the marbles from their original location in Greece to London had sparked great controversy, as no less visible a figure than Lord Byron criticized what he saw as a blatant theft motivated by the desire to glorify British imperial power and cultural achievement.[3] In "Chapman's Homer," Keats points out the colonization inherent in the act of translation and equates the experience of reading that text with Cortez's march across the

New World to discover the Pacific Ocean (however inaccurate the facts in the poem may be). In "Ode on a Grecian Urn," the urn signifies not just in the image on its exterior but in its value as a product, a vessel containing the silenced remains of an individual. The urn represents not only the affluence and artistic achievement of Greek society but also the power of a British empire that owns such an artifact. Furthermore, as a product, as a thing, the urn is both self and Other, emblematic of the British (and ancient Greek) center as well as of the periphery of the Mediterranean space of modern Greece. Faulkner's marble faun is also a product, a type of Elgin marble that signifies Greek, British, and even American imperial power much like a component of bricolage, which Lévi-Strauss argues has a current mythical value but also retains the value of its former signification.[4] One has a Greek statue in one's garden because one has the power to have it; such a possession represents a translation of empire.

The other evident source for the poem may be located in Donatello, the faun figure in Nathaniel Hawthorne's novel *The Marble Faun*. Although the narrative is set in Italy, Nancy Bentley and Anna C. Brickhouse have shown that it encodes American constructs of race. Half man and half goat, the faun evokes the dark Other, whether Native, African, or Latin American. It is important to remember that by the Middle Ages, the chief of the goat-men, Pan, had been reworked into Christian iconography as Satan. The sexual freedom, revelry, and drunkenness that the goat god signified in pagan culture became redefined as sins in Christianity. As Jeffrey Burton Russell argues, this new "symbolism was intended to show the Devil as deprived of beauty, harmony, reality, and structure.... Among the common bestial characteristics given [demons] were tails, animal ears, goatees, claws, and paws ..." (131), and demons "were blacks, who were popularly associated with shadow and the privation of light" (49). Such conflations of Satan, goats, and blackness informed New World definitions of the Other whether they were the red natives of the new land or the imported black slaves. Zora Neale Hurston effectively illustrates the transformation of the goat as a racial signifier in her play *The First One*, in which she presents her own version of the story of Ham's curse. In the play, Ham is the whitest of Noah's children and is lauded for his Dionysian lifestyle. He is, in fact, repeatedly referred to as "a young male goat." But when Noah curses him with blackness, those very celebrated Dionysian values are transformed into traits of evil, rebelliousness, and, of course, blackness. Such a transformation of the meaning of Dionysian values occurs in the changes in the character of Hawthorn's Donatello when he murders Miriam's tormenter.

The Faulknerian marble faun therefore represents a body that registers a complex set of racial and cultural signifiers because its Otherness is counterbalanced by and finally even subsumed in its selfness. A creature from Greek narrative, the faun may be seen as an extension of the Greek Revival begun in Britain and foundational in the construction of the United States and particularly salient in southern architecture. The Classical Revival began in England in the 1750s as a result of archeological activities in Greece, which were aspects of the larger British imperial project.[5] With the Revolution and the break from England, American leaders in part borrowed from England's focus on classical antiquities and, Talbot Hamlin argues, partly looked away from that influence to the superseding "inspiration of the ancient classic world of Greece and Rome" (3). Hamlin further notes that the United States's interest in Greece and Rome was particularly strong as part of "the enthusiasm which the whole Western World, and particularly the new republic, showed for the struggles of Greece during her wars of independence" (xvi–xvii).[6] Classical influences can be found in architecture from the nineteenth century (especially buildings constructed between 1820 and 1860) throughout the East Coast, especially in Philadelphia, Boston, and New York. And with one of the most visible figures in this movement being a Virginian, Thomas Jefferson, the southern states particularly embraced this architectural form.[7] Jefferson became enthralled with classical art and culture, as is exemplified in Monticello, and southern architects such as Robert Cary Long and his son Robert Cary Long, Jr., followed suit. However, southern appropriations of this architectural style seem particularly pointed in establishing a heritage of empowerment for, as William T. Ruzicka explains, the

> specific occurrence of Greek Revival architecture in the American South was not, as in the Northern states, a matter of style, but rather the particular response of a culture which understood itself to be a repetition and not an imitation, a recurrence rather than a recreation of ancient Greece, and fortuitously found the architectural style proper to its image. (6)

Faulkner's faun thus stands as a racially and culturally hybrid figure. On one hand, he represents the white imperialist, set in the formal garden, who shows cognizance of the power of the god of his kind, "Here Pan's sharp hoofed feet have pressed / His message on the chilly crest, / Saying—Follow where I lead, / For all the world springs to my reed" (Faulkner, *Marble* 13). At the same time, however, the half-goat status of the faun makes the creature half Other. Just as he is the production of an Apollonian art form, created in a solid medium, he nevertheless desires the Dionysian fluidity of the earth, the freedom of sound instead of the chill of silence. He regrets that he must be like the Keatsian "unravished bride of quiet," lamenting that the "whole world breathes and calls to me / Who marble-bound must ever be" (12), and coaxed by a blackbird's song that echoes the alluring melody of the Keatsian nightingale tempting him to enter a world of motion and excitement. This realm is the mythological realm of paganism, full of sexual freedom and Bacchic pleasure. The faun is both self and Other, its licentious goat-drives, its Satanic impulses, its "dark" desires now predominant, striving to overcome and choke out its Apollonian whiteness, and emerge as the Other.[8]

This Other passes; carved of white marble, the faun may in fact be viewed as a "counterfeit" Other.[9] This body is an extension of the white aristocratic South's hybrid body, an ostensibly white entity that marginalizes itself, containing the Other within its own milky epidermis by pillaging its darker pigments and stealing the Other's rhetoric of defeat and oppression. Indeed, it is from the southern slaves that those aristocratic whites being reconstructed after the Civil War took the rhetoric of the oppressed to articulate their victimization by what they saw as northern imperialism in Reconstruction, as is evidenced in the performative narratives of such post-Reconstruction writers as Irwin Russell, Joel Chandler Harris, and especially Thomas Nelson Page, who enact the very performative techniques their black framed narrators employ.[10] The Faulknerian/southern body represents a site of contending narratives of hegemony and counterhegemony, or imperial impulse and resistance to that impulse. Indeed, the marble faun evokes a number of United States and southern United States icons of various imperial significations. On one hand, the statue participates in the iconography of the wooden cigar-store Indian, a carved and now static Native American body, conquered and solidified into a clichéd trophy and relic of the white hegemony that vanquished it. At the same time, the faun evokes the Confederate soldier statue, which is a symbol of the deification of southern soldiers erected in defiance of Reconstruction. In this southern context, the faun particularly highlights what Toni Morrison identifies as an Africanist presence in the very Jeffersonian pastoral model upon which southern agrarianism is built. This model—what Lucinda MacKethan calls "the dream of Arcady"—is based on Greek pastoral, and yet that Greek pastoral champions a pagan world of Dionysian values that white aristocratic southerners associated with the very race they abhorred even as they paternalized it. Blackness—the Other—exists within the very construct of agrarian whiteness that the aristocratic white narrative promotes.

The bridge between this image/trope of whiteness in the poetic work of *The Marble Faun* and Faulkner's later fiction may be located in his early story "Black Music." The racial overtones of the story are suggested by the title, which echoes Sherwood Anderson's *Dark Laughter*, a novel that accentuates stereotypes of African Americans as Dionysian and which, as Thadious Davis has shown, influenced Faulkner's depiction of black characters and culture.[11] A frame narrative, the storytelling in the piece takes place in Rincon, which the narrator describes as a port "less large even than one swaybacked tanker looming above the steel docks of the Universal Oil Company" (Faulkner, *Collected* 799). It is a space located in the global South against the backdrop of a southern-informed global economy with poor white overtones, being a thinly disguised Standard Oil Company—Rockefeller's economic empire attacked for its ruthless tactics.[12] The story's frame narrator seems a racially empowered figure, presumably a Universal Oil Company boss who indulges his curiosity about the locals during his off time. The frame actually contains two narratives: the first is told by someone on roughly equal footing with the frame narrator who represents an ambiguous "they," possibly workers in the oil company as they are self-professedly "white"; the second narrative is told by a mysterious ex-draughtsman named Wilfred Midgleston, whose coming to Rincon was precipitated by an experience in which he believed himself to have been transformed into a faun.

The first frame introduces the second frame and is significant because of its racialization of Midgleston. The narrator of the first framed story asserts that Midgleston "came from the States" because he stole money and fled the authorities. Midgleston is "a white man," the narrator affirms; yet after "sponging on us white men" (of whom the narrator is a representative) until they "got tired of it he took to sponging on these Spigs. And a white man has got pretty low when he's got so stingy with his stealings that he will live with Spiggotties before he'll dig up his own money and live like a white man" (799–801). Although white, Midgleston is not *completely* white but rather hybrid: he is one of the "men a little soiled and usually unshaven" who live in the port (802). The first framed story's narrator himself is one of these individuals—a somewhat shady person who has apparently stolen money and run away to Rincon to hide out. And he possesses some disdain for the frame narrator whom he addresses and who is not one of the "down-at-heel compatriots [of this] informant," who are "unavoidable in the cantinas and coffee shops, loud, violent, maintaining the superiority of the white race and their own sense of injustice and of outrage among the grave white teeth, the dark, courteous, fatal, speculative alien faces" of Rincon's natives (802).

After learning why Midgleston is in Rincon, the frame narrator finally catches up with the man and, after buying him a meal, convinces him to tell his story. Midgleston begins by assuring the narrator that his reason for being in the port "ain't what you think. . . . I never stole any money" (804). Instead, he is here and will not return home because he "done something. . . . Something that ain't in the lot and plan for mortal human man to do. . . . At one time in my life I was a farn" (805). When the narrator asks what a "farn" is, Midgleston answers:

> A Farn. Don't you remember in the old books where they would drink the red grape wine, how now and then them rich Roman and Greek senators would up and decide to tear up a old grape vineyard or a wood away off somewheres the gods used, and build a summer house to hold their frolics in where the police wouldn't hear them, and how the gods wouldn't hear them, and how the gods wouldn't like it about them married women running around nekkid, and so the woods god named . . . Pan. And he would send them little fellows that was half a goat to scare them out— (805)

At this point, the narrator realizes that Midgleston is talking about a *faun*, and Midgleston notes that "the Bible says that them little men were myths.

But I know they ain't.... Because for one day in my life I was a farn" (805). The term is rife with implication, sounding much like a colloquial (especially southern) pronunciation of "foreign," which in the Faulknerian context means Other, not white, outside the bounds, friendliness, and protection of the community; and it is a term that appears often throughout Faulkner's work.

Midgleston explains that he once worked for an architect in New York City and was sent to a "tract [of land consisting] of a meadow, a southern hillside where grapes grew, and a woodland" in Virginia with plans for a sort of aristocratic Greco-Roman pleasure dome (806). This plot of ground had a history; first, a New England goatherder used the land to grow grapes but moved away when one of his rams broke the man's leg. Then an Italian man began to "gather the grapes and make wine out of them" (806); after "doctoring" the wine and getting rich from its sale, he died when his truck full of grapes wrecked in a storm. Now a rich New York couple named Van Dyming wants to build a neo-Acropolis, with its own Coliseum and amphitheater. This Greek- and Roman-informed construct represents a translation of empire from those ancient civilizations through the British and now the American imperial impulse; this project also represents an effort to build another Monticello in the Virginia countryside. But Midgleston uses the body of mythology that fuels the Van Dymings' imperial project against itself as he explains that the gods "used me [to dismantle the Van Dymings' project] . . . just as they used that ram on that New England fellow, and that storm on that I-talian" (809). On the train headed toward the Van Dymings' future estate, Midgleston sees

> animals inside the fence . . . when all of a sudden it felt like I had been thrown off the earth. I could see the bank and the fence go whirling away. And then I saw it. And just as I saw it, it was like it had kind of exploded inside my head. . . . I saw a face. In the air, looking at me across that white fence on top of the bank. It was not a man's face because it had horns, and it was not a goat's face because it had a beard and it was looking at me with eyes like a man and its mouth was open like it was saying something to me when it exploded inside my head. (811)

Some men on the train revive him with whiskey, and when he arrives at his destination and steps off the train he relates that "it was all green, the light was, and the mountains," and he exclaims, "Let her rip" (812) as he goes to buy a whistle, "a tin one, with holes in it" and then, as he makes his way to the Van Dymings, he begins to undress (812–13).

When Midgleston arrives at the Van Dymings', he unchains a bull that is kept in the pasture and then begins chasing Mrs. Van Dyming around the yard in a scene that re-creates the frieze on Keats's urn. Midgleston produces a newspaper clipping to tell the story for him, the headline of which reads, "MANIAC AT LARGE IN VIRGINIA MOUNTAINS[:] PROMINENT NEW YORK SOCIETY WOMAN ATTACKED IN OWN GARDEN" and goes on to say, "Mrs. Carleton Van Dyming Of New York and Newport Attacked By Half Nude Madman And Maddened Bull In Garden Of Her Summer Lodge" (814–15). This heading is followed by "pictures and diagrams" and a story in her words about how she had expected the draughtsman but instead encountered a wild man chasing her with a long knife (presumably the whistle—who knows who is lying?). The narrative ends with her standing against a tree terrified while the bull circles her and Midgleston raises the "knife" to his lips to blow, at which point she faints, thus creating a tableau in which, true to the Keatsian urn, the principals never actually touch. The gods' use of Midgleston was successful, as the article goes on to note that the Van Dymings immediately moved away and sold their land. Midgleston himself flees the scene of his exuberant dalliance, working his way southward until he reaches Rincon, where he leads the life of a tramp, sleeping under a piece of tarred roofing paper in a house that belongs to the Universal Oil Company.

Although "Black Music" is not explicitly "southern" in the typically Faulknerian sense, the narrative of imperialism and the larger context of oppression in the global South infuse it with recognizable southern themes. Trapped by the industrial-material center of New York/Park Avenue, Midgleston moves steadily southward through Virginia to New Orleans and then to Rincon. As he treks further south he grows "darker," beginning with the less-than-white hybridity of being a faun; indeed, his assault (apparently perceived as an attempted rape) on Mrs. Van Dyming seems to invest him with the "black beast" stereotype, another racist notion that resembles the African American-as-goat figuration. And, again, Midgleston emerges as something less than white in Rincon, where he is hybrid, Other, and foreign to whiteness and imperial power. His trek through the circumambience of hybridity in the U.S. South represents the site of his transformation from bourgeois white northerner to global southern Other who refuses to bow to capitalistic imperial impulse in the very face of one of its symbols—the Universal Oil Company.

The marble faun figure as a trope of whiteness fraught with hidden hybridity reappears in Faulkner's first two novels as he made his way deeper into the art of writing fiction. In *Soldiers' Pay*, Januarius "Jones' face [is] a round mirror before which fauns and nymphs might have wantoned when the world was young" (58), and his eyes are described as "clear and yellow, obscene and old in sin as a goat's" (67). The novel opens with Jones in the garden of Rector Mahon, and, like the marble faun, he wants to escape the formal garden for the fluid freedom of the forest and the promise of sexual encounter. As the novel progresses, he first attempts to seduce Cecily Saunders and then tries his luck with Margaret Powers and finally finds himself reduced to chasing the nymphlike maid, Emmy. Faulkner has already described Emmy as an earthy emissary of Dionysian expression, as she and Donald have made love in the forest before he left for the Great War. Fascinated by and attracted to her as a poor white with a status of servitude, Jones calls her "Cinderella" (133) and is last seen in the novel pursuing her "like a fat satyr, leaping after her, hopelessly distanced" (286). As with Midgleston and Mrs. Van Dyming, Jones and Emmy reenact the image on the Grecian urn. While Jones as a character descends from the marble faun, the imperial impulse seems largely absent from his intentions or his function in the text, although it should be noted that his mastery of Latin designates him as a sort of neoempowered Roman, and Faulkner associates that language with imperialism in the text, particularly when Joe Gilligan reads to Donald Mahon from Gibbons's *History of Rome*, quipping that in doing so he and Mahon will "bust up a few empires" (279).

Faulkner's second novel, *Mosquitoes*, opens with Talliafero admiring Gordon's marble statue of a torso that seems neither or both male and female—yet another of Faulkner's variants on the marble faun, only androgyny replaces a racial ambiguity in this image. Still, the whiteness of the image is significant, especially in the context of a generation of counterfeit Others and false nonwhites as Faulkner traces the exploits and nonexploits of an eclectic group of artists, would-be artists, and nonartists during their excursion onto Lake Pontchartrain. The primary figure of hybridity and imperial design in the novel appears in the form of Al Jackson, about whom Fairchild spins tall tales and who hearkens back to the conquering general Andrew Jackson while also being part fish, a poor-white "fish rancher." Meanwhile, the "foreigner" Other in this novel is the Italian Pete, whom Major Ayers (the quintessential white British imperialist) describes as "one of your natives . . . red Indians" (65). Pete seems the most readily colonial subject on the yacht, a "subaltern" who, in Spivak's terms, cannot "speak," trapped as he is on a yacht where the main activity is "[t]alk, talk, talk: the utter and heartbreaking stupidity of words" (186).

This wooden Indian Pete figure finds further development in Jewel Bundren in *As I Lay Dying*. "Still staring straight ahead," Darl says of Jewel, "his pale eyes like wood set into his wooden face, he crosses the floor in four strides with the rigid gravity of a cigar store Indian dressed in patched overalls and endued with life from the hips down" (4). Jewel is the familial hybrid child of the Bundrens, the son not of Anse but of Reverend Whitfield. And like the static Native American statue and the marble faun, Jewel maintains a rigidity in bearing: although he stays in motion, Jewel finds himself trapped in the quagmire of Anse's "ethics"; his need and desire for freedom and motion particularly appear in his violent reactions to Cash, who, in his patient constancy in his work in the plastic medium of wood, represents the Apollonian opposite of Jewel's dynamic Dionysianism. Indeed, Jewel would have himself and his mother "on a high hill and me rolling the rocks down the hill at their faces, picking them up and throwing them down the hill faces and teeth and all by God until she was quiet and not that goddamn adze going One lick less. One lick less and we could be quiet" (15). Just as his mother believes "that words are no good; that words dont ever fit even what they are trying to say at" (171), Jewel hardly speaks, his single monologue being even shorter than his mother's and his speaking elsewhere in the novel primarily cursing.

The marble faun as image of whiteness and the complexities of imperial impulse represents a particularly important factor in Faulkner's imagination when he turned back to north Mississippi in his fiction to work out his imperial saga *Father Abraham*, the manuscript of which features a drawing of Pan very similar to one Faulkner drew for *Mayday*.[13] When this material reached full realization and saw print ultimately in *The Hamlet*, the goat emerged as a unit of currency as Faulkner explores both the Satanic and Dionysic aspects of the goat-man in a pastoral setting fraught with the crisis of an invading capitalistic system manipulated and attenuated to the point that its every loophole finds itself exploited to fullest effect. Flem Snopes is certainly the god of goats, a Pan who is able to out-Satan Satan. V. K. Ratliff may be the long-standing champion of Yoknapatawpha County and the shrewdest of traders, but it is Flem Snopes who literally gets his goats on his way to becoming emperor of the hamlet. Flem is, in fact, the new Frenchman of Frenchman's Bend, perhaps not foreign enough to be considered European but definitely a colonizing outlander, his home being a far-away place: nothing less than Hell itself. Indeed, the novel's constantly repeated expletive "Hell Fire" and Ratliff's having been taken during the goat deal inform his vision of Flem's swindling Satan. Son of a barn-burner, Flem is utterly unperturbed by Satan, whom he cheats not only out of his soul but out of Hell itself; as Satan, whom Ratliff refers to as "*The Prince*," fades from power amid "*bright, crown-shaped flames*," he yells, "*Take Paradise! . . . Take it! Take it!*" (873). As the goat god Pan, Flem actually precedes Satan as icon. The Prince learned how to use his pitchfork "on Chinees and Dagoes and Polynesians, until his arms would get strong enough to handle his share of white folks" (871), but Flem, descendant of the marble faun, is neither and both white and nonwhite and wields both identities to achieve his imperial goals.

As goat god, Flem must have his goddess, and her name is Eula. With her "eyes like cloudy hothouse grapes" (738), Eula Varner's "entire appearance suggested some symbology out of the old Dionysic times—honey in sunlight and bursting grapes, the writhen bleeding of the crushed fecundated vine beneath the hard rapacious trampling goat-hoof" (817). Yet, like the marble faun, she represents a static entity, as "[s]he seemed to be not a living integer of her contemporary scene, but rather to exist in a teeming vacuum in which her days followed one another as though behind soundproof glass, where she seemed to listen in sullen bemusement, with a weary wisdom heired of all mammalian maturity, to the enlarging of her own organs" (817). She maintains the doubleness that characterizes the faun: "[t]here was one Eula Varner who supplied blood and nourishment to the buttocks and legs and breasts; there was the other Eula Varner who merely inhabited them, who went where they went because it was less trouble to do so" (822). She is Emmy reborn, a nymph-turned-goddess, the product of "one blind seed of the spendthrift Olympian ejaculation" (867). In fact, she is the daughter of a faunlike man who even in old age regularly meets a woman in a "sylvan Pan-hallowed retreat" for lusty fornication during which he "would not even remove his hat" (861). Her father is also the established head of Frenchman's Bend (the old Frenchman's plantation itself a colonial project now in ruins), and Eula, caught in the colonizing gaze of the men in the hamlet, finds herself transferred as goods from one figure of power to another—from her father the suzerain to Flem the colonizer.

A character who shares similarities with Flem (primarily his silent and relentless work ethic) and who emerges as an important incarnation of the marble faun is Joe Christmas. Connected by name to the hybrid figure Christ, Christmas and the people he encounters throughout *Light in August* suggest that he may be white trash, Hispanic, African American, Italian, and, above all, a "foreigner." Still, he passes as just white—the dietitian herself realizes that he "*will look just like a pea in a pan full of coffee beans*" (130) when removed to an all-black orphanage. Christmas is one of a host of hybrid white-Others in the novel; for example, Joanna Burden is a white woman who is also "a foreigner whose people moved in from the North during Reconstruction. A Yankee, a lover of negroes, about whom in the town there is still talk . . . that lingers about her and about the place: something dark and outlandish and threatful" (46–47). And even though Gail Hightower is a white man, he is also a foreigner whose skin is the slightly off-white "color of flour sacking" (78); when he leaves his congregation amid newspaper photographers after his wife's death, his face hidden behind a hymn book "looked like the face of Satan in the old prints" (69). Christmas too has "the face of Satan" (205), recognized as "the devil! It's Satan himself" (322), the incarnation of the goat-figured black beast rapist, who, like Wilfred Midgleston, grows "darker" when Joe Brown accuses him of raping and murdering Joanna. And yet, again, Joe Christmas is a figure of whiteness—a figure whose racial instability makes him all the more threatening as he struggles to negotiate the white to almost-white shades of his skin color while alternately embracing and rejecting the perspective and experience of the Other.

Faulkner constructs another "foreigner" on the hybrid antitype of Christ in the character of the corporal in *A Fable*. All of the men who mutiny with him are "not merely like foreigners but like creatures of another race, another species," but "three of the four were not Frenchmen, that is, because now the crowd itself had discerned that the fourth one was alien still somehow even to the other three" (681)—of "middle-European nationality" (784). The corporal's outsider status threatens the entire stability of the impetus of fighting for the father/ motherland that the novel designates as the sustaining force of war. But he is not just a foreigner, as he is the hybrid offspring not only of a mountain woman but also of the French Generalissimo himself. Although a character whose very identity remains fluid, identified as at least two other soldiers already confirmed as dead at different times and places, the corporal in the end becomes transformed into a literal monument to and of nationalism when the army inters his corpse in the Tomb of the Unknown Soldier.

Absalom, Absalom! offers a similar "French foreigner," a black beast rapist who passes as a white imperialist—Charles Bon. Mr. Compson alternately describes the New Orleans native as both an Oriental and Occidental figure. Mr. Compson first imagines Bon "lounging . . . in the outlandish and almost feminine garments of his sybaritic privacy" (76)—"a hero out of some adolescent Arabian Nights who had stumbled upon (or rather, had thrust upon him) a talisman or touchstone" (76). On the other hand, Mr. Compson thinks that maybe Bon exists "behind [a] barrier of sophistication" (74)—the "youthful Roman consul making the Grand Tour of his day among the barbarian hordes which his grandfather conquered" (74), whose sophisticated letters to Judith Sutpen are "the metropolitan gallant's idle and delicate flattering" (102). Bon thus emerges as another descendant of the marble faun: he is a counterfeit Other, a white man made dark who emerges as hero, villain, and victim at various moments throughout the text. And when in Quentin's and Shreve's narrative Henry kills "the nigger that's going to sleep with [his] sister" (286), Wash Jones reports to Rosa Coldfield that "Henry has done shot that durn French feller. Kilt him dead as a beef" (106).

Quentin—a partial creator of the narrative of Charles Bon's racial hybridity—is himself perhaps one of the most intriguing of Faulkner's counterfeit Others, partly for the reciprocities between the character and

Faulkner himself. Clearly a white aristocratic male southerner, he seems even more a metropolitan figure than his fellow Mississippians, as Herbert Head observes in *The Sound and the Fury*, he does not "look like these other hicks" (108). At Harvard, however, he becomes himself marginalized; the three boys whom he encounters on the last day of his life think "[h]e talks like they do in minstrel shows . . . like a colored man" (120). Quentin most famously casts himself as caught between the tortured poetics of victimizer and victimized in *Absalom, Absalom!* in which he plays the role of the tragic southern Other in relation to what the white aristocratic South views as its imperial oppressor—the North. The crisis of the unreconstructed white male southerner replicates the crisis of the oppressed African Americans, poor whites, and women of postbellum southern society so that the narrative of the Other finds itself subsumed in Quentin's narrative of tragedy within whiteness. In fact, Quentin presumes to speak for all southern experiences in his weighty and yet ironic and even self-deconstructing lines regarding the South: "I dont. I dont! I dont hate it! I dont hate it!" (Faulkner, *Absalom* 303). The effect of his self-Othering is that it masks, with its mix of nostalgia and tragedy, the very real tragedy of the novel's true Others.

The image of the marble faun thus threads its way throughout Faulkner's work as one of whiteness filled with the instabilities of hybridity. And Faulkner shows the ways this seemingly blank palette is a site of pigment-mixing, the location of instability ironically hidden behind its very overwhelming glare which can be as terrifying as the images of whiteness in other United States writers' works, such as Poe's *Narrative of Arthur Gordon Pym* and Melville's *Moby Dick*. Particularly striking are the subtle ways in which Faulkner kneads this image in its various incarnations, rendering Wilfred Midgleston an object of pity, Januarius Jones a grotesque, Flem Snopes a triumphant racial trickster, Joe Christmas a tortured soul caught in a matrix of racial constructs, and Quentin Compson a manipulator of Otherness. Likewise, Faulkner's female descendants of the marble faun emerge in impressive variety, as Emmy like Midgleston can escape the bonds of her status and immerse herself in the fluidity of the forest and Eula finds herself entrapped by male-generated narratives of her as a static and unattainable icon while Joanna's whiteness seems merely secondary to her status as "Negro-loving" Yankee foreigner. Through this trope of whiteness and hybridity, Faulkner found ways to articulate in a single body the shifting perspectives of subject and object, self and Other, oppressor and oppressed as well as the ways they may be masked by what Western and United States narratives would posit as an inexpugnably stable construct.

GENEALOGIES OF WHITE DEVIANCE

The Eugenic Family Studies, *Buck v. Bell*,
and William Faulkner, 1926–1931

—JAY WATSON

The historian C. Vann Woodward once suggested that "[a] Hemingway hero with a grandfather is inconceivable" (31). Woodward was indirectly alluding to what he considered to be the absence of a thick historical awareness in Hemingway, Dreiser, Anderson, and numerous other American writers of their generation. As a counterexample to this ahistoricist tendency in American letters, he pointed to "Southern novelists" who fashion their characters "as an inextricable part of a living history and community" (37), and above all to William Faulkner. For Woodward, the presence of grandfathers, and of "uncles, aunts, cousins, and in-laws" (31) in the work of Faulkner and his regional cohorts—in short, the work of a genealogical imagination—signaled the presence of a genuinely historical consciousness that was key to Woodward's definition of southern distinctiveness (15–16). Another historian, Richard H. King, has drawn on Freudian paradigms to argue that genealogy offered Faulkner and other writers of the southern renaissance a framework for constructing and interrogating a mythic "family romance" of the white South centered on bonds of affection and rivalry among fathers, sons, and grandfathers (20–38). As King sees it, a critical engagement with genealogy is a must for Faulkner characters seeking to graduate from a monumentalizing attitude toward authority and the past into a more properly historical one. And more recently, George Handley has proposed genealogy as the master trope of New World plantation literature in the postslavery era, perhaps the only discursive strategy with the breadth, flexibility, depth, and currency to illuminate the intergenerational, interracial, and powerfully gendered networks of filiation and affiliation that informed plantation relations in the Americas. As Handley explains, New World planters turned to genealogy as an instrument of hegemony, "an ideological and metaphorical tool of exclusion" (15) that helped legitimate and consolidate the "landowning social power" (3) of the plantocracy by writing blacks and other peoples of color out of the national family (15). In the hands of postslavery novelists like Faulkner, however, genealogy can alternately serve as a subversive "biological tool" that directs attention to "the ellipses of the planter's scheme" and works to "expose planter authority as illegitimate" (17). For Faulkner and other New World writers, then, a genealogical vision proves a vital resource in the effort to further the work of decolonization in Plantation America. The master's tool *can* dismantle the master's house.

There is, then, no shortage of scholarly attention to the genealogical dimensions of Faulkner's best work.[1] I want to suggest, however, that an important source and context for Faulkner's emphasis on genealogy, and for his use of genealogical tropes and structures in his writing, has gone entirely uncommented on in Faulkner studies: the mainstream U.S. eugenics movement, which enjoyed widespread cultural influence during Faulkner's formative years. From our twenty-first-century vantage point, we can too easily dismiss eugenics as a refuge for crackpots, pseudoscientists, and Nazis, but as critic Daylanne English explains, it was "a central national ideology" in the U.S. during the 1910s and 1920s (14), "so widely accepted that it might be considered the paradigmatic modern discourse" (2). Indeed, writes English, "so pervasive" was eugenics ideology during this period "that it became nearly invisible ... for the vast majority of the U.S. population, simply 'true'—just common sense" (33). And a major element of this common sense was genealogy. For genealogy also served as an exclusionary tool for the eugenics movement, which, as we will see shortly, developed a new social-science methodology around the practice. So I find it enormously suggestive that this movement was heading south to a new place, turning its attention to a new regional growth area it had previously neglected, at precisely the same time that William Faulkner was turning his attention northward from his New Orleans novel *Mosquitoes* to begin delineating the contours of a fictional Mississippi county in a series of works that also represent *his* first attempts at genealogical narrative. The two paths—Faulkner's personal odyssey and the eugenics movement's southern swing into the nation's region[2]—converged upon a common geographical setting (the rural upland South), a common problematic (the social specter and racial riddle of deviant whiteness), and a common set of core motifs and methods, including what one scholar of eugenics has labeled "family-tree technology" (Rafter, *White Trash* 16). It is significant that Faulkner's birth as a genealogical novelist coincides with his invention of Yoknapatawpha, but just as significant that both of these developments coincide with the eugenics movement's "discovery" of a new social crisis and policy focus: the southern white problem family.

GENEALOGIES OF DEVIANCE

Eugenics had mid-nineteenth-century intellectual roots in the work of Darwin and Francis Galton, but the movement gained a new visibility and credibility in the United States with the publication in 1877 of *The Jukes: A Study of Crime, Pauperism, Disease and Heredity*, by Richard Dugdale. Dugdale's book inaugurated a new social-science genre, the family study, that Nicole Hahn Rafter calls "the most influential product" of the eugenics movement "in terms of ideological impact" (*White Trash* 2). The family studies arose in response to a social problem that represented a crisis for eugenics advocates: how to account, in terms consistent with their beliefs about evolution and race, for the presence of whites—anointed in contemporary science and anthropology as the superior race—in prisons, hospitals, poorhouses, asylums, and elsewhere among the ranks of the nation's unfit? Family studies methodology "solved" this problem by constructing elaborate genealogies that framed undesirable social traits as products of heredity, passed down through family bloodlines by defective progenitors thought to possess bad "germ plasm," the contemporary term for genetic material. Blaming white deviance on heredity allowed eugenics advocates to sidestep environmentalist explanations that might have focused on social injustice and economic inequalities in the modernizing nation, *and* to salvage white supremacy by tracing white problem traits to lineal rather than racial failings. The strategy also led seamlessly to a policy objective: "if those afflicted with 'bad germ plasm' could be prevented from 'breeding,' society would be cleansed of social problems" (Rafter, *White Trash* 1). This emphasis on negative eugenics—preventing the propagation of the unfit through means that included sexual segregation, marriage restrictions, and sterilization—came to dominate the movement by the turn of the century.

English calls the family studies "a new interdisciplinary genre: a mixture of short story, personal narrative, travel narrative, sociology, and statistics" (28). For the half-century after Dugdale published his "Jukes" study, they were almost exclusively located in the northeastern or midwestern states, often near institutional centers of eugenics research and leadership such as Charles Davenport's Eugenics Record Office (ERO) in Cold Spring Harbor, New York, or the Training School for the Feeble-Minded at Vineland, New Jersey (where Elizabeth Kite and Henry Goddard began the study of the infamous "Kallikak" family). They focused overwhelmingly on rural rather than urban whites; as Rafter notes, sounding a little like Karl Marx, "the degeneracy of country life" is their "dominant theme" (*White Trash* 7). In these rural enclaves, family studies researchers employed an extremely loose conception of "family" to construct sprawling clans or "tribes" that often spanned four or five generations and whose horizontal reach was just as expansive. Among these families they "discovered" a liberal (and methodologically shaky) inventory of undesirable social and moral traits they considered to be genetically transmissible: alcoholism, criminality and violence, "pauperism" (understood as deserved rather than undeserved poverty), prostitution and "harlotry" (promiscuity, licentiousness), shiftlessness, "nomadism" (geographical wandering), physical infirmity, and "feeblemindedness," a term originally used to designate mental retardation but employed more and more widely over the years until it became an umbrella term that could encompass practically any or all of the other traits and was indeed thought by many eugenicists to be biologically linked to them. In constructing this biological white underclass as an ideological receptacle for deviance, the family studies "created a powerful myth about the somatic nature of social problems" (Rafter, *White Trash* 2).

They also inadvertently opened up a rift in U.S. whiteness, attesting to the ways in which it differed internally from itself.

One way to chart the movement's turn to the South in the 1920s as a field for eugenics research and legislation is to follow the career of a single figure, Arthur H. Estabrook, whom Nathaniel Deutsch characterizes as the most prolific of the family studies authors (102). Trained as a fieldworker at Cold Spring Harbor the summer before the ERO officially opened in 1910, Estabrook quickly made a name for himself as the author of a 1915 follow-up study of Dugdale's Jukes and then embarked on another follow-up of an equally infamous clan from eugenics history, Indiana's so-called "Tribe of Ishmael," whom the Reverend Oscar McCulloch had made the focus of an 1888 family study. Then, in the 1920s, Estabrook traveled to Amherst County, Virginia, to conduct the research that resulted in the 1926 book he coauthored with Ivan E. McDougle, *Mongrel Virginians: The Win Tribe*, one of the last of the published family studies but the first to focus on rural southerners. And in 1924, he was called back to Amherst County to serve as an expert witness in a court case designed to test the constitutionality of the state's new eugenic sterilization act, a case that eventually made its way before the U.S. Supreme Court and resulted in what is now regarded as one of the worst decisions in the Court's history: *Buck v. Bell* (1927).

The Virginia law, closely following the model eugenic sterilization bill drawn up by Harry Laughlin in his *Eugenical Sterilization in the United States* (1922), empowered state institutions such as the Virginia Colony for Epileptics and Feeble-minded in Lynchburg to sterilize "probably potential parent[s] of socially inadequate offspring" (quoted in Lombardo 290). For the test case, the Colony superintendent selected Carrie Buck, a sixteen-year-old native of Charlottesville who was assigned to the Colony in 1924 following a diagnosis of feeblemindedness. By the 1920s, feeblemindedness had come to be understood in highly gendered terms that often had little to do with intelligence: in a man, shiftlessness, lack of industriousness, or other indications of unsuitedness to labor could prompt a diagnosis of feeblemindedness, whereas in women the focus was on promiscuity, prostitution, illegitimacy, or other signs of sexual immorality.[3] Carrie Buck, then, fit the bill, having recently borne a daughter out of wedlock. As legal scholar Paul Lombardo has meticulously shown, the Virginia Colony officials who were the defendants in the test case made their case for sterilizing Carrie Buck by employing a crude version of family studies methodology to fashion her as a member of a dysgenic, multigenerational enclave of feeblemindedness and vice. Summoning up the social and moral specter of the Jukes and Kallikaks (to whom Buck's family was explicitly compared at the trial [Lombardo 5–6]), and manufacturing evidence by means of hearsay, innuendo, and the diagnostic liberties taken by expert witnesses such as Estabrook, the defense argued that Buck was the illegitimate, feebleminded child of a feebleminded mother, Emma Buck (also an inmate at the Lynchburg Colony), and that Carrie's illegitimate daughter, eight-month-old Vivian, already exhibited the telltale signs of the condition herself. The defense, in other words, enlisted genealogy to make its case for the hereditary nature of feeblemindedness and for Carrie Buck as a dangerous carrier of this defective trait, a potential mother of morons[4] in need of neutering for the public good. The power of this genealogical argument and its attendant discourse was evident in the wording of Justice Oliver Wendell Holmes, Jr.'s majority opinion for the Supreme Court, which ruled eight to one in favor of the bill. After comparing the statute to a recently upheld vaccination law in Massachusetts, Holmes concluded acerbically, "Three generations of imbeciles are enough" (quoted in Lombardo 287).

A word or two is perhaps in order here to explain the specific emphasis in the *Buck* case (and in Holmes's opinion) on *three* generations of deviance. The rediscovery in 1900 of Mendel's work on the laws of inheritance had a profound effect on the eugenics movement. After around 1912, writes Rafter, the family studies became increasingly preoccupied with the mechanisms of genetic transmission, the *how* as well as the presumed *fact* of heredity (*White Trash* 9). Feeblemindedness, for instance, came to be understood by Henry Goddard and others as a single-gene recessive trait (Rafter, *Creating* 141–42). But with this conclusion came a new anxiety: recessive traits do not always express themselves in the offspring of carriers but are capable of skipping a generation (or more) and thus going undetected by eugenics reformers eager to prevent their spread in the general population (see Kevles 164–65, 197–98). We can sense this anxiety behind the observation by Edward M. East, a contemporary eugenicist whose *Heredity in Human Affairs* was published in the same year as the *Buck* decision, that "[t]he recessive abnormalities are the curses of mankind" because "one cannot tell when they are going to crop out" (92), or that defects "of the recessive type ... may lie hidden for a series of generations" (22). So East worked out what critic Ashley Lancaster has called a generational timeline for the detection of feeblemindedness (Lancaster 31). After identifying the trait as recessive (East 44), East goes on to argue that the product of "one defective and one normal germ-cell will be of normal mentality." He is attempting, rather simplistically, to evoke the way a recessive trait remains unexpressed in a heterozygous carrier. "Possibly he or she will not be as well provided with brains as a 'pure' normal," East writes, "but true feeblemindedness will never be in evidence." In the union of "two such cross-bred persons," however, feeblemindedness will resurface "occasionally" in the children ("about 25 percent" of the time). Three generations are enough, then, to document a hereditary line of feeblemindedness. This same sort of quasi-Mendelian reasoning was at work behind the strenuous efforts of the defense in the *Buck* case to identify feeblemindedness in a third Buck generation: baby Vivian's diagnosis (however implausible) would not only establish the transmissibility of Carrie's alleged defect; it would also render Carrie's own diagnosis that much more airtight. Eugenics researchers typically worked hard in their genealogical charts and diagrams to demonstrate this kind of generational continuity in the traits they studied.

Buck v. Bell was followed by a resurgence of eugenic sterilization legislation in the U.S., especially in the South. Mississippi's bill, which according to historian Steven Noll followed the Virginia statute "word for word" (*Feeble-Minded* 71), was approved by the state house of representatives on Tuesday, April 10, 1928 (Larson 117–18)—only two days, that is, after a severely retarded man who has undergone a crude and historically before-the-fact version of compulsory sterilization sits howling in a horse-drawn buggy on a Mississippi town square, in the closing sequence of Faulkner's fourth novel.[5] Three of the novel's four narrative sections, in fact, are set within a week of that red-letter day in Mississippi eugenics history. But before turning to *The Sound and the Fury*'s extensive dialogue with eugenics themes and techniques, I want to pause for a few pages to explore Faulkner's first fictional forays into Yoknapatawpha County, which were also, significantly, forays into the genealogies of white dysfunction that also lay at the heart of the eugenic family studies.

FATHER ABRAHAM AND UNCLE FLEM

In 1926, having followed Sherwood Anderson's advice and returned to Oxford from his *wanderjahr* in New Orleans and Europe, Faulkner embarked on his first Yoknapatawpha narrative, the comic fragment *Father Abraham*, which remained unpublished during his lifetime but which supplied material he would recycle in "Spotted Horses" (1931), *The Hamlet* (1940), and other published fictions. In describing the project for an Oxford *Eagle* reporter, the novelist's friend Phil Stone could easily be referring to one of the eugenic studies commissioned by Davenport's ERO: "something of a saga of an extensive family connection of 'poor white trash'" (quoted in Meriwether n.p.). Faulkner's choice of a name, Snopes, for this clan is not simply (as many have noted) a tongue-in-cheek allusion to the Scopes trial of 1925, which called attention to the backwardness and anti-intellectualism of rural and small-town southerners. It also resembles the denigrating pseudonyms fabricated by the authors of the family studies to "protect" the identities of their subjects: Jukes, Nams, Zeroes. Moreover, with his allusion to the "hillcradled cane and cypress jungles" of Frenchman's Bend (14), Faulkner evokes the same sort of southern rural hill country locale featured in Estabrook and McDougle's exactly contemporaneous family study, *Mongrel Virginians*, the book that brought family studies methodology to the South. Faulkner's account of this rural "neighborhood" as characterized by bootlegging, violence, and sexual immorality (16) marks the hills as a hotbed of vice that flouts middlebrow mores. There the Snopeses, whom the narrator refers to as a "race" (19), exhibit many of the social and moral failings that contemporary eugenicists believed to be genetic defects. "Shiftless" and "rootless," they are dull and clannish. Combining the dysgenic threat of nomadism with an unnerving fecundity, "they move and halt and move and multiply and marry and multiply like rabbits" (20). On the same page they are explicitly compared to "mold on cheese."

They are also equipped with the bare outlines of a genealogy. Only five Snopeses appear onstage in *Father Abraham*. All are males—Flem, Eck, Eck's son Admiral Dewey (known as "Ad"), I. O., and I. O.'s son Clarence. Their wispy genealogical connections are complemented, perhaps even clarified, by hierarchical ones. At the top of the heap stands "Uncle" Flem (14), whose title, much like "Uncle" Billy Varner's (16) among the village folk, announces him as a founder figure, a kind of patriarch at the head of his enclave. If that "Uncle" additionally designates a specific family relation to his kinsmen I. O. and Eck, then the latter two figures form a second generation rather than simply functioning as serial successors and placeholders who move into the niches in the local economy vacated by Flem. If so, then Ad and Clarence represent a third generation of—well, not imbeciles, exactly (though the hulking, dim-witted Clarence gives one pause [see 69–70]), but certainly figures who in various ways lie askew of normative whiteness in Yoknapatawpha.

What is more, Flem's "descendants" in this loose genealogical structure fall into an equally loose approximation of the "good" (normal) and "bad" (dysgenic) lineages that Goddard traced to a common patriarch in his 1912 study of the Kallikaks. This dual-lineage focus, which Goddard saw as "a kind of controlled experiment" devised by nature (Rafter, *Creating* 143), represented a major innovation in family studies methodology at the time.[6] It is echoed in *Father Abraham* by the contrast between Eck and Ad on the one hand, and I. O. and Clarence on the other. The former two are affable, honest, well-meaning, even innocent—sturdy male subjects pulling their weight economically and ethically in Frenchman's Bend. The latter two are explicitly dishonest and consequently, like Flem, elicit distrust in others: I. O. applauds Flem for hoodwinking the locals by selling them a worthless string of Texas ponies (64–65), while Clarence steals candy from the Varner general store (69–70). As such, *Father Abraham* poses—though it does not attempt to solve—the same riddle that Goddard explored in his Kallikak genealogy: how successful and defective branches of a family lineage can be traced through a common ancestral figure.

Faulkner's title works to reinforce these eugenically inflected associations. Eugenicists were well aware that they were following biblical precedent in their preoccupation with genealogy and the sins of the fathers. Indeed, the family studies sometimes read like parodies or perhaps travesties of the Hebrew Bible, with each dysgenic "begat" more disastrous than the last and the genetic defects of the ancestors visited upon their posterity to the third and fourth generations (Lombardo 38–39). Faulkner follows suit, with the comparison between his poor-white patriarch and the supreme example of the genealogical founder in all scripture: Abraham, father of Israel. And not only that—Father Abraham, like Uncle Flem, presides over a Kallikak-like dual lineage: the "chosen" line that runs, with God's special favor, through Abraham's legitimate son Isaac, and the illegitimate bloodline, destined for pariahhood, that becomes the tribe of Ishmael.[7] Though the manuscript remains unfinished, its eugenic implications only incompletely worked out, Faulkner draws on a variety of textual devices and strategies to experiment, tongue firmly in cheek, with a quasi- or pseudoeugenic narrative stance that presents the Snopeses not simply as a ragtag assortment of marginal whites but as a genealogy of deviance.

"THEY AINT MY SARTORISES. . . . I JUST INHERITED 'EM"

One way to look at the "genesis" of Faulkner's apocryphal county is as a kind of twin birth, for by the end of 1926 the novelist was at work on a companion to *Father Abraham* in ushering Yoknapatawpha into being. In this ersatz genealogy of the Mississippi fiction, *Flags in the Dust* (completed in September 1927) resembles the proverbial healthy white baby, focusing on the elite Sartoris family and its aura of romance and glamour, while *Father Abraham*, preoccupied with the socially marginal and more or less stillborn as a text, looks more like the runt of the litter. It is tempting, in fact, to impose a Kallikak-like "family" structure on the two narratives, with *Flags* focusing on the eugenically sound and *Abraham* the eugenically unsound branches of Yoknapatawpha's white "tribe." *Flags*, in fact, flirts with this comparative approach in its own right. Alongside its account of the well-born Sartorises, the novel features a Snopes narrative of its own, the sordid story of Byron Snopes, whose path crosses disastrously with both the Sartoris family and their elite cohorts, the Benbows. Sexually perverted and "half-insane" (764), thieving, wandering, and mendacious, this "hillman of indeterminate age" (545) is a walking library of dysgenic traits. Drifting into Jefferson, he pauses long enough to pen an anonymous series of obscene letters to Narcissa Benbow, peer into her bedroom window by night, and break into her house to pilfer a pair of her underthings, before lighting out for points unknown with an undisclosed but substantial sum of money he has liberated from old Bayard Sartoris's bank (763–73). As backdrop to Byron's story, we learn that of his clan, whom the narrator presents collectively, in terms shaped by *Father Abraham*, as a lineage, "a seemingly inexhaustible family which for the last ten or twelve years had been moving to town in driblets from a small settlement known as Frenchman's Bend" (678). "[B]rought . . . household by household, individual by individual, into town" by their kinsman Flem (again compared to "Abraham of old"), "incoming Snopeses . . . multiplied and flourished" (679) in a nightmare scenario that could have been lifted straight from the pages of an ERO bulletin or family study.

The only problem with the politically soothing prospect of casting the poor-white Snopeses as *kakos* to the Sartorises' *kalos* is the hint of doubt raised by *Flags* itself about the Sartorises' eugenic credentials, the health and integrity of the family bloodline. Far more meticulous than *Abraham* in its presentation of genealogical information, *Flags* invites the reader to reconstruct a Sartoris lineage that stretches across five generations, from Colonel John (plus his brother, "the Carolina Bayard," and his sister, Virginia Du Pre), to John's son Bayard (referred to as old Bayard in the novel), to Bayard's son John (and his wife, Lucy Cranston Sartoris), to John and Lucy's twin sons, young Bayard and Johnny, down to young Bayard's and Narcissa Benbow's infant son, Benbow Sartoris, who gets himself born on the same day his father perishes in a spectacular airplane crash (864). The Sartoris ranks include planters, bankers, and military officers, builders of empire at home and abroad—to all appearances, a gallery of the eugenically fit. War has claimed the lives of a few, such as the Carolina Bayard and young Johnny, and irrevocably marked others, such as Colonel John and young Bayard (whose plane crash compulsively repeats his brother's death in air combat in World War One). Indeed, *Flags* comes close at times to an anxiety prevalent among eugenicists about the dysgenic effects of war, its nasty, counter-Darwinian habit of promoting the survival of the unfit by carrying off the soundest human stock, the best and the brightest, in disproportionate numbers (see, for instance, East 249). "Funny family," muses Horace Benbow about the Sartorises. "Always going to wars, and always getting killed" (674).

This special talent for living fast and dying young—for an early, violent, glamorous end—seems to lie at the heart of the mysterious "doom" that hovers over the Sartoris line and lends its dark, romantic aura to Faulkner's narrative more generally (788). Over and over, the Sartoris men are singled out for tragic, showy destinies that highlight their grand, reckless gestures. They are, as Faulkner might have put it, splendid failures; "They never get into the papers but one way," observes Aunt Jenny (866). This can work to obscure the otherwise glaring fact of that failure, the irrefutable evidence that generationally, genealogically, the family legacy—or perhaps its defective trait—is decline. The men seem to die younger with each new generation; the twins Johnny and Bayard don't even make it out of their twenties. (Old Bayard, as his title implies, is the exception who proves the rule, outliving his son and one of his grandsons and only narrowly missing outlasting the other.) This is no doubt why the genealogical enterprise as it is actually depicted in the novel is linked so intimately with death. In his day, Colonel Sartoris openly scoffed at the pretentiousness of genealogy, calling it "poppycock" (615). But among his descendants there are two scenes of explicit genealogical activity in *Flags*. Upon young Bayard's return from the war, his grandfather climbs to the attic, unlocks a large chest full of Civil War memorabilia and other musty family heirlooms, and hauls out a "huge, brass-bound bible" (614). He then makes two additions to the Sartoris family tree inscribed therein. Both new entries record deaths: Johnny's in combat, and young Bayard's first wife Caroline's in childbirth, only a few weeks before the Armistice (616). Duly chastened by "the stark dissolving apotheosis of his name" (615), old Bayard goes on to comment ruefully on the impending "extinction" of the family lineage (624), a prophecy more or less borne out at novel's end, when *Flags* arrives at its second major site of genealogical endeavor, the Jefferson cemetery (868–71). Here at any rate the family name seems to be thriving. But the monumentalizing work of the headstones and marble pillars and "pompous genealogical references" (870) that adorn the Sartoris plots is overshadowed by the broader aura of death. At the end of the day (and the novel will indeed conclude at the end of a day), this graveyard genealogy offers bleak confirmation of the extinction rather than the perpetuation of a lineage—witness to yet another lost cause, this time a eugenic one.

This is the context in which *Flags* refigures the ineffable Sartoris doom in pointedly biological terms, as a "virus" passed down the generations from "that one which dominated them all," Colonel John Sartoris (870). To reframe the family founder as a fountainhead of contagion is an irreverent move, no doubt, but also, I would suggest, a eugenically freighted one. The viral trope, after all, cannot be taken literally: a man cannot pass a virus down to great-grandsons he never lived to see. Rather, the germ invoked here is probably closer to the "bad germ plasm" of eugenics discourse. If so, the Sartoris "virus" signals the corrupting effects of defective heredity. The strong implication, then, is that the family fatality assumes genetic form. As usual, Aunt Jenny sums it up best. "Sartoris," she observes. "It's in the blood.... No earthly use to anyone" (795). None of this bodes well for baby Benbow at the novel's conclusion. Five generations of Sartorises may be enough. Seen in this eugenicist light, the narrative's early account of its "upland country" setting (547), "lying in tilted slopes against the unbroken blue of the hills," may simply signal the onset of yet another dysgenic drama among the nation's white rural hillfolk—Sartorises not excepted.

If *Flags* thus raises doubts about the eugenic fitness of relatively unadulterated white bloodlines at either end of the social spectrum (Sartoris and Snopes), the novel also delves into the eugenic implications and consequences of social, racial, and biological mixture. It does this, however, in a roundabout way. Ironically, the Eugenics Record Office originated as an offshoot of the American Breeders Association, an organization dedicated to the improvement of agricultural stock; apparently, the intellectual leap from the pedigrees of prize animals to the genealogies of degenerate American families was a viable one for Charles Davenport and other Progressive-era thinkers like him. Faulkner brings these connections full circle by bringing into his narrative a pair of dubious animal pedigrees that arguably represent a subtle thought experiment in genetic hybridity. We can start with the novel's well-known encomium to the lowly mule, a tour de force of mock-heroic hyperbole. "Father and mother he does not resemble, sons and daughters he will never have" (780). Call him, if you will, a mongrel Mississippian. Cross-bred and "celibate" (i.e., sterile), "[o]utcast and pariah," "perform[ing] alien actions among alien surroundings," this "object of general derision" serves as a living emblem of unfitness, and he is moreover positioned against a material landscape whose features were already by Faulkner's time coming to signify the white-trash cultural habitat: "rusting cans and broken crockery and worn-out automobile tires on lonely hillsides." If the social anxiety generated by this biological anomaly is thus affiliated with the white underclass, we should remind ourselves, in light of the mule's inability to reproduce, that it is the elite Sartorises, and not the working-class Snopeses or MacCallums featured in the novel, whose lineage has funneled down to a sole surviving male specimen.[8]

Not coincidentally, it is at the remote MacCallum homestead in the Yoknapatawpha hills, where young Bayard goes to seek refuge from the guilt and shame of causing his grandfather's death in an automobile accident, that *Flags* conducts its other bizarre exercise in animal husbandry. Seeking to create a new superbreed of hunting dog, "with a hound's wind and bottom, and a fox's smartness and speed" (827), this family of woodsmen has mated its bluetick hound, General, with a domesticated red fox named Ethel. "Hit's a experiment," one of the sons explains, and the result once again, as with the mule, is a case study in hybridity as genetic disaster: "No two of them looked alike, and none of them looked like any other living creature—Neither fox nor hound; partaking of both, yet neither; and despite their soft infancy, there was about them something monstrous and contradictory and obscene" (828). And dysfunctional: when the MacCallum patriarch dangles a pork rind before them as a bait line, the pups fail to detect it by sight or track it by scent and wind up blundering into the cabin wall, where they remain in "voiceless confusion" until human help arrives (829). "Now, what do you think of them, fer a pack of huntin' dawgs," the old man asks Bayard. "Cant smell, cant bark, and damn ef I believe they kin see." It's the canine equivalent of feeblemindedness: sheer, genetically grounded incompetence.

Appearances by Ethel—first with the MacCallum hounds and then with her motley litter—frame Bayard's brief interlude with the family (813–14, 837), but the significance of this juxtaposition—the degree or even the conceptual basis of correspondence between the grotesque pups and their poor-white breeders—is difficult to pinpoint. These are the same MacCallums, after all, whom Faulkner will celebrate in later short fiction as "tall men": sturdy, proud, and self-sufficient, natural aristocrats in the American grain.[9] That hindsight makes it hard to read the puppies as an image of their human keepers. Yet the text does hint at an analogy between the two. Noting the "bafflement" and "grave horror" with which General contemplates his dysgenic issue, Mr. MacCallum voices his sympathy: "Well, I dont blame the old feller.... Ef I had to look around on a passel of chaps like them and say to myself Them's my boys—" (829). But the exasperation he attributes to General resurfaces only pages later in the old man's words about his own chaps, which echo the language in which he enumerated the inadequacies of the pups: "I be damned ef I aint raised the damdest smartest set of boys in the world. Cant tell 'em nothin', cant learn 'em nothin'; cant even set in front of my own fire fer the whole passel of 'em tellin' me how to run the whole damn country" (835). The point of all this remains unclear. Are the MacCallums the hill-country answer to the Snopeses, an exemplary enclave of rural white homogeneity and authenticity? Are they, like their reengineered foxhounds, a ragtag—if seemingly benign—collection of Mississippi mongrels? It doesn't help matters that Faulkner places the MacCallum patriarch, Kallikak-style, at the head of dual lineages—fathering five boys with his first wife and another with his second—or that all of the sons, from twenty-year-old Buddy to fifty-five-year-old Jackson, seem to have opted for a bachelor's life with their father over marriage and a lineage of their own. What seems indisputable, though, is the anxiety and confusion surrounding questions of purity and hybridity in *Flags*, even when displaced into nonhuman contexts and forms.

It is worth noting that this confusion was a relatively late development in the family studies literature. Early family studies authors showed little concern with the specter of racial mixing. The thing they truly feared was the prospect of defective whiteness "passing" as normal in the general white population and thereby adulterating the white gene pool.[10] The heyday of the eugenics movement in the U.S., from 1877 to 1930, overlaps significantly with the era of legalized segregation. As a result of Jim Crow law and custom, the incidence of miscegenation during this period was by all indications down from the slavery era (see Williamson, *New People* 88–91, 188–90). As a result, the family studies were far more likely to focus on the dangers of inbreeding than of race-mixing; some researchers considered "consanguinity" (by which they typically meant unions between cousins) and incest (between siblings or parent and child) to be genetically transmissible defects (Wray 71). The major exception to this rule? Estabrook and McDougle's *Mongrel Virginians*. As Deutsch (129), Matt Wray (81–82), and others have detailed, *Mongrel Virginians* was conceived as a deliberate effort to throw the rhetorical and ideological muscle of eugenics research behind Virginia's Racial Integrity Law of 1924. The bill, passed at the same session of the state legislature as the sterilization law upheld in *Buck*, placed new restrictions on racial intermarriage. To demonstrate the need for this new law, Estabrook and McDougle sought out subjects who would illustrate the pernicious social effects of race-mixing. Traveling to upland Amherst County (which they rechristened "Ab County," opening their study by creating a fictional Southern county out of an actual one, in a move Faulkner was repeating the same year), they unearthed a sprawling, multigenerational, triracial horde they dubbed the Wins (White-Indian-Negro). Predictably, given the political agenda of the authors, the Win "tribe" proved to be a hotbed not only of miscegenation but of classic dysgenic traits such as feeblemindedness (or "poor mentality"), insanity, and epilepsy; promiscuity, illegitimacy, and prostitution; shiftlessness, dishonesty, and thievery. Curiously, the authors also noted a "high incidence of consanguinity" (152) in this otherwise dangerously heterogeneous clan.

Much as some historians have argued for a distinctively southern form of medical practice shaped by the region's racial institutions and ideology (see, for instance, Breeden), there is a case to be made for *Mongrel Virginians* as introducing a distinctively regional variant on the white-trash family study in which concerns about inbreeding and race-mixing compound rather than contradict one another. If so, this southern turn in the eugenic imaginary, already hinted at in *Flags*, finds more explicit expression in Faulkner's next novel, *The Sound and the Fury*, where the twin shadows of incest and miscegenation haunt the interior life of a southern family whose claims to whiteness grow more dubious with each succeeding generation.

AMERICA'S WORST FAMILY?

In his comprehensive 2009 study of Indiana's "Tribe of Ishmael," Deutsch demystifies the discursive strategies employed by researchers like Oscar McCulloch and the ubiquitous Estabrook to vilify the Ishmaels as (in Deutsch's words) "America's worst family." Indiana's rich and ignominious role in U.S. eugenics history may resonate behind the state's cameo appearances in *The Sound and the Fury*.[11] Indiana, after all, is where a desperate Caddy Compson goes in search of a respectable marriage that can salvage her reputation in the wake of her unwanted pregnancy, and the fiancé she finds at French Lick, Herbert Head, hails from South Bend. Faulkner, however, hardly needed to look beyond the borders of Mississippi to dream up a eugenic nightmare like the Ishmael tribe. For in *The Sound and the Fury*, he has arguably constructed his own version of America's worst family right at home in Yoknapatawpha County. Don't take my word for it—listen to Jason Compson: "I haven't got much pride, I cant afford it with a kitchen full of niggers to feed and robbing the state asylum of its star freshman. Blood, I says, governors and generals. It's a dam good thing we never had any kings and presidents; we'd all be down there at Jackson chasing butterflies" (230); "Like a man would naturally think, one of them is crazy and another one drowned himself and the other one was turned out into the street by her husband, what's the reason the rest of them are not crazy too" (233); "I says no thank you I have all the women I can take care of now if I married a wife she'd probably turn out to be a hophead or something. That's all we lack in this family, I says" (247).

Nothing else in the Faulkner oeuvre compares with the collection of eugenically stigmatized social traits assigned to the Compson family. The list could begin, like the novel, with Benjamin, the poster child for feeblemindedness in modern American literature. If we can trust the anonymous African American voice that offers an alternative perspective on Benjy's thirty-third birthday ("You mean, he been three years old thirty years" [17]), what contemporary eugenicists would have called Benjy's "mental age" would actually classify him as an *imbecile* (with a mental age of three to seven years) rather than, as the *Macbeth* allusion in the novel's title would suggest, an *idiot*, the term intelligence testers reserved for individuals with a mental age of two or below (Deutsch 112; Kevles 78). Consistent with period attitudes toward the retarded, Benjy's eugenic threat is sexualized, as becomes clear when his inarticulate overtures toward the Burgess girl are interpreted as a sexual attack. Though the episode predates present events in the novel by many years (Mr. Compson is still alive at the time, as his discussion of the crisis with Jason reveals [52]), the fate assigned Benjy in the wake of the Burgess encounter, with its overtones of eugenic sterilization *and* racial lynching,[12] is surely on some level a response on Faulkner's part to the public discussions of eugenic sterilization legislation going on in Mississippi as the novelist worked on the early parts of his manuscript—and during the very week, month, and year in which three of the novel's four narrative sections take place. In this context, the Compsons' own efforts to contain Benjy's perceived genetic and sexual menace, first by restricting him to the fenced-off family homeplace, then by putting him under the surgeon's knife, resemble nothing so much as the eugenic measures devised and implemented at state facilities for the mentally retarded such as Mississippi's recently opened School and Colony for the Feebleminded in Ellisville, tracing the same arc from institutional segregation to compulsory sterilization. Seen in this light, the Compson house looks more and more like a contemporary mental institution in its own right, with the novel's opening view "[t]hrough the fence" (3), and its repeated attention to that fence over its first several paragraphs, evoking an inmate's longing gaze past the perimeter of his confinement toward freer, greener pastures beyond.[13] Indeed, from a strictly eugenic standpoint, Benjy's castration could be understood as a tactical improvement on clinical vasectomy (the method of male sterilization most closely associated with sterilization legislation) rather than a crude forerunner of it. For while vasectomy helped ward off the emergence of future generations of defectives, it did nothing to prevent the licentiousness and lust thought by many eugenicists of the period to be genetically linked to feeblemindedness—an irony noted from within the eugenics movement itself.[14] Indeed, some eugenics advocates actually preferred castration as a more comprehensive way to address the problem.

But feeblemindedness is merely the first in a long line of defective traits that plague the House of Compson. Mr. Compson and Uncle Maury are both miserable alcoholics, and Benjy briefly follows in their footsteps when T. P. introduces him to the "sassprilluh" stored in the cellar for Caddy's wedding (20–22, 37–40). Jason is a habitual liar and a thief. The self-pitying Mrs. Compson is an invalid who suffers from either a chronic physical infirmity or a mental one; Maury's "health is bad" as well (44). The elder Quentin fixates on particularly intimate versions of "consanguinity" with his sister as he spirals downward toward madness and suicide. "Nomadism" appears to run rampant in the Compson family, with runaway daughters Caddy and Miss Quentin joined by peripatetic sons like Quentin and Jason, who drift through the urban and small-town spaces of sections two and three. These were all traits attributed to "bad germ plasm," "defective heredity," or the work of recessive genes during the heyday of eugenics literature and social policy.

Moreover, the Compson family closely reproduces the gendered canons of social deviance that structured eugenic ideology. The men's problems all point, in various ways, to their unsuitedness for a modern bourgeois work regime, to a basic absence or failure of industriousness: from Quentin's school truancy (admittedly a problem for both Quentins) to Jason's numerous breaks from the hardware store to forge checks or chase his niece around town (despite his own protest that he "likes work" [196]), to Maury's economic parasitism, to Mr. Compson's drinking (Jason ruefully observes that "after a while Father wouldn't even come down town anymore but just sat all day with the decanter" [233]). Female deviance, on the other hand, is rooted in the reproductive rather than the productive realm. The Compson girls, Caddy and daughter Quentin, exhibit the "traits" of promiscuity and illegitimacy, the telltale symptoms of sexual immorality that led many sexually adventurous (or simply sexually active) girls of their era, irrespective of intelligence, to be diagnosed as "morons" (like Carrie Buck), sent to institutions for the feebleminded, and/or surgically sterilized.[15] Indeed, Jason envisions something along precisely these lines for his sister and niece. Reflecting on Benjy's castration—and very possibly influenced by the political debate over sterilization building in his home state at the very moment he is speaking—he adds, "they never started soon enough with their cutting, and they quit too quick. I know at least two more that needed something like that, and one of them not over a mile away, either" (263; and see 253).[16] The inordinate time and energy the Compsons spend worrying about and trying to control the sexuality and fertility of the family daughters mimics contemporary anxieties about "moron" girls and the "harlots" and "prostitutes" that populate the family studies. Jason, in fact, at one point accuses Caddy of prostitution (209), but if we follow the practice of some eugenic authors and define "family" loosely enough to include a figure like Jason's Memphis consort Lorraine ("a good honest whore" [233]) within the Compson genealogy, then that "defect" is already covered.

Other aspects of Compson family structure dovetail suggestively with motifs from eugenics discourse. Faulkner's decision to bless (or curse) Mr. and Mrs. Compson with the specific number of four children, for example, makes this group of siblings precisely the right size to function as a kind of living laboratory or natural experiment in the distribution of genetic traits. Recall that, in the simplistic understanding of Mendel's laws that characterized the eugenics movement into the 1920s, defective traits were thought to be single "unit characters" carried on recessive alleles. That meant that dysgenic traits could skip a generation, carried but not expressed by heterozygous parents capable of passing the defect along to their offspring. Statistically, the chance of this happening in the next generation—of the trait resurfacing in the child of heterozygous carriers—would be "about 25 percent," as Edward East noted (44). This is why Henry Goddard, for example, could write that such unions yield "three normals to one defective" (quoted in Rafter, *Creating* 143); or Harry Laughlin could argue that the presence of "as few as one in four 'hereditary degenerates' born to a family" would implicate the parents as carriers eligible for sterilization under his Model Law (Lombardo 142); or Joseph DeJarnette, an expert witness at the *Buck* trial who displayed a decidedly less than expert grasp of the matter, could explain that "in breeding people, a man that has a certain quality of mind will breed one-fourth a certain way" (quoted in Lombardo 123). The Compson sibling cohort perfectly accommodates this one-in-four structure—a case study in Mendelian mathematics. Starting with the superficial fact that only one out of the four siblings is female, we could go on to observe that many of the group's more eugenically unsavory traits follow the same distribution pattern. One out of four is an imbecile. One out of four dreams of committing incest. One out of four is a thief. One out of four is promiscuous and bears an illegitimate child. One out of four might be considered insane. One in four is a demonstrated alcohol abuser. Poor Mr. and Mrs. Compson! The demographics of sibling deviance point a devastating finger of genetic blame in their direction.

What is more, the Compson "tribe" features the same three-generational structure that played such an important role in the *Buck* case. This is as true in 1898, when the household includes Mrs. Compson's dying mother, as in 1928, when it includes Caddy's bastard daughter. It is really the women of the family, then—and not, as in *Flags* and *Father Abraham*, the men—who form the basis of its trigenerational schemes, once again echoing *Buck*, whose notorious "three generations of imbeciles" were all from the female line.[17] So if we pause for a moment to ask why Miss Quentin is so desperate to cash the fifty-dollar money order she expects from her mother, the echoes of *Buck* may grow even stronger. Jason recounts the scene:

> "Tell me what you've got to have money for," I says.
> "I've got to have it," she says. She was looking at me. Then all of a sudden she quit looking at me without moving her eyes at all. I knew

she was going to lie. "It's some money I owe," she says. "I've got to pay it today."

"Who to?" I says. [...]

"It's a girl," she says. "It's a girl. I borrowed some money from a girl." (214)

If this flimsy explanation is no more satisfying to the reader than to Jason, then why *does* Quentin need the money? Could it possibly be for the same reason that Lafe MacCallum gives Dewey Dell Bundren ten dollars to carry with her to Jefferson in *As I Lay Dying*? To take care of an unwanted pregnancy? The wording of the passage hints loudly at the possibility: why do you need the money, Jason asks; "It's a girl," Quentin announces. Is Caddy's sexual history repeating itself here in full, all the way down to illegitimate conception? If so, then eighteen-year-old Quentin in 1928 would find herself in the same role that the Virginia authorities erroneously assigned to sixteen-year-old Carrie Buck in 1924, that of an illegitimate daughter with an illegitimate child of her own, the crucial link in a three-generational chain of deviance. And the analogy with *Buck* would only grow firmer should that unborn child indeed prove to be—like Vivian Buck—"a girl."

But however we choose to understand Quentin's predicament, *The Sound and the Fury*'s attention to female generational linkages (a new focus in the Faulkner oeuvre) leads the novel to another issue that preoccupied the eugenics movement: the disastrous social consequences of bad mothering. As Rafter and others have shown, the bad mother is a stock figure in the family studies literature. In the movement's gendered "genealogical imaginary" (Yukins 166), mothers were usually considered more responsible than fathers for the transmission of genetic defects to their children, just as "moron" girls were thought to be more dangerous as a sexual threat and genetic menace than their male counterparts.[18] These beliefs affected eugenics policy: evidence suggests that sterilizations were performed at a higher rate on women than on men (Noll, "Far Greater" 38–39, 49–50). Whether as sources of defective traits such as feeblemindedness, vectors of congenital illnesses such as syphilis, or indifferent or incompetent nurturers, mothers bear the brunt of the blame for the unfitness that eugenics researchers inevitably found in the deviant individuals and groups they studied. Dugdale, for instance, traced the problems of his white-trash Jukes back five generations to a group of six sisters (Dugdale 37), one of whom (rechristened "Ada Juke" by Dugdale) was already infamous in social-science literature as "Margaret, Mother of Criminals" (Lombardo 8–9; and see Yukins 174). The dual-lineage methodology of Goddard's Kallikak study virtually guaranteed the "discovery" of a bad mother as the source of genetic ruin, since the "good" and "bad" branches of the family stemmed from a single Revolutionary-era sire but two distinct consorts—one, "a Quaker woman of sound family" (Rafter, *White Trash* 75), who produced an upstanding line of responsible citizens, while the other, a "feebleminded tavern wench" (Lombardo 124), presided over a genealogical Hall of Shame. The *Buck* case sounded a similar note. Superintendent Priddy concluded that the "line of baleful heredity" responsible for Carrie's alleged defects came through her mother, Emma (quoted in Lombardo 110), and at the trial, Estabrook went farther to speculate, with little apparent ground, that Emma had inherited feeblemindedness from *her* mother (Lombardo 129).

Few voices in Faulkner sound the bad mother theme as stridently, and with such a sense of betrayal, as Quentin Compson in section two of *The Sound and the Fury*. It is his distinctive eugenic motif and obsession as sterilization is Jason's.[19] Thinking of his own raising, he condemns Mrs. Compson as a nonentity—"*If I'd just had a mother so I could say Mother Mother*" (172)—only to wish she were more of one when his thoughts turn to Caddy's upbringing: "*My little sister had no. If I could say Mother. Mother*" (95). He even fantasizes about *being* a mother, or more precisely about not being one, holding the paternal phallus at bay to prevent the dysgenic conception of Caddy's seducer, Dalton Ames (80). These associations reach a crescendo in Quentin's nightmarish image of the maternal body as biological prison. The Compson parents sometimes indulge—in the presence of their children—in a kind of eugenic accounting or scorekeeping, alternately claiming and disclaiming specific traits for the paternal Compson and maternal Bascomb lineages. Mrs. Compson, for instance, attempts to disavow genetic responsibility for Benjy, Quentin, and Caddy—and later for her granddaughter—by chalking up their shortcomings to "bad blood" (104; cf. 260, 299) that she implicitly attributes to her husband's line. Quentin, however, isn't buying, vilifying Mrs. Compson as a literal matrix of eugenic horror:

> When I was little there was a picture in one of our books, a dark place into which a single weak ray of light came slanting upon two faces lifted out of the shadow.... It was torn out, jagged out. I was glad. I'd have to turn back to it until the dungeon was Mother herself she and Father upward into weak light holding hands and us somewhere below them without even a ray of light. (173)

In an important essay that takes its title from this passage, Noel Polk has also identified the bad mother as a signature element of Faulkner writing at this stage of his career (see Polk, "The Dungeon"). But Polk's Freudian analysis has less to say about how the novelist's running dialogue with eugenics discourse throughout this period helps give this figure its special biological menace, the "shadow" that reaches from the mother's body to enshroud her children. For Quentin to remember or perhaps just to imagine the page that bears this picture and the maternal space it delineates as "torn out" of the volume in which it appears smacks of eugenic violence against the mother's body—a sterilization procedure displaced into a less overtly invasive form.

For the Compsons, the price of the family's numerous offenses against eugenic standards of social propriety is racial anxiety about and within the bloodline. As Wray and Rafter have shown, to fall under the scrutiny of eugenics researchers was for many families to fall afoul of, if not altogether out of, whiteness itself. The family studies in particular contributed to the development of what Wray calls the "stigmatype" (23) of a white-trash social *and racial* identity that loosely overlapped but did not coincide with normative middle-class U.S. whiteness. On several occasions in *The Sound and the Fury* the Compsons express concern that the family's claim to whiteness has been compromised. The behavior of the girls in particular, first Caddy and then Quentin, elicits racial doubt and suspicion. Caddy is chided by her mother for the unladylike way she carries five-year-old Benjy around the house: "You'll injure your back. All of our woman have prided themselves on their carriage. Do you want to look like a washerwoman" (63). This is a racially charged as well as class-inflected image: in the world of white privilege Mrs. Compson invokes (but no longer fully occupies), black women do the washing, as evidenced by the 1928 scene in which the interplay between Luster and the unnamed figures "washing down at the branch" (14) clearly identifies the latter as African American. Quentin is more explicit in pointing out the racial overtones of his sister's sexual behavior: "*Why wont you bring him to the house, Caddy? Why must you do like nigger women do in the pasture the ditches the dark woods hot hidden furious in the dark woods*" (92).[20] Jason picks up the theme in remarks to his niece: "Everybody in this town knows what you are.... But I've got a position in this town, and I'm not going to have any member of my family going on like a nigger wench" (189).[21] We begin to sense the enormous social and racial pressure that falls on the daughters of elite (or once-elite) white families like the Compsons, the burden of preserving, and *embodying*, the racial integrity of the family name. Nor are the Compson men exempt from racial suspicion. Quentin sounds like a black man ("like they [talk] in minstrel shows") to three boys he encounters near the river in Cambridge (120). And then there is Benjy, whose plight in so many ways evokes that of the black man in the South: stripped of his birth name and given a biblical name in its place, castrated for an alleged sexual assault on a white girl, confined to the grounds of a former plantation and condemned to dependency there. Small wonder, then, that the family is haunted by fears of racial falling. More and more, it seems, with each new generation, to be a Compson is to be (in Wray's words) not quite white. As with the Compson horse that breaks Quentin's arm—"a blood horse ... [i]n the stable ... but under leather a cur" (112)—an elite pedigree is no guarantee of eugenic fitness in Faulkner's version of the family study.

THE HILL FOLK

Where attention to eugenic issues is concerned, Faulkner's next published novel, *As I Lay Dying*, picks right up where *The Sound and the Fury* leaves off. Again we encounter a copious inventory of dysgenic traits exhibiting the differently gendered criteria of deviance: Darl Bundren's madness, the illegitimate pregnancies of Addie and Dewey Dell, Anse's temperamental unsuitedness to labor ("he tells people that if he ever sweats, he will die" [17]), the idiosyncratic work habits of his boys, threats (no longer, as in *The Sound and the Fury*, merely idle) to send family members to Jackson, physical disfigurements like Anse's hump (86, 170), and so on. We might even speak of a clan proclivity for nomadism expressed in Dewey Dell's wandering past the turnrow with Lafe (27), Jewel's nocturnal ramblings, or the whole family's slow drift across the Yoknapatawpha landscape as the novel unfolds. Dewey Dell's unborn child brings to the Bundren household a trigenerational sweep, once again transacted through the female line, with whose eugenic implications we are by now familiar. And the bad mother theme resonates through Addie's wasted physical condition and candid admissions of adultery and maternal indifference, Dewey Dell's animosity and resentment toward her own fetus ("God gave women a sign when something has happened bad" [58]), Darl's dada refrain that "Jewel's mother is a horse" (95)—the nearest thing, phonetically, to calling her a whore—and his remark to younger brother Vardaman that when it comes to mothers, "I haven't got ere one" (101). Vardaman's mother, of course, is a fish—cold-blooded and alien (84). Indeed, whereas Quentin Compson fixates on the mother as biological dungeon, Addie Bundren's putrefying corpse hints at an even deeper level of horror: the mother as biological slough.

For the remainder of this section, however, I want to focus on three aspects of the novel that carry Faulkner's ongoing dialogue with eugenics forward onto new ground. We can start with *As I Lay Dying*'s physical and social topography. More decisively than any of the Faulkner narratives that precede it, *As I Lay Dying* is set in the rural, working-class, white hill-country world of the eugenic family studies. The text obsessively notes that the Bundrens are hill folk. The novel's opening section follows Darl and Jewel from their bottomland cottonfield up "the bluff" to the family homestead (4). So steep is this bluff that portly Doctor Peabody, summoned from town just in time to preside over Addie's death, has to be pulled up by rope, prompting his wry commentary on the spectacle of "[a] man seventy years old, weighing two hundred and off pounds, being hauled up and down a damn mountain" (43). Far more than "Sartoris" or "Compson" and roughly on a par with "Snopes," the Bundren surname evokes the patronizing pseudonyms of family studies literature; indeed, in the same year that Faulkner published *As I Lay Dying*, the Reverend Ira Caldwell published a five-part study in the journal *Eugenics* about an especially abject band of Georgia whites he dubbed the "Bunglers" (Miller 125–27, Palmer 135–36). Finally, the social demographic featured in the novel includes nary a

Compson, Sartoris, or any other representative of Yoknapatawpha's planter elite. The nearest equivalent the novel can produce is probably Peabody, from the county's professional class. This too is consistent with the family studies, focusing on poor whites but written by middle-class professionals.

At the same time, the novel's innovative structure bears striking affinities with family studies methodology. As Rafter (*White Trash* 2) and Wray (71) explain, the fieldwork for these studies typically included numerous interviews with family members, friends, neighbors, more distant acquaintances, doctors, and other public functionaries. The authors then compiled these field notes into more polished narratives, often with a strong analytical and statistical dimension. On the page, the sixty interior monologues that comprise *As I Lay Dying* read like field interview material transcribed from the oral information-gathering stage of this process, ranging from brief, cryptic remarks ("My mother is a fish") to extended meditations and reminiscences, such as Darl's lyrical account of the river crossing (141–49). While it could be argued that the monologues of *The Sound and the Fury* perform a similar function—like lengthy depositions from some sort of legal or social casework involving the Compsons—the number and diversity of the informants in *As I Lay Dying* much more directly evokes family studies research. Seven of the fifteen narrators are Bundrens themselves, joined by neighbors (Tull, Cora, Armstid), acquaintances (Samson), a doctor (Peabody), a minister (Whitfield), and a pair of total strangers from Mottson (Moseley) and Jefferson (MacGowan): more or less the complete range of subjects canvassed in family studies fieldwork. The task of constructing a larger narrative framework for these voices, however, and of arriving at an overarching social and moral interpretation of the Bundrens—of writing up the field notes—falls to the reader, an ingenious way, perhaps, of enlisting readerly participation, or collusion, in the eugenic enterprise.

When we take up this challenge, the story that emerges is in several key respects a tale of the Progressive era in U.S. society and culture, a period that was not coincidentally the high-water mark of the eugenics movement in America. In a highly original reading of the novel, Patrick O'Donnell frames the Bundrens' journey to Jefferson as a socially and politically fraught encounter between an unruly, "nomadic" family (86)—with its pockets of privacy and interiority, transgression and madness—and the modern state apparatus: the Bundrens' gradual negotiation with, discipline by, and incorporation into "the State and its striations, its systems of communication and exchange" (93). From the moment the road—the publicly funded project for which Anse reserves such special venom (Faulkner, *As I Lay Dying* 35–37)—presents itself before the Bundren homestead, the family and its members are pulled inexorably toward the defining institutions, spaces, and representatives of the state, in "an extensive series of encounters" with "doctors, police, clergy, and merchants" (O'Donnell 86); "county health and sanitation laws" (88); officials from the state mental hospital (87); the public sphere more broadly considered as a zone of gossip and scandal, "communal discussion and advice" (86); the law and custom of "contractual obligations" (86); and lastly, with the introduction of the new "Mrs Bundren" on the novel's closing page, "the public institution of marriage" (87).[22] Small wonder, then, that the Bundren "pilgrimage comes to a halt in front of the Jefferson courthouse" (86). For O'Donnell, the novel ultimately dispels the "fantasy" of a strict division between public and private—of the family as a haven of "inwardness" and "desire"—by portraying the Bundrens in Althusserian terms, "as a commodified entity that works ... according to the law" (93).

O'Donnell is less interested, however, in probing the links between the tale he excavates and its particular historical and cultural context. (His concept of "nomadism," for instance, comes not from the family studies but from Deleuze and Guattari.) But the problematic he describes, the "negotiation and legitimation of the family's continuance within the bounds of state authority" (84), lay at the very heart of Progressive-era ideology, with its emphasis on the state's right and *need* to intervene in the private realm (the home, the family, the body) in the name of the public good. A very similar "negotiation" was at work in eugenics discourse and policy, which also subjected individuals and families to specific forms of state discipline and control, and indeed in the family studies themselves, which, as the movement's leading arm of knowledge production, directed an especially pernicious form of knowledge/power against their rural subjects, often with the explicit purpose of justifying even more egregious forms of state encroachment such as institutionalization and sterilization.[23] O'Donnell's account of this negotiation process is cautiously neutral: the Bundrens pay a cost for their entrance into the state apparatus—Addie and Darl are the price of admission—but the remaining family members receive benefits as well, such as a "civic" identity and the legitimacy it entails (87). But it is worth pointing out that for many marginal white families like the Bundrens, and indeed for all of the groups featured in the family studies, the encounter with the state—its penal and criminal justice systems, its social services, hospitals, and mental health networks, its moralizing ministers—was an unmitigated disaster, marked by disempowerment, stigmatization, and invasive violence. The closing sections of *As I Lay Dying* bear witness to this disempowerment and dependency: to be sure, the Bundrens' arrival in Jefferson brings access to new opportunities and pleasures, but family members are also shown borrowing money, bumming shovels, being sexually exploited, and enduring the gentle and not-so-gentle ridicule of townfolk like Doctor Peabody.

There is also a racial dimension to this process that O'Donnell never really addresses. During the Progressive era, the modern state with which the Bundrens find themselves "negotiating" was to a very real degree what sociologists Michael Omi and Howard Winant call a white "racial formation," as U.S. nationalism and U.S. whiteness went largely hand in hand throughout the period. In his contribution to this volume, Peter Lurie suggests that the Bundrens' townward odyssey doubles as a movement toward and into whiteness, an introduction to new modern strategies and resources for comprehending, pursuing, and consolidating a normative (and national) white racial identity (151–52). But in many ways, the family's racial trajectory is just the opposite of the path Lurie describes. For as the Bundrens travel father and father from their home, farther from the friends and neighbors who know and share something of their life and history—and as the stench from Addie's corpse becomes more and more intolerable—their behavior seems more and more outrageous and incomprehensible in the eyes of the strangers they meet along the way. They grow more and more abject, trashier and trashier, less secure than ever in their grip on whiteness. Fittingly, then, their bodies darken on the journey. Vardaman and Dewey Dell's legs appear black as they lie on a pallet on the Gillespie family's porch, half in and half out of the moonlight (216); later that night, Jewel's back turns black "like a nigger's" from the greasy homemade ointment applied to the burns he suffered while rescuing Addie's coffin from their hosts' burning barn (224); Cash's foot turns black, also "like a nigger's," beneath the cement cast in which the family has ludicrously attempted to set his broken leg; and later, as Peabody prepares to remove the cast, and "sixty-odd square inches of skin" in the bargain (240), Cash is still not quite white, with a "face about the color of blotting paper." This fall from racial grace reaches a kind of nadir at the bottom of a hill outside Jefferson, where a trio of African Americans recoil in "outrage" at the odor emanating from the Bundren wagon—black people commenting derisively on the way white people smell (229). The irony underscores the role of modernizing, urbanizing environments like Jefferson in accentuating the racial marginality and misperformance of the rural white underclass that peoples the eugenic family studies. Along with its genealogy, the Bundren story bears out Wray's account (65–95) of how poor-white social deviance was constructed by the eugenics movement as a thoroughly racialized and racializing phenomenon, as the mark of a degenerate, biologically alien population at once within and out of step with "the white race."

"CRIMPS AND SPUNGS AND FEEBS"

It can be easy to miss, but *Sanctuary* (drafted before *As I Lay Dying* in 1929 but published after it, in 1931) contains its own narrative of a family of rural white hill folk drawn into the clutches of the state apparatus. Much as the road catalyzes the Bundrens' townward march and inevitable arrival under the thumb of the state, here it is a telephone, one of O'Donnell's "systems of communication and exchange," that starts the Goodwins along the road to Jefferson (in the sheriff's car) and into their own round of negotiations with the modern state. This is in all likelihood the same road from Frenchman's Bend that the Bundrens were unable to take to town because the bridge over the Yoknapatawpha River was washed out. But in most other respects, when the Goodwins come to town in *Sanctuary*, it's *As I Lay Dying* all over again, all the way down to the corpse.

This clan is worth a closer look, since it dominates the first hundred pages of the novel before dwindling down to a more nuclear configuration, and a more secondary role, in Jefferson. It is headed by the bootlegger Lee Goodwin and his common-law wife, the former Memphis prostitute Ruby Lamar. The Goodwins are joined at the Old Frenchman Place, the antebellum ruin where Lee has set up his operation, by Pap, a decrepit old man, and by Lee's assistant, Tommy. Despite his name, Pap's precise place in the Goodwin genealogy remains unclear. "I never knew who he was, who he was kin to," recalls Horace Benbow of his visit to the Frenchman Place in the novel's opening chapters (110). "Maybe not to anybody." (Indeed, Horace briefly wonders whether Pap might just come with the house.) Tommy, whose degree of kinship with Lee, Ruby, or Pap is also unspecified—*Sanctuary* can be as hazy in its evocations of family ties among its poor-white subjects as the family studies themselves—isn't just hill folk but an out-and-out hillbilly: barefoot and in overalls, with an affinity for "fiddle music" (78), "a sunburned thatch of hair, matted and foul" (10), "a soft short beard like dirty gold in color," and a jug of moonshine at the ready. On the long, lurid night that Temple Drake and Gowan Stevens spend at the Frenchman Place, the Goodwins are joined by Popeye, a Memphis gangster who markets Lee's liquor, and by a drunken accomplice named Van. For this one night the bootlegging clan reproduces the structure of Temple's elite Jackson family (see 289–90), with Pap serving as the underclass equivalent of her elderly father, Judge Drake; Lee, Tommy, Popeye, and Van standing in for her four brothers; and Ruby functioning as a more worldly version of virgin Temple herself. But there is a classic eugenic third generation present as well at the Frenchman Place: the Goodwins have a son, an infant Ruby keeps in a cardboard box in the kitchen "so the rats cant get to him" (18).

A hillbilly, a gangster, a good-hearted hustler, a bootlegger, a worthless old man—Faulkner is clearly flirting with various forms of white-trash caricature at the Frenchman Place, and with eugenic stigmatypes as well. The household teems with defective or deviant traits. In addition to the general atmosphere of criminality and violence, Pap is both blind and deaf, traits that were sources of eugenic concern in the 1920s, when there were in fact efforts to introduce sterilization legislation for the blind (Black 145). Slow-witted Tommy clearly evokes period conceptions of feeblemindedness; he is the obvious object of Ruby's remark that she cooks "for crimps and spungs and feebs" (9), and on another occasion he is described as wearing an expression of "imbecile glee" (47).[24] Ruby's own Manuel Street past attests to her sexual immorality, and—once again following the gendered schemes of deviance promoted by eugenics literature—Lee's *lumpenproletariat* status places him in an eccentric relation to the bourgeois economic regime and its models of productive male labor. In this context it is telling that "nowhere" around the Frenchman Place is there "any sign of husbandry—plow or tool" (41), and "in no direction" any "planted field in sight." In addition to being bootleggers, Goodwin and Van are drunks. Even the baby is sickly and weak, a suggestive symbol—if not an outright symptom—of genetic dysfunction and decline. (And Popeye is a whole other ball of wax we'll get to later.) To Temple's anxious question, then, of whether the bootleggers are "just like other people" (56), *Sanctuary* would appear to answer, "Not on your life."

In the novel's shift to new settings in the aftermath of Tommy's murder and Temple's corncob rape at the Frenchman Place and its emphasis on the increasingly interimplicated predicaments of Temple and Horace, we can lose sight of the way that Ruby's phone call to the sheriff to report "[a] dead man" in her barn is the beginning of the end for the Goodwins, the inaugural event in the dismantling of this trashy clan by the intrepid forces of the state. That the Goodwins don't have a phone—that Ruby must walk two miles to the Tull household to use one—is symptomatic of the extent to which they have up to this moment remained off the grid, outside the state's elaborate mechanisms of scrutiny and surveillance. That all changes with the phone call. And it is equally symptomatic that once this machinery kicks into gear and the trek toward town begins for the Goodwins, the first member of the clan to reach Jefferson is actually Tommy, laid out on a cooling board in the front room of a funeral parlor on the town square (112–13). Hypervisible, helpless against whatever indignities the townfolk or legal officials may have in store for it, Tommy's corpse signals what is in store for the other Goodwins transported to Jefferson, especially Lee, who winds up a spectacle and a dead man himself by the end of his brief tenure in town.

Indeed, the three principal Goodwins, like the Bundrens before them, are pulled into a comprehensive network of institutional and state power that, in Foucauldian terms, finds their poor-white delinquency and difference useful indeed.[25] Lee, of course, enters the penal and criminal justice systems, on a treadmill from the county jail to the county courthouse and back again. Every item of material evidence at his trial signifies rural deviance: a "bullet from Tommy's skull" (269) evokes violent crime, "a stoneware jug containing corn whiskey" conjures up bootlegging and drunkenness, and a stained corncob (283) hints not just at backwoods outhouse etiquette but also—as the District Attorney, with the help of two other public functionaries, "the chemist and the gynecologist" (283), manages to insinuate—at a far darker and more aberrant scenario. Meanwhile, Ruby and the baby are assigned to Horace Benbow's one-man version of the social services sector, shuttled from lodging to lodging, advanced small sums of money, examined by medical authorities when the child's health worsens (135). All three become the subject of commentary by local ministers (128), and malicious gossip circulates throughout Jefferson's private homes and public spaces to supply an additional level of social control. In some ways, the journey of hayseeds Virgil Snopes and Fonzo Winbush to barber's college in Memphis (188–99) is a comic version of this white social trajectory from rural sanctuaries to the urban corridors of state power.[26] But there's nothing comic about the Goodwins' situation in Jefferson. The family is utterly undone. Indeed, we can already sense the social pressure that mounts behind the encounter between the modern state and poor-white clans like the Goodwins when Ruby identifies herself on the phone to the sheriff as "Mrs Goodwin" (105) rather than as Ruby Lamar—a concession to middlebrow sexual mores that the District Attorney will later attempt to exploit at Lee's murder trial, where, after Ruby allows herself to be summoned to the witness stand as "Mrs Goodwin," he attempts to maneuver her into conceding that Lee is merely her common-law husband (269–70). (Tommy similarly falls afoul of the coroner over the matter of *his* last name [113].) Finally, at the other end of the disciplinary spectrum, there is Pap, never seen again in the novel after the state comes calling for his keepers, apparently left to fend for himself back in the hills.

As in *As I Lay Dying*, the white-trash odyssey into civic space that is depicted in *Sanctuary* carries distinct racial overtones. Both Temple and Horace describe Popeye as a "black" man over the course of the novel (7, 42), but the aura of blackness that gathers around Lee Goodwin has far more destructive consequences. As a bootlegger during a period when alcohol was a source of racialized sexual anxiety in the white imagination (Williamson, *Rage* 142), Goodwin would have been a racially suspect figure even before the sensational allegation at his trial that he has raped a white woman. Certainly his fate at the hands of lynchers the night after the allegation surfaces in court (295–96) demonstrates the degree to which he has forfeited his claims to whiteness and become associated in the town's white mind with the black beast rapist of southern racist mythology. The mob not only burns Goodwin but also, the novel strongly implies, mutilates and perhaps rapes him as well, thus closing out Goodwin's Jefferson journey with an ironic recapitulation of the same crimes—murder and sexual assault—that prompted it in the first place. Meanwhile, Ruby and her son are tarred with a similar brush, slipping farther and farther down Jefferson's racial ladder until the only white person who will offer them a place for the night is an unhinged old crone known for trafficking in spells with African American customers (200).[27] And the cloying, estranging materializations of whiteness at work in the novel's descriptions of the baby's "blueish eyelids," "lead-colored cheeks," and "color of weak milk" (120, 160) further emphasize its distance from a normative white racial identity.

As an addendum to its account of what, with a nod to southern eugenics history, we might call the Good-Win Tribe, *Sanctuary* unveils a sociological case history in its final chapter that reads like a succinct family study in its own right. Though it takes place in the urban environment of Pensacola, the story of Popeye's birth and early childhood exhibits many of the stock features of family studies narrative. His father's itinerant lifestyle as a professional strikebreaker (303), along with his mother's upbringing in the transient atmosphere of a boardinghouse (302), hints at nomadism as a family trait that later expresses itself in Popeye's travels to "Mobile and then New Orleans and then Memphis" and back home to Florida (309). A different sort of wandering leads the mother into fornication, illegitimate pregnancy, and a case of syphilis she passes along to her child (304). Popeye is developmentally disabled from birth, precisely the sort of child who in the early decades of the twentieth century would have been diagnosed as feebleminded: at age three, he "looked about one" (305), and "he did not learn to walk and talk until he was about four years old" (304). In keeping with period anxieties about the feebleminded, Popeye turns out to be a moral delinquent as well, a sociopath who cuts a pair of pet birds and "a half-grown kitten" to pieces with scissors (309) and shuttles through the social services system, with stops as "a kind of day-pupil at an institution" (308) and as an inmate at "a home for incorrigible children" (309), before graduating to a life of crime and a second career as a sexual pervert and predator who menaces the genetic integrity of the highborn (singling out elite Temple as his first "serious" girlfriend). Moreover, if all this weren't bad enough, Faulkner throws a third generation into the mix, in the person of Popeye's maternal grandmother, a pyromaniac and sociopath in her own right, who goes out in a Bertha Mason–style blaze of glory after setting the boardinghouse on fire—a true madwoman in the attic. In this context, the grandmother's earlier remark to a policeman who comments on her cracked sense of humor—"I bring down the house" (307)—could be read as a grim genealogical pun, the confession of a classic eugenics-era bad mother. With nomadism, licentiousness, illegitimacy, disease and invalidism, and violent crime all lurking in the family tree, the House of Popeye is built on decidedly dysgenic foundations.

When Popeye finally runs up against the law in Alabama—arrested, tried, and sentenced to death for a murder he did not commit (309)—he is treated to much the same parade of state and civic functionaries that Lee Goodwin encountered on being brought to Jefferson: policemen, lawyers, judges, jailers, ministers, and a sheriff who does double duty as Popeye's executioner (309–16). It's the same date with institutional destiny and social control that was the explicit agenda of the family studies, lying in wait for white trash whenever it came to town. Indeed, when we bear in mind that the gap between Popeye's actual and "mental" ages would have classified him as feebleminded, his execution begins to look less like a legal punishment for wrongdoing, a talionic eye for an eye, than like a eugenic elimination of the unfit. There were among eugenics advocates of this period some who did not flinch at the prospect of euthanizing the unfit. The brothel madam Reba Rivers comes close to such a sentiment in *Sanctuary*. Of Ruby's unfortunate baby and the dire future that awaits it, she comments, "It better not been born at all. . . . None of them had" (212). And only a few pages later, Horace Benbow makes the theme chillingly explicit, as he reflects on a disillusioning interview with Temple in her brothel room.

> Better for her if she were dead tonight, Horace thought, walking on. For me, too. He thought of her, Popeye, the woman, the child, Goodwin, all put into a single chamber, bare, lethal, immediate, and profound: a single blotting instant between the indignation and the surprise. And I too, thinking how that were the only solution. Removed, cauterised out of the old and tragic flank of the world. (221)

Horace's imagery directly invokes the "lethal chamber" of turn-of-the-century eugenics debate, proposed as a method of euthanasia well before it was adopted for criminal executions ... and for Nazi genocide (see Black 247–51). If *The Sound and the Fury* envisions the liberal use of compulsory sterilization and *As I Lay Dying* dramatizes the impact of institutional segregation, it falls to *Sanctuary* to predict the inexorable drift of a eugenic imaginary toward the final ("the only"?) solution.

THE FAULKNER FAMILY STUDIES

The discourse of eugenics represented a complex, ambivalent cultural legacy for Faulkner as he wrote his way into Yoknapatawpha and the genealogical structures at its imaginative core. During these germinal years, he created a significant cohort of characters, and indeed entire family lines, that exhibit nearly the entire range of social traits identified by the eugenics movement as hereditary defects, and he created other characters who speak and/or think in the conceptual language of eugenics. This is hardly to say, however, that his relationship to eugenics discourse was a passive or uncritical one. For the narratives I have examined here also engage eugenic tropes, classifications, and discursive strategies in order to expose, interrogate, or challenge them. For one thing, they recognize the significant—if not necessarily all-determining—role of environment alongside heredity in the formation of behavior, including the deviant behaviors the eugenicists liked to blame on bad genes. This is the subtext of the accusation Miss Quentin levels at Jason at the Compson dinner table—"If I'm bad, it's because I had to be. You made me" (260)—a claim that the novel on the whole bears out. By the same token, Darl Bundren's madness arguably owes as much to his early childhood environment, the sibling structure and parent-child dynamics that Addie so cynically manipulates, as to any genetic predisposition to mental illness. And Popeye's case history in chapter 31 of *Sanctuary* is no less persuasive as an anatomy of a pathological childhood social environment than as a study in three generations of defective heredity.

Moreover, as novels like *Flags in the Dust* and *The Sound and the Fury* demonstrate, Faulkner was willing to direct family studies methodology toward the analysis and critique of elite white bloodlines like the Compsons and Sartorises as well as toward more conventional accounts of the rural poor. The family studies genre originated with Francis Galton's celebratory account of "hereditary genius" among elite English families, including his own (English 6), but by the turn of the century the focus had shifted to the white underclass, where it remained through the 1920s and into the Depression years. As he fictionalized the form, however, Faulkner also expanded its range to permit a critique of southern ruling-class ideology. By assigning genealogies of deviance and decline to the regional elite, he undercut their claims to legitimacy, power, and privilege. Including racial privilege. Indeed, the presence of a Gibson "genealogy" in *The Sound and the Fury*—three generations of hardworking, churchgoing, respectable African Americans who bear legitimate children, sound of mind and body, and who by and large meet the challenges of their modernizing world—works precisely to underscore this point, to model black fitness as a foil to Compson unfitness, the white family's fundamental inability and unwillingness to face the demands of a new century.[28]

Finally, Faulkner brings to his family studies an emphasis on and respect for the interiority of his subjects that was typically absent from eugenics discourse. Rafter has criticized the "relentless objectification" at work in the family studies literature, its

> insistence on turning people into things. That members of the bad families may have had their own points of view on the conditions and activities described in these works seems not to have occurred to the authors.... By denying their subjects an independent point of view, the authors denied them authority over their own lives. The "defectives" lost their voice, as the authors assumed the ability to speak for (or, rather, against) them. (*White Trash* 24–25)

Similarly, in his history of *Buck v. Bell*, Lombardo offers a withering indictment of the process of silencing and objectification at work at the trial, as Carrie Buck's own attorney colluded with the defense to deprive his client of a voice (see especially 135, 147–48, 155–56). Faulkner's experiments with interior monologue in the late 1920s should be seen and appreciated in this context. By introducing this narrative strategy into his family studies of the

Compsons and Bundrens, he "ventilated" the genre, opening it up to the perspectives, thoughts, sensations, and emotions of its marginalized white subjects. In *The Sound and the Fury* and *As I Lay Dying*, the feebleminded receive a voice ("Caddy smelled like trees"), an unwed mother can gain a hearing ("I feel like a wet seed wild in the hot blind earth"), and the white poor talk back to the structures of authority that encroach on their rural world ("Durn that road").

Historians are in general agreement that the influence of the eugenics movement waned in the U.S. after around 1930, as, in Daniel Kevles's words, "the number of books and articles published on eugenics steadily declined" (170).[29] This was certainly true of family studies research, which according to English had already reached its peak between 1915 and 1917 (145). It might be more accurate, though, to say that family studies methodology, and in particular its genealogies of white deviance, didn't disappear from the scene in the 1930s so much as migrate into new disciplinary territory— from sociology and law into imaginative literature—and that by doing so it was able to extend the eugenic inroads into southern territory established in the twenties by *Mongrel Virginians* and *Buck v. Bell*. Examples of this trend could include such classics of southern poor-white representation as Erskine Caldwell's *Tobacco Road*, Grace Lumpkin's *To Make My Bread*, Agee and Evans's *Let Us Now Praise Famous Men*, and Steinbeck's *Grapes of Wrath*. Seen in this light, the Faulkner family studies should be understood as an important transitional oeuvre linking eugenics literature to fiction and memoir in an evolving cultural response to the whiteness of a different color percolating into the national imagination from below the Mason-Dixon Line.

QUEERING WHITENESS, QUEERING FAULKNER

Hightower's "Wild Bulges"

—ALFRED J. LÓPEZ

I.

I should clarify from the outset that I am not a Faulknerian by any stretch, and so am not interested in producing a reading of Faulkner's novels that "solves" their many ambivalences and inconsistencies, their hints and feints toward a critique of race, class, and gender as repressed but active discourses at work in the Jim Crow South. Such an analysis would lie beyond not only this essay but also my own expertise. Rather, I wish to use a particular character in a particular novel—the defrocked minister Gail Hightower, from *Light in August*—as a way of opening an inquiry into how current approaches to whiteness studies, especially those attuned to the ways in which gay and lesbian whites are somehow "marked" by their distance from heteronormative whiteness, may prove useful to the reading and interpretation of U.S. southern literature generally, and Faulkner in particular.

It is axiomatic in whiteness studies that whiteness derives much of its power paradoxically from its invisibility—the idea that whiteness is not a "race," that it is in fact nothing at all—the "powerful position ... of being 'just' human," as Richard Dyer deftly puts it (2). One result of the invisibility of whiteness as an ethnic, racial, or class position is that it assumes the role of a universal discourse of "civility" and even "humanness," which then sits in judgment of the nonwhite world; thus other races, ethnicities, and sexualities exist as *gradations* of distance from the idealized, invisible norm of heteronormative bourgeois whiteness.[1] As Dyer further explains, "White power ... reproduces itself regardless of intention, power differences and goodwill, and overwhelmingly because it is not seen as whiteness, *but as normal*" (10; emphasis added). In such a model, as Matt Wray and Annalee Newitz among others have pointed out, regional categories within a larger hegemonic national identity, such as southernness within a U.S. context, always already constitute a "mark" of difference, the damning mark of a regional difference that also represents an irreducible distance from the unspoken, invisible norms of whiteness.[2]

Sexuality operates as one possible parameter of such difference, and thus distance, from heteronormative whiteness. As I have argued elsewhere, one significant feature common to many colonial queer white texts, especially those with an element of bildungsroman (but really any coming-into-self-knowledge narrative), is the protagonist's burgeoning realization of desire for the racial Other, thus contradicting the official dictates and unofficial norms of both racial purity and heteronormativity. As Dyer explains, "[This desire] is the felt connection between gays and ethnic minorities, as much as romantic and sexual encounters with non-white men" (6)—the idea of a shared condition of markedness in relation to heteronormative whiteness, rather than the fact of any sexual encounter itself, overrides other considerations of transgression or taboo. I want to open the essay with the question of whether queer moments in U.S. southern texts such as *Light in August* reveal precisely this kind of oppositional cultural logic. Gail Hightower's queerness represents a sort of thread of connectedness that runs through *Light in August*, one which aligns him with other marginalized whites (Byron Bunch, Lena Grove) and others of more ambivalent racial and sexual subject positions (Joe Christmas, who claims to be black, may be part Mexican, and slips in and out of active and passive sexual roles throughout the novel).[3] More importantly, in chapter 20 of Faulkner's novel, Hightower himself comes to a limited, incomplete reckoning with his long-suppressed sexuality, a reckoning that offers as intimate a portrait as one may find in U.S. southern literature of the divided, repressed psyche of closeted gay whiteness in the Jim Crow

South. One could in fact argue that *Light in August* itself represents a sort of theoretical intervention, a reinscription of queer histories into modernization, into a neocolonial society trying to reinvent itself as an oppositional regional identity. The ambivalence of its ending, however—its awkward final embrace of the sham heteronormative couple Byron Bunch and Lena Grove in particular—also suggests how difficult it may be to effectively combine whiteness studies and queer theory in the context of U.S. southern literatures. Both queer studies and whiteness studies, of course, emerge out of projects of opposition and resistance. It is not for nothing, for instance, that Christopher Lane announces his desire that queer theory will shatter Britain's colonial legacy, once and for all (13); and as I have argued elsewhere, whiteness studies begins precisely from the proposition of exposing or dismantling whiteness as an implicitly privileged subject position, by rendering it both visible and subject to critique (López 14). With this essay I propose to carry these emancipatory projects into the realm of U.S. modernist southern literature (beginning with Faulkner as arguably its avatar and canonical representative) in a manner that may suggest possibilities for further work beyond my present scope. With that goal in mind of initiating a critical conversation whose eventual parameters and conclusions I cannot claim to know, I write, as Gayatri Spivak has written in a different context, for a future reader.[4]

II.

A comprehensive analysis of suppressed gay and lesbian elements in Faulkner, or even a queer reading of *Light in August*, lies beyond the bounds of this essay. For now I will focus on a single character in Faulkner's novel, not Joe Christmas (whose ambivalent racial and even gender positions drive much of the novel's critique of race and heteronormative masculinity in the Jim Crow South) but Gail Hightower, the disgraced Presbyterian minister whose interstitial position between whiteness and blackness, bourgeois and working-class Jeffersonian, and marginal position relative to even the events of the narrative render him a perfect candidate for the kind of analysis of marginalized or "marked" queer whiteness I seek to demonstrate.

In a novel (for Faulkner, an oeuvre, really) full of "marked" white characters—the condition of "markedness" here being understood to signify a distancing from the ideal of bourgeois middle-class northern/western whiteness, by virtue of taint from a racial, class, geographical, or linguistic identification—Hightower nears a distancing mark beyond that shared by his erstwhile congregation. Their imaginary link to ideal whiteness is mediated by their status as southerners, and in the South by virtue of their being Presbyterians rather than Baptists; Hightower, however, bears the additional shame of being an abolitionist from a family of abolitionists, and of having suffered a domestic scandal. But there is something more: the rumors, swirling around Hightower ever since he loses his congregation, of black lovers and "queer" relationships with blacks. For just as membership in the whiteness club depends on more than mere pigmentation, the fact that Hightower's "skin is the color of flour sacking" (78) becomes irrelevant once the congregation deems him unworthy in other respects. "Queer" in this context, as any historically conscious study of Faulkner would point out, is not a sexual referent but a cultural one; "queer" in the world of Faulkner's Jeffersonians simply means deviant.[5] But this adherence to a 1930s understanding of Hightower's "queerness" serves only to foreclose on the possibility of queering Hightower—and the novel itself—today. And as *Light in August*'s penultimate chapter makes exceedingly clear, Hightower spends his life concealing his homosexuality from his wife, his congregation and fellow townspeople, and even from himself.

If there is a closet in Faulkner's novel, I would argue that this structure's metaphorical parameters are neatly framed by the window in which Hightower sits from dusk to nightfall every night, and through which he comes to confront, however elliptically, the suppressed desires that paradoxically both define and destroy his life and render him the "fifty-year-old outcast who has been denied by his church" (49). I will thus limit my focus for the remainder of this essay to chapter 20 of *Light in August*, in which the defeated, demoralized Reverend Hightower sits once again—perhaps for the last time in his life—in the window and has his moment of near-reckoning with both his disempowered whiteness and his lifelong repressed homosexuality. I say "near" because in the end Hightower turns away from a true self-confrontation, rendering his would-be reckoning a missed opportunity or *tuché*, in the Lacanian sense of a missed encounter with the real—a recurring cycle of approach and evasion that preserves the fantasy of a pristine, chaste, youthful whiteness that has sustained him through the years.[6] As we shall see, by the end of chapter 20 that fantasy remains intact only for Hightower; for readers of *Light in August* as well as its characters, any illusion of a stable hegemonic order based on a system of fixed race, class, and gender identities finds itself in crisis long before Hightower's elliptical confession of his homosexuality, a crisis that the closing chapter's depiction of an anxious, provisional façade of heteronormativity (in the nonrelationship of Lena Grove and Byron Bunch) does little to assuage.

III.

Chapter 20 opens after the climactic event of *Light in August*, the horizon of expectation and dread toward which arguably the entire narrative has been moving almost from the moment of its protagonist's first appearance: Joe Christmas's lynching in chapter 19 in Hightower's home (464–65). The text offers no explanation of why Christmas chooses Hightower's house to make his last stand from the pursuing mob, and perhaps on the level of plot we may believe such a turn to have come about spontaneously or randomly. Structurally, however, Christmas's murder and mutilation on Hightower's kitchen floor triggers the extended reverie that comprises all of chapter 20.

In the dusk of the aftermath of Christmas's death Hightower finds himself, as he does every other evening, sitting in his front window, the street outside his house "framed by the study window like a stage" (466). The street in fact functions nightly, has functioned for years, as the site of Hightower's recurring fantasy visions of young men and thundering hooves, much as he had once used his pulpit as a site from which to repeatedly rehearse differently the symptoms of the fears and neuroses that had plagued him since childhood.[7] Psychoanalysis teaches us that the symptom recurs endlessly and compulsively, part of the subject's vain attempt to regain a lost coherence that the traumatic primal scene has ruptured. For Hightower, first pulpit then study window serve as the mise-en-scène—literally the "frame"—through which the wish fulfillment of his suppressed lifelong desires finds its outlet. Let us note in passing that in Freud the "framing" of a dream scene in this manner always calls attention to its artifice—its quality of performance on the "stage" of the sleeping subject's briefly liberated unconscious. Freud's most famous case study, his analysis of the "Wolfman," contains just such a "staged" dream scene that underpins all of that subject's repressed incestuous longing for his father.[8] In Hightower's case, the street is very much the "stage" upon which the homoerotic fantasies that so dogged his brief preaching career continue to be acted out.

But what exactly is the content, the pathogenic nucleus, of Hightower's suffering? What is the content of the repressed that insists on returning at the same time every evening, acting itself out as a nightly vision in "the final copper light of afternoon" (466)? As in Freud's Wolfman, what matters is not the content of the vision/dream itself but the latent or displaced signified to which it corresponds. Hightower's thoughts as he sits in the window quickly wander from the vision itself, of young cavalrymen and "trumpets" and "falling horns" and the "beginning thunder" of horse hooves, via his dead wife to his childhood. Or more to the point: to his father.

The irreducible ground of Hightower's psychic conflict—what the narrative calls the "truth or as near truth as he dare approach" (467)—begins to emerge as he reminisces about his childhood impressions of his parents. But Hightower spends less time pondering the fate of his chronically ill mother than his father's contradictory character: a minister who went to war with the Confederates, yet "had owned no slaves" (467). The young Gail Hightower watches his parents struggle and suffer in the name of a political, economic, and cultural system in which they themselves do not participate and from which they draw no benefit: "[His father] would neither eat food grown and cooked by, nor sleep in a bed prepared by, a negro slave" (468). The senior Hightower's fighting for and continuing to live within a society to which he himself is an outsider is a contradiction whose complexities are no doubt beyond the young Gail at the time. But young Hightower will gain that insight, will grasp the horror of its meaning completely and utterly at a particular moment of epiphany, his affective response to which will mark him forever in his own mind as an outsider, alienated from his people and even from himself. It is a moment of awful self-knowledge from which, as we shall see, the young boy will never really recover.

Before we arrive at that moment of self-reckoning, however, it is important to point out one other characteristic of Hightower's father that he shares with someone else in the novel. Like Byron Bunch, the elder Hightower "was riding sixteen miles each Sunday to preach in a small Presbyterian chapel back in the hills," and receives the same ridicule from his own father (Gail Hightower's grandfather) that Bunch endures from his peers (468). The significance for my larger reading of this parallel between characters who also share an intimate affective bond with Hightower will become apparent later on. For now let us simply note the parallel, and the grandfather's laughter—which Hightower's father endures as "if it had been shouts or curses" (468)—and set it aside.

The trigger for Hightower's primal scene, the irreducible ground and pathogenic nucleus of all that troubles and besets him for the rest of his life, lies waiting after his father's return from the Civil War for twenty-five years—appropriately enough for a psychoanalytic reading, dormantly, latently—in a trunk in the attic. The very seed of Hightower's lifetime of psychic suffering, the senior Hightower's "somber frock coat," which he never wears again after his return from the war, lies fallow "until one day his son opened the trunk and took it out and spread out the careful folds in which it had been arranged by hands that were now dead" (468). Of course this is a popular and profound theme in mythology, as well as in popular banal entertainments of all sorts: from Pandora's box and Aladdin's lamp to the *Lord of the Rings* trilogy and *Jumanji*. Such themes always have as their referent the Faustian cautionary tale of the desire for forbidden knowledge and its consequences, often knowledge that some previous explorer has wisely attempted to hide for the good of the future, that none other should stumble across its like again. But the dangerous object is never hidden well enough, and always finds its way into another dupe's hands. (This is also consistent, of course, with the canonical psychoanalytic concept of repression: nothing is ever repressed completely or permanently.)

So the young Hightower ("'I was eight then', he thinks") opens the trunk and finds the coat. But the first sensory perceptions that the now-old man remembers involve smell: "It seems to him that he can still smell the rain, the moist grieving of the October earth, and the musty yawn as the lid of the trunk went back" (468). The first sight of the coat strangely triggers an immediate association not with his father—no "oh my, this must be his coat"—but with his now-dead mother: "Then the garment, the neat folds. He did not know what it was, because he was *almost overpowered by the evocation of his dead mother's hands*" (468–69; emphasis added). I will return to these tactile elements in a moment, because I must first establish the latent sexual nature of the child's symbolic encounter with the paternal phallus while standing in the place of the dead mother. The text signals the child's realization of this horror—of realizing his own attraction to his father and desire to replace the mother by the act of *undoing* the mother's act of folding and packing the coat—by a simple reflexive act: the child becomes nauseous.

As any careful reader of *Light in August* will have noted by this point in the text, nausea accompanies virtually every sexual act and situation in the novel: Joe Christmas's repeated vomiting, first as a child (122) and later in his abortive first encounter with the waitress/prostitute Bobbie (188–89); Christmas's being "sick" after his later violent encounter with a prostitute who fails to express revulsion at sleeping with a Negro (225); and most disturbingly, the vomiting of the men who witness Grimm's castration of the dying Christmas in the novel's grisly climactic scene (464–65). Thus the young Hightower's becoming "a little sick" at the sight of his father's coat in the attic—and especially at the sight of a patch of "blue, dark blue," which for the boy signifies his father's violent killing of a Union soldier—unmistakably signals the situation's repressed sexual content (469). That the boy experiences the feeling "of hushed and triumphant terror which left him a little sick" while standing in the place of his dead mother—the realization of which has already "overpowered" him—further confirms this primal moment of queer vertiginous pleasure and self-loathing. In short, it is an unmistakable moment of *jouissance*, in the Lacanian sense of enjoying the symptom. The young Hightower is simultaneously thrilled and revolted by both the implicit violence that the blue patch signifies and the sexual transgression implied by his own usurpation of the mother's place. In another uncanny parallel with Freud's Wolfman—a case whose real title, let us remember, refers to a history of infantile neurosis—for young Hightower the satisfaction of viewing (and *smelling*) the father's coat is paradoxically also the source of the anxiety, the former being the patient's masochistic longing for sexual satisfaction from his father, the traces of which the adult Hightower's dream/vision of the cavalry charge exhumes in distorted (but not sufficiently distorted) form.[9] Further, the young Hightower's history of intestinal symptoms that predate the primal coat scene—the "organs [that] required the unflagging care of a Swiss watch"— provides an instructive analogue to similar symptoms developed by Freud's patient later in his adult life (469).[10]

Finally, it is worth mentioning two more perhaps minor points, if only in passing. First, the possible relevance of the adult's keen recollection of the smells, which he articulates in descriptors that would have been unavailable to the boy—make very clear the sexual significance that he now attaches, however latently or elliptically, to the primal scene. Water images, as psychoanalysis teaches us, translate quite readily from rain into both tears and semen, a connection made easier to grasp by the narrative's further description of a "moist grieving" (468).[11] Second, the visual and olfactory description of the "musty yawn as the lid of the trunk went back" (468) is a profoundly sexual image, albeit a distorted one; one has only to turn the horizontal image of the opening lid to the more vertical one of parting legs—and perhaps the "musty yawn" that a young boy would imagine the legs of an older adult emitting as they part—to see how clearly such an image informs the child's sense of being "overpowered by the evocation of his dead mother's hands"—the censored version reads— "which lingered among the folds" (469).[12]

Reading the opening of the trunk in this context allows us to understand the calculated ambiguity with which the following paragraph begins:

> That evening at supper he would be unable to eat. Looking up, the father, now a man nearing sixty, would find the child staring at him with terror and awe *and with something else.* Then the man would say, "What have you been into now?" and *the child could not answer,* could not speak, staring at his father with on his child's face an expression as of the Pit itself. (469; emphasis added)

Of course we can now clearly identify the "something else" with which the child stares at his father: horror and loathing at his own repressed, never to be requited sexual desire. The child's expression "as of the Pit itself"—that invocation of eternal damnation and punishment—now becomes intelligible as an expression of guilt and shame, the child's self-damning interpretation of the father's relatively innocent query: What have you been into now? Of course the child cannot answer: to do so would break not only the spell of *jouissance* but the boundary of what is unutterable, inadmissible even to himself, much less to the father with whom he has such a distant, even icy relationship.

The rest of the paragraph renders even more transparently both the sexual nature of the child's neurosis and its object:

> That night in bed he would not be able to sleep. He would lie rigid, not even trembling, in his dark bed while the man who was his father and his only remaining relative, and between whom he and himself there was so much of distance in time *that not even the decades of years could measure, that there was not even any physical resemblance,* slept walls and floors away. (469–70; emphasis added)

In this passage the most palpable terror is proximity to the father—or rather the father's proximity to his bed—and the much-obsessed-upon distance functions paradoxically as both obstacle to and protection from the potential acting out of the child's incestuous fantasy. The description of the child lying "rigid, not even trembling" obviously enough signifies terror or fear, but his self-conscious stillness simultaneously underlines his fear of both being noticed and losing control of his own body—as if there were no telling what lascivious gesture or motion his body might make if he were to lose focus for even a second on its rigid stillness. The rest of the passage displays a conflicted, contradictory mix of closeness and distance. The boy reminds himself that the man sleeping "walls and floors away" is in fact his "only remaining relative," and thus sexually unavailable. But what of the awkward denial of the father's relation to him contained in the fantasy that "there was not even any physical resemblance," as if not looking alike would sufficiently qualify blood ties to permit the relation with the father that he so desperately desires?

Read in this burgeoning context of incestuous desire and queer self-loathing, the young Hightower lives out a recurring cycle of *jouissance* and nausea, nights of unbearable insomnia and unrequited desire followed in the morning by "one of his intestinal fits," a cycle that the child sets in motion once again by returning to the attic and "the coat ... [to] touch the blue patch with that horrified triumph and sick joy" (470). The only way the child can find to break the recurring and debilitating symptom is to transfer his feelings onto a safer, more distant object, and to channel his illicit desires, however incompletely and inadequately, into a more acceptable and conventional form. Thus instead of admitting to the Negro servant (but how could he?) the true nature of his illness, the boy asks to hear about his grandfather's war exploits: "Tell again about grandpa. How many Yankees did he kill?" (470) Transferring his repressed sexual energies onto this safer object and form allows young Hightower to lose momentarily his sense of "terror" and the "triumph" of *jouissance*, and indulge in a simpler, more generalized feeling: "[it] was pride" (470).

This transference of the neurosis into a more acceptable sense of family "pride" in the grandfather's life and exploits, however, proves fleeting, at least in the adult Hightower's consciousness. After a brief history of the grandfather's and father's contentious relationship, and a gesture of admiration of the former's gruff charm and "simple adherence to a simple code," Hightower concludes that the elder Hightower had misread his father: "'But sanctity is not the word for him', the son's son in turn thinks" (472, 473). Tellingly, the qualities that Hightower emphasizes in his reading of his father form an uncanny echo of his own divided psyche, despite the very different economic, political, and cultural circumstances in which each has lived:

> [A man] had to guard and protect that little *not only from nature* but from man too, by means of a sheer fortitude *that did not offer, in his lifetime anyway, physical ease for reward*. That was where his disapproval of slavery lay, *and of his lusty and sacrilegious father*. The very fact that he could and did see no paradox in the fact that he took an active part in a partisan war and on the very side whose principles opposed his own, was proof enough *that he was two separate and complete people one of whom dwelled by serene rules in a world where reality did not exist*. (473; emphasis added)

Two moments in this passage stand out within the context of the queer reading I am building. First, Hightower articulates an understanding of social life as something lived *against* nature—one's own nature included. Thus Hightower sees his own father as having lived an "unnatural" life by virtue of the latter's having willingly repressed his true "nature" as part of a compromise formation to enable him to remain in the society. Second, but more important for my reading, is Hightower's description of his father's coping mechanisms in terms that can be described only as a closet: the very idea of living as "two separate and complete people," only one of whom can exist manifestly in the world, speaks to a dissocation common among trauma victims, a distancing from traumatic reality so comprehensive and extreme that it amounts to the construction of an entirely different *life*—or a mask or outward shell of a life, as it were. Finally, although these do not read as a single articulation in the passage, Hightower's acknowledgment of the "sheer fortitude" required to live a life so intensely closeted that the subject cannot allow himself even the possibility—entertain the thought— of "physical ease [read 'relief,' 'discharge'] for reward," coupled with his wistful tribute and simultaneous denial of his "lusty and sacrilegious" grandfather—adjectives that the grandson never in his life dared to apply to himself—together complete the poignant portrait of a man looking back with deep regret on a lifetime of closeted chastity and devout self-denial.

Hightower continues his musings as he dreams of the "phantoms" that he now realizes have shaped his life: his father and mother, and the Negro slave that comes to live with him after his grandfather died. Yet the language of one particular passage within this part of the narrative reiterates the structure of the attic scene: Hightower again displaces the mother and takes her place—more specifically, he shares her place with her—as part of his recurring wish fulfillment of incestuous longing for the father. What begins with a meditation on his dying mother's eyes ("two eyes which seemed daily to grow bigger and bigger") gives way to an abstruse, nearly indecipherable passage that may be a rape fantasy, but certainly effaces its own meaning by the use of an utterly vague pronoun:

> They were the house: he dwelled within them, *within their dark and allembracing and patient aftermath of physical betrayal*. He and she both lived in them like two small, weak beasts in a den, a cavern, into which now and then the father entered—that man who was a stranger to them both, a foreigner, almost a threat: *so quickly does*

the body's wellbeing alter and change the spirit. He was more than a stranger: he was an enemy. (475; emphasis added)

We can see that the language of the passage describes not sex, but violence: "physical betrayal." But beyond the opposition of the father as "threat" and "enemy" to Hightower and his mother lies the fact that again he has at least partially displaced her—strategically at precisely the moment at which the opportunity to be "entered" presents itself. The thrill of violence has carried over from the boy's primal scene with the coat into the present fantasy of being raped, in the manner of a "small, weak" beast, as he imagines that perhaps his mother is. The italicized passage "so quickly does the body's wellbeing alter and change the spirit" only reinforces the distorted logic of the passage; although on a literal level Hightower here means the changing physical fortunes of his mother, a more psychoanalytically attentive reading would yield the plausible conclusion that a lifetime of living "unnaturally" has, in Hightower's mind, altered and changed his own "spirit." To what degree, then, is the enemy really located within Hightower's own fractured, dissociated psyche? His recollection of the "phantoms" that have mediated his entire life may yield not only Hightower's lifelong relation to the phantoms but also the possibility that they mark the very parameters of Hightower's closet—that is, their lingering existence in his life as wish fulfillments and fantasies suggests their relation to the original pathogenic nucleus.

In the space remaining I want to examine the idea of the "phantom" or, more specifically and perhaps tellingly, of the phantom that Hightower doesn't originally count but adds on, as if in passing, later. After listing the three phantoms (father, mother, Negro mammy) Hightower states in the following paragraph: "This was the third phantom. With this phantom the child ('and he little better than a phantom too, then,' that same child now thinks beside the fading window) talked about the ghost" (477). That child from long ago is, as he asserts and psychoanalysis confirms, the place to which he must return in order to confront and undo all that he has been suffering from all these many years. Paradoxically, but fittingly as this meditation takes on the quality of a deathbed confession as well as an analysis, Hightower thinks of his boyhood self as containing the source of both his suffering and his release: "[My] only salvation must be to return to the place to die where my life had already ceased before it began" (477).

Let us note too that the violence and horrors of war are not the problem, although that is what the manifest form of the symptom might lead us to believe. The young Hightower "found no terror in the knowledge... No horror here..." (478). So the pathogenic nucleus must lie somewhere else. Where? Let us examine the place where Hightower does not wish to go, the trace of a blocked memory: "'[I]t's no wonder,' he thinks, 'that I skipped a generation. It's no wonder that I had no father'..." (477–78).

In the following paragraph, we have another of the urns that Diane Roberts points out tirelessly in *Faulkner and Southern Womanhood*, as the young Hightower envisions his future life taking shape "like a classic and serene vase" (478). But the rest of the passage promptly undercuts this idyllic vision, as Hightower declares his desire to be "sheltered from the *harsh gale* of living and die so, peacefully, with only the far sound of the circumvented wind" (478; emphasis added). The pun on Hightower's first name, Gail (as in a harsh gale), is obvious enough, although we may ask ourselves how he expects to be sheltered from the gale/Gail when it is not attacking him from without, but from within. It is himself, I would argue, his own nature, that he wishes to be sheltered against and have circumvented, and the seminary is what Hightower had hoped would give him that. Again, as in chapter 8, the vision of the vase deconstructs itself, but this time in a way that exposes the artifice of Hightower's social façade. The rumblings of a troubled unconscious constitutes his own harsh gale/Gail buffeting the top—the mind, brain—of the Hightower. And yet the big white "ghostly" head, bandaged, knows that "there are more things in heaven and earth too than truth," perhaps paraphrasing Hamlet but more importantly revealing a truth that a different grammar will yield: there are more truths—or, to be precise, another truth—than that which is manifested in the "heaven and earth" schema of his chosen religion (479). Here the relation between the automaton (those elements or signifiers that repeat in the subject's psyche) and the *tuché* (the real behind the repeating signifier that the subject always misses, or grasps only partially: in this case Hightower's lifelong repression of his homosexuality) begins to emerge. There are indeed "more things in heaven and earth" than Hightower, even at this late stage, is willing or indeed able to confront.

One of the automatons or recurring signifiers in chapter 20 is Hightower's wife, or "woman." The text's portrayal of her as a "harassed gambler" who is "savagely" plotting a marriage for apparently social and material reasons, or perhaps to escape from some horror that she never names ("All of it! All! All!") is not flattering (480). But the fact that Hightower turns to this language of marriage as an escape for his wife belies his own interest in "marriage and escape" (481). But from what? Perhaps from the "harsh gale" in his own head, buffeting the Hightower and ruining its efforts to achieve calm, peace. We might also think of Mrs. Hightower's proposed campaign of "abasement and plotting" in terms of Hightower's own "abasement," the false heterosexual life he is plotting to live for the sake of achieving his desired position: "*Yes. I see. I see now. That's how they do such, gain such. That's the rule. I see now*" (482). (We might also note in passing the close resemblance of "gain" in this passage to gale/Gail.) And when the passion disappears from his wife (whether it was ever there in him remains an open question), Hightower takes it "without much surprise and perhaps without hurt" (482).

What does take Hightower very much by surprise, even as he muses by the window, is the emergence of the house and the overwhelming vision of death and blood and sweat and repressed desire—emanating very much from the idea of the house—that permeates the rest of the chapter. Hightower wants more than anything else to move into a particular house—a house in which he can sit in the window and gaze upon his beloved fantasy scene of "boys riding the sheer tremendous tidal wave of desperate living. Boys. Because this. This is beautiful. . . . Here is that fine shape of eternal youth and virginal desire [repetition of the urn image] which makes heroes" (483). Certainly the passage and image are demonstrably homoerotic, but that is not my point here. I'm more interested in the "house" that he must inhabit in order to properly enjoy those "boys" and their "virginal desire." Youth, love, repressed homosexuality born of a forbidden erotic attraction to his male ancestors—all of these lie latent and barely repressed within Hightower's reverie. In fact, the fantasy is so overwhelming to Hightower even now, so "unbelievable," that he must suppress it "lest paradoxical truth outrage itself" (484)—lest he be forced to confront his own long-suppressed desires, now being awakened by his unrequited love for Byron and his wonder at the beautiful, bloodied man who died on his kitchen floor.

The same paragraph continues into Hightower's fantasy of the "boys" in action, which is again very erotic: "the trees uprearing against that red glare as though fixed too in terror . . . you can feel, hear in the darkness horses pulled up short, plunging; clashes of arms; whispers overloud, hard breathing, the voices still triumphant . . ." (484). And then there are the bugles. Not trumpets, now—bugles. Freud tells us that the dream-work can scramble or distort its true meaning in any number of ways, but that one of those ways is by scrambling letters in a word.[13] Thus by a simple displacement of two letters in the word "bugles" it becomes "bulges." If you read the word back into the sentence it is transparent to the point of being comical: behind them the rest of the troops galloping past toward the rallying bulges. It is an easy enough thing to joke about, until we consider that choice of words. It is "bugles" here and nowhere else in the chapter until the very end (elsewhere it is "trumpets," except for the last sentence). One very plausible explanation for this change may be that the other visions imply a romantic, almost medieval vision of southern knighthood, while this scene portrays more of the actual heat of battle. But I do not think that a close reading of the other scenes would necessarily confirm such an interpretation. I cannot claim to know why Faulkner chose "bugle" for this particular moment of the text instead of "trumpet," but "bugle" in the middle of a very erotically charged scene easily translates to "bulge." Throw in the fact that these particular men are hungry—"the *white* gaunt faces of living scarecrows" (484; emphasis added)—and connect this back to Joe Christmas's own vision of hunger and denial in the scene of the field peas and molasses in chapter 10 and we can also see how issues of appetite and denial of those appetites remain latent here as well. We may at least note in passing the narrative's structural parallel between hungers and repressed contents here: Christmas's association of the aroma of the field peas with his white adoptive father's inexplicable ability to resist eating them, and Hightower's imaginative link of the "white gaunt faces" on the horses with not only the dead grandfather but the beautiful mixed-race man who lies castrated on his kitchen floor. The implied relationship, in short, between indulging forbidden appetites—whether sexual or gastronomic—and violence and death could not form a more ominous cautionary tale for Hightower. (I will return briefly to this point in my conclusion.) Let us note finally that Hightower's grandfather is killed, at least according to the Negro servant's version of the story, in the act of stealing chickens—a term that not only ties in nicely with the erotic component of hunger and suppressing appetites but also calls up the venerable gay slang term for older homosexuals who seek young boys: "chicken hawks."[14] Finally, the possibility that "a woman, likely enough the wife of a Confederate soldier . . . a woman in a bedroom" may have shot the grandfather appeals to the grandson's sense of guilt and self-loathing, and the perverse enjoyment (*jouissance*) he draws from these: "I like to think so. It's fine so" (485). It is telling, however, that the final shred of heteronormative masculinity to which the young Hightower clung as a boy—his sole remaining source of "pride" being his grandfather's war exploits—should be so cruelly undermined, and that the adult Hightower should take such perverse pleasure in the queering.

Throughout chapter 20 Hightower works to make sense of, to construct a narrative out of, his life—or rather "the sum of his life" intertwining with "the suspended instant out of which the soon will presently begin" (486). He knows himself to be a sinner, but more importantly, he comes closer here than anywhere else in the chapter to telling us explicitly what his desire really is. It is a knowledge that has already destroyed his marriage and, he believes, his wife's life: "Perhaps in the moment when I revealed to her not only the depth of my hunger but the fact that never and never would she have any part in the assuaging of it," he muses, he committed his greatest sin; not in acting out his latent desires, but in being responsible for his wife's misery and eventual death: "I became her seducer and her murderer, author and instrument of her shame and death" (488). Or, she was his. It is not a thought that emerges in the chapter as such, but it is the reading of many members of the defrocked minister's erstwhile congregation. As we have seen, so much of Hightower's testimony in chapter 20 is distorted, inverted, and displaced that it becomes habitual to read his every utterance and thought this way.

Hightower's final psychical act of simultaneous introspection and self-protection both distances him from the grisly prospect of having been complicit in his wife's death and subsumes and condenses—in short, deflects—all of the anxieties and fears connected with his own closeted queer nature and his deep despair at having used his wife as "an instrument to be called to Jefferson" at the expense of her happiness and eventually her life (489). This last breathtaking act of condensation sweeps away not only the complexities of his own repressed sexual longing for his father (then) and Byron Bunch (now), but his guilt and shame at believing himself implicated in his wife's death into a single overarching image: "I have been a single instant of darkness in which a horse galloped and a gun crashed" (491). This single fantasy of his grandfather's riding and dying on a charging horse—even if his end came in the role of "chicken hawk"—simultaneously overpowers and displaces every other facet of Hightower's loves, desires, and fears. And of course this is not a new defense strategy of the minister's unconscious but one it learned long ago: as the child who willed himself to forget the dark desires and nausea invoked by an old trunk and a forbidden queer love by displacing them onto conspicuous displays of pride over his grandfather's war exploits. The final grim paradox generated by the obsessional neurosis brought about by a lifetime of repressing his homosexuality is that even this moment of heteronormative masculinity turns out to be just another overdetermined queer moment: the grandfather as a "chicken hawk," punished for his indulgence of a deeply felt but illicit hunger, just as the racially ambivalent man lying dead and castrated in his house pays the ultimate price for his own indulgences and transgressions. And inextricably imbricated with this moment of bitter epiphany is, I would argue, this parallel structure of *markedness*, between a man ostracized and repressed by heteronormativity and another destroyed by race. This metonymic relation, intuited but never articulated by Hightower himself, comes closest to fruition in the fractured moment—a stunning, blurting-out of sudden spontaneous allegiance—in which Hightower tries vainly to stop Christmas's lynching: "'Men!' he cried. 'Listen to me. He was here that night. He was with me the night of the murder. I swear to God—'" (464). Although it is a gesture that makes no sense in terms of the actual relations between the characters as allowed for in Faulkner's plot—Hightower and Christmas, after all, do not know each other, never exchange a word in the novel—Hightower's is an attempt to protect one whom he intuits as sharing a common condition, if not an actual subject position, in relation to heteronormative whiteness. As such, I would argue, this moment in *Light in August*, as much as any other, constitutes a theoretical intervention into the nature of such bonds, however fleeting or abortive. I say "abortive" because Hightower is fixed back into his place in the very next sentence, spoken by one of the (presumably heterosexual) white men who have come to lynch the fugitive Christmas: "*Jesus Christ! . . . Has every preacher and old maid in Jefferson taken their pants down to the yellowbellied son of a bitch?*" (464;

emphasis added). Hightower, in that moment outed in a cruel, casual manner that he himself cannot fathom, relents to both Christmas's death and his own queerness, and forfeits his now-failed attempt to forge that bond in the face of such naked white aggression and power. Read in this way, Grimm's outburst perhaps forms the very trigger, along with Christmas's lynching, of Hightower's death meditation in chapter 20.

What surprise, then, that Hightower himself finally shrinks from the implications of his own self-exploration, deciding eventually, "*I don't want to think this. I must not think this. I dare not think this*" (490) before retreating into a final fantasy vision of his beloved "boys" with their "wild bulges" —I mean "bugles"—thundering off into the distance, perhaps taking his consciousness and his life with them.

PASSING AS MISCEGENATION
Whiteness and Homoeroticism in Faulkner's *Absalom, Absalom!*

—BETINA ENTZMINGER

In Faulkner's *Absalom, Absalom!* two paired male relationships, that of Quentin and Shreve in the novel's present and that of Henry and Charles in the novel's past, couple the sexual taboos of homosexuality and miscegenation. I offer here a reading of *Absalom, Absalom!* similar to Deborah McDowell's famous reading of Nella Larsen's *Passing*. McDowell explores the connection between passing for white and passing for straight, arguing that the "more dangerous story—though not named explicitly—[is] of Irene's awakening sexual desire for Clare" (xxvi). Corinne Blackmer points out that "[s]ince the term 'passing' carries the connotation of being accepted for something one is not, the title of the novel [*Passing*] serves as a metaphor for a wide range of deceptive appearances and practices that encompass sexual as well as racial passing" (100). Like *Passing*, *Absalom, Absalom!* overtly explores the "deceptive appearances" that resist society's attempts at racial classification. Furthermore, *Absalom, Absalom!* invokes a shadow theme about the complexities of desire. As Richard Dyer wryly puts it, "[T]he problem with queers is you can't tell who is and who isn't" (*Culture* 97).

In Faulkner's novel, the obvious homoeroticism of Charles's and Henry's relationship is mirrored by the homoeroticism between Quentin and

Shreve. Both Quentin and Henry, however, young men brought up in the patriarchal South, divert their attention away from their homosexual desires onto a more open topic for their time and region: the taint of black blood. Blackness is offered as the final answer for which the narrators and readers search to explain why Henry kills Charles. The novel shows race to be a simplifier and (as in McDowell's reading of *Passing*) the safe(r) zone that permits evasion and/or erasure of homosexuality. However, repressed desires and homosexual panic lead to hysteria and self-destruction in both Quentin and Henry. This repressed homoeroticism finds veiled expression in the narrative structure of the text itself. By blurring the boundaries and emphasizing the interconnections of race, gender, and sexuality, Faulkner reveals that hierarchical categories are arbitrary, they serve to facilitate denial, and they are mutually imbricative, relying on each other to function.[1]

Faulkner uses narrative in this novel and others to suggest a blurring of social boundaries and binaries, including those of desire. As Heide Ziegler points out, "Quentin Compson listens to Rosa Coldfield while talking to himself. He also speaks and listens at the same time, when he and Shreve identify with Henry Sutpen and Charles Bon: telling and listening merge; they become indistinguishable activities" (645). This fusion of speaking and listening suggests the possibility that other binaries—male and female, gay and straight, black and white—are not as rigid as our culture represents them. Alex Vernon argues that

> [w]hile the story turns on the historical Southern taboo of racial intermixing, Faulkner artfully incorporates generic miscegenation into the novel's structure. The narrative structure of *Absalom, Absalom!* can be viewed as a "cross-breed" of several literary forms, including (among others) the naturalist novel, biography, autobiography, and the oral tale largely associated in the American South with black culture. . . . Its narrative miscegenation ultimately unsettles the South's erroneous yet fundamental insistence on strict black-white speciation. (155–56)[2]

Absalom, Absalom! emphasizes the lack of definitive borders between black and white (Charles passes for white and the reader and characters "discover" that he has black blood only near the end of the novel), between the past and present (the narrative shifts in time without demarcation or warning), between individuals (the narrative also shifts without demarcation or warning from one narrative voice to another), and even between thoughts themselves (as sentences are often unpunctuated and blend into one another). Through these techniques, the narrative's blurring and crossing of boundaries unsettles the culture's insistence on seeing other types of difference, such as those related to race, gender, and sexuality, in black and white.

The whiteness to which the novel's young southern males are born or aspire and which shapes their view of themselves and their society is coded as masculine and heterosexual. As Mason Stokes points out in *The Color of Sex*, "[W]hiteness works best when it attaches itself to other abstractions, becoming yet another invisible strand in a larger web of unseen yet powerful cultural forces" (13). Dyer elaborates, "If race is always about bodies, it is also always about the reproduction of those bodies through heterosexuality" (*White* 25). White supremacy merges with compulsory heterosexuality because white supremacy involves dominance and control over women and blacks, and to be penetrated by another suggests submission or passivity.[3] From a white supremacist point of view, the white male body is that which possesses and penetrates; the black body, like the female and the homosexual body (which the dominant culture perceives as feminized), is that which is penetrated and possessed. The taboo against homosexuality resembles that against miscegenation, Faulkner's ostensible focus, because both often necessitate "passing," both can often involve "coming out"— risking the danger of public exposure of both color and desire, and both fail to reproduce biologically the whiteness our society values above all else. Historically, as Warren Hedges notes, "[d]isruption in racial categories also destabilizes categories of gender; blackface and cross dressing ... went hand in hand" in the late nineteenth century, for example (231).[4]

The dominant culture continues to link its fears of homosexuality with its fears of blackness. Closer to Faulkner's time and culture, the motto of the KKK was "Don't be half a man, join the Klan" (Altman 200). The implication here is that all truly white and truly masculine people have the same agenda to protect their privileged status, and all of those people who don't belong under white robes are not real men and not real whites. Once again, conventional masculinity merges with whiteness. Even today—though possibly to a lesser extent—U.S. society considers both whiteness and heterosexuality normative, invisible. As Other, blacks and homosexuals have historically faced similar oppression in our society.[5] In his 1971 study *Homosexual: Oppression and Liberation*, Dennis Altman quotes a letter from the gay black writer James Baldwin to his nephew: "You can only be destroyed by believing that you really are what the white world calls a *nigger.*" Altman adds, "So it is with the homosexual" (71). In both cases, the oppression involves the dominant group's projection of undesirable qualities onto the oppressed.

As a southerner, Faulkner was well acquainted with racial oppression, but he was also familiar with the gay culture of the early twentieth century. In 1915, Havelock Ellis published his famous study *Sexual Inversion*, which documents that a distinct gay culture did exist during Faulkner's time and was known to those outside the group. Many critics note Faulkner's close friendships with homosexuals in Paris and New Orleans. And the theme of homoeroticism is one that Faulkner explores in other works. For example, Neil Watson observes in *Go Down, Moses* "the triple threat of forbidden desires, the explicit interracial and incestual taboos juxtaposed with the implicit, still unnameable taboo of homoeroticism" (205). Richard Godden and Noel Polk reread the ledgers in "The Bear" to uncover a repressed tale of homosexual desire in the family chronicle that they believe explains Ike's rejection of his birthright as convincingly as the more accepted reading of the patriarch's past interracial incest. Michelle Ann Abate explores homoerotic imagery in *The Sound and the Fury*, and Duvall examines male homosexual panic in *Light in August*.

Compulsory heterosexuality was also a practice with which Faulkner was familiar. Either he or his publisher deleted four scenes showing same-sex erotics from his early novel *Mosquitoes* (Gwin 132). But in *Absalom, Absalom!* even the characters notice that something is omitted, or at least unacknowledged. As Mr. Compson says, "They are there, yet something is missing" (80), and Henry says to Charles, "You give me two and two and you tell me it makes five and it does make five" (94). The "something missing" to which Mr. Compson refers is the information that explains why Henry shot Charles. The something extra to which Henry alludes (the extra that allows two and two to make five) is Bon, the extra son who introduces dangerous racial and (I argue) unspoken sexual tensions. As Quentin and Shreve struggle to justify events of the past and Mr. Compson records all that doesn't add up, Faulkner suggests an ambiguity of desire. The unexplained, the silence in the narrative, suggests the closet that often conceals homosexual desire. As Eve Kosofsky Sedgwick points out in *Epistemology of the Closet*, our culture often links homosexuality to absence and silence, labeling such desire "unspeakable," a "love that dare not speak its name" (202). While the characters sense an absence that may be queer, the novel foregrounds unnamed homoeroticism for the reader. Throughout the first half of *Absalom, Absalom!* Faulkner plainly suggests the homoerotic attraction between Charles and Henry, complicating the question of sexuality and desire. Faulkner tells us many times that "Henry loved Bon" (71) and that Quentin and Judith "had been seduced almost simultaneously by a man whom at the time Judith had never even seen" (73). Faulkner at first implies a young man's love and admiration for an older, more sophisticated friend, but soon the descriptions of these characters and their relationship become noticeably sexual and the gender distinctions blur:

> And it would be hard to say to which of them [Henry or Judith] he [Charles] appeared the more splendid—to the one with hope, even though unconscious, of making the image hers through possession; to the other with the knowledge, even though subconscious to the desire, of the insurmountable barrier which the similarity of gender hopelessly intervened;—this man whom Henry first saw . . . in the slightly Frenchified cloak and hat which he wore, or perhaps . . . presented formally to the man reclining in a flowered almost feminised gown . . . this man handsome elegant and even catlike and too old to be where he was, too old not in years but in experience. (75–76)

Charles's physical appearance and demeanor suggest the feminine, and his experience differs so markedly from that of other young men as to have aged him prematurely. Henry fantasizes about Charles Bon ("by whom he [Henry] would be despoiled, choose for despoiler, if he could become, metamorphose into the sister, the mistress, the bride" [77]) as he would about a lover, and the greatest barrier to their union is their similarity of gender. In fact, Henry's growing love for Charles is described as his "corruption" at the hands of the older man (91).

In the relationship between Charles and Henry, the woman, Judith, is ancillary. Faulkner tells us that Charles "paid Judith the dubious compliment of not even trying to ruin her, let alone insisting on the marriage either before or after Sutpen forbade it" (78). And the author suggests, "Perhaps in his fatalism he [Charles] loved Henry the better of the two, seeing perhaps in the sister merely the shadow, the woman vessel with which to consummate the love whose actual object was the youth" (86). The way the woman functions in this relationship is not unusual. Stokes asserts that "[w]hite supremacy ... can be usefully understood as a homosocial network that commodifies and appropriates the bodies of white women and black men in order to consolidate both whiteness and heterosexuality as governing ideologies, ever present abstractions, condensed forms of panic, and political structures" (18). Stokes's explanation practically reiterates Faulkner's description of his triad of characters:

> [I]t was not Judith who was the object of Bon's love or of Henry's solicitude. She was just the blank shape, the empty vessel in which each of them strove to preserve, not the illusion of himself nor his illusion of the other but what each conceived the other to believe him to be—the man and the youth, seducer and seduced, who had known one another, seduced and been seduced ... before Judith came into their joint lives even by so much as a girlname. (95)

We see here a homosocial bond reified through the body of the female, an object of exchange our culture uses, as Claude Lévi-Strauss points out in *The Elementary Structures of Kinship*, to solidify partnerships between men (115). Faulkner's repetition of the word "seduced," however, suggests more than a homosocial bond; it suggests sexual desire. Judith functions as a decoy, providing acceptability to the closeness of the two men, and as a token to be exchanged, a sign of their affection for one another.

Judith's whiteness is essential to her symbolic function in this relationship. As Faulkner tells us, Quentin has grown up in a South in which there are three classes of the "opposite sex"—"ladies, women, females—the virgins whom gentlemen someday married, the courtesans to whom they went while on sabbaticals in the cities, the slave girls and women upon whom that first caste rested and to whom in certain cases it doubtless owed the very fact of its virginity" (87). Because Judith is a white lady, no sexual activity is expected or permitted in her relationship with Bon. The asexuality of their interactions ensures that her liaison with Bon does not deprive Henry of the erotic energy of this triad, and the potential for sexuality (when they "someday marry") permits an outward show of proper heterosexuality. This sexual categorization of women explains why Bon's involvement with the octoroon mistress makes so little sense to Mr. Compson as a reason for Henry's murder of Charles. Because she is a woman of mixed race, Charles's sexual involvement with her would not only be expected, but assumed, and a ceremony between them that holds no legal weight would not likely trouble Henry. Perhaps the certainty of sexuality between Charles and this woman also explains why the relationship inspires little emotional interest for Quentin: "In fact, Quentin did not even tell Shreve what his father had said about the visit. Perhaps Quentin himself had not been listening when Mr. Compson related (recreated?) it that evening at home" (268). The assumption of a heterosexual union detracts from the homoerotic potential of Henry's and Bon's relationship in a way that the asexual bond with Judith does not, and it is this homoerotic potential that fascinates the two young Harvard men. Judith's whiteness also makes possible the four years probation in which Charles and Henry depart together to decide if and when they will rejoin the sister/bride who waits at home. The war held white women captive and passive, unlike white men, who could go off to fight, and unlike free blacks, who could attempt to flee for the North.

Judith, however, is not just any white woman. She is sister to both men in this exchange. In addition to miscegenation, Faulkner links homoeroticism to another more overt taboo—incest, forming what Watson has labeled in *Go Down, Moses* a triple threat. Similar to Henry, in *The Sound and the Fury* Quentin Compson fantasizes about his sister's lover Dalton Ames, casting himself in a feminine role at the moment of intercourse between Dalton's parents: "If I could have been his mother lying with open body lifted laughing, holding his father with my hand refraining, seeing, watching him die before he lived" (80). If we read *Absalom, Absalom!* with *The Sound and the Fury* in mind, we can assume that the Sutpen legend's incestuous intricacies also enthrall Quentin.[6]

Why does this *combination of taboos* recur in Faulkner's works? Michael Davidson's term hemophobia, which describes human fears of and obsessions with blood, suggests the way the prohibitions against miscegenation, incest, and homosexuality correlate: "Bleeding disorders raise concerns about the porousness of boundaries, the vulnerability of the bodily envelope, the infection of bodily fluids—concerns that parallel phobias about sexual deviance and racial mixing" (44). Each of the taboos relates to blood and bloodlines, the passing on or failure to pass on traits that we deem desirable or undesirable, and their association does not occur solely in literature. According to Claude Lévi-Strauss, "[I]ncest . . . combines in some countries with its direct opposite, interracial sexual relations, an extreme form of exogamy, as the two most powerful inducements to horror and collective vengeance" (10). But as Kalpana Seshadri-Crooks asserts, the combination of these taboos actually makes some forms of incest permissible: "The strict separation between those who were kin (racially similar people) versus slaves (racially dissimilar people) rendered the incest taboo void *a propos* the latter group. . . . The prohibition of miscegenation should above all be understood as the tenacious refusal to grant legitimacy in order to preserve the possibility of incest" (42–43). Faulkner illustrates this possibility explicitly in "The Bear" where the patriarch, Carothers McCaslin, has a daughter, Tomasina, with his slave Eunice and then later impregnates Tomasina, causing Eunice to commit suicide. McCaslin's actions are legally permissible due to his racial dominance over Eunice and Tomasina. The scenario becomes more complicated in *Absalom, Absalom!* only because the man is black and the woman is white, someone whom the culture deems too valuable to bear illegitimate offspring, and legitimacy is made impossible by both the incest and the miscegenation taboos.

How does the third prong of this triple threat, homosexuality, figure into the dynamic described above? Perhaps the prohibition against miscegenation *facilitates* unacknowledged homosexuality as it does unacknowledged incest. In reinforcing the notion that black men are not really "men," antimiscegenation laws may have made homosexual acts with black men seem less transgressive, in the same way that incest with slave offspring was not really considered incest. Often, in masculinist culture, the effeminized position, the penetrated, is offensive, but penetrating another man is sometimes considered a sign of dominance over him and does not necessarily indicate that the penetrator identifies himself as homosexual.[7] For example, Maurice Wallace reads a threat of homosexual rape in the climactic fight scene with Mr. Covey in Frederick Douglass's 1845 *Narrative of the Life of Frederick Douglass*:

> Unmistakably, the portrayal of Covey, enraged by the slave's insubordination ripping the slaveboy's clothes from his body "with the fierceness of a tiger" (102), is a graphic recapitulation of Anthony's savage assault on Hester.... Douglass musters a physical strength heretofore unrealized in resisting Covey. The latter's violence is counteracted by the former's as one's phallic will—Douglass's—overcomes and 'feminizes' the other's—Covey's. If, in this scene, Douglass is a slave made a man, then Covey, by the designs of a historic fiction of binary exclusivity in matters of race and sex, is a man made a slave/woman. (92–94)

By linking the taboos against miscegenation, incest, and homosexuality, Faulkner suggests that the triangulation of these arbitrary boundaries on desire permits the simultaneous maintenance and breaking of taboo by the dominant power group.

Faulkner points out a similar social implication between the taboo against racial mixing and the taboo against homosexuality. After the four years of denial that *Absalom, Absalom!* figures as the Civil War, Charles and Henry finally come together, the phallic "pistol lying yet across the saddle bow unaimed" as they approach the gate of Sutpen's Hundred. Henry finally penetrates Bon with a bullet after warning him not to cross the barrier. Earlier Henry had placed himself in the feminine role, fantasizing that Charles might despoil him as "the sister, the mistress, the bride" (77). In switching from the stereotypically feminine to the stereotypically masculine role, Henry acts out his conflicted emotions. The result is fatal whether this scene is read as a symbolic consummation of Henry's homosexual desire or, alternatively, as an enactment of his homosexual panic. According to Sedgwick, homosexual panic arises when the intense male social bonds that male entitlement demands become difficult to distinguish from the "most reprobated bonds" of homosexuality. The similarity of the two bonds, one socially mandated and one socially prohibited, causes confusion and fear that one's peer and perhaps even oneself may be a homosexual. The fear and confusion leads to violence against those perceived to be a homosexual threat (185–86), but the absence of a clearly visible marker of homosexuality leads to hypervigilance lest we fail to recognize "them" and thereby implicate ourselves in their sins. Faulkner points out that the same difficulty complicates the distinctions between black and white, suggesting that both hierarchical binaries are artificial: that which we abhor may often be unrecognizable, and it may therefore be everywhere or nowhere. So, the social abjection of blackness and/or homosexuality creates hysteria and is ultimately untenable.

Crossing the gate at Sutpen's Hundred is a symbolic penetration and a transgression of conventional social boundaries. The phallic gun and the threatened homestead suggest the violence enacted against those who bring the possibility of homosexuality too close to home. In the next chronological scene, Judith learns she cannot marry Charles because Henry has killed him. Charles's penetration by another man has made the marriage impossible. On a figurative level, the direct consummation of homoerotic desire, bypassing the female, is destructive to both heterosexuality and whiteness because whiteness has been socially construed to connote virility and dominance. Quentin and Shreve eventually arrive at the conclusion that Charles is part black to explain Henry's action because a white man could not be penetrated in this way. Quentin's and Shreve's labeling of Charles as black simultaneously reinforces stereotypes of blackness as passive/feminine and provides them with "black"-tinted spectacles to shield them from the uncomfortable recognition of homosexual desire.

In the second half of the novel, Faulkner suggests that Quentin's and Shreve's fascination with Henry's and Charles's story stems at least in part from identification. As the college students re-create the tale in the present, their identities merge with those of the young men from the past: "four of them and then just two—Charles-Shreve and Quentin-Henry" (267). Faulkner links the two pairs further through homoerotic descriptions of Quentin and Shreve as they struggle to understand Charles's and Henry's mysterious conduct. As they talk, Shreve sits half-naked, a fact that Faulkner notes repeatedly. Shreve has a "naked torso pink-gleaming and baby-smooth, cherubic, almost hairless" (147). And "from the waist down the table concealed him; anyone entering the room would have taken him to be stark naked" (177). Here Faulkner suggests the gaze of another who might enter the room and note Shreve's "stark nakedness," thereby implicating the two in something improper. Dyer points out that we don't often see naked white male bodies in film because "a naked body is a vulnerable body" (*White* 146). And "a sense of separation and boundedness is important to the white male ego" which does not risk "being merged into other bodies" (152). Faulkner repeatedly associates Shreve with Charles, another feminized male. The concealment of Shreve's lower body further suggests secret, forbidden activity. Shreve's actions and Faulkner's descriptions of them often seem vaguely sexual: "soon he will raise the window and do his deep-breathing in it, clenchfisted and naked to the waist, in the warm and rosy orifice above the iron quad" (176). "Warm and rosy orifice" seems an oddly sexual way to describe an open window, and a phallic stiffness resonates from the "iron quad." *The Sound and the Fury* also suggests a homoerotic tie between the two roommates. A fellow Harvard student jokingly describes Shreve as Quentin's husband, and Quentin notes that Shreve twice touches his knee as they ride in Mrs. Bland's car; here Quentin twice moves his knee away (147–48). In *Absalom, Absalom!* Faulkner suggests that, as they ponder the unexplained aspects of Charles's and Henry's relationship, Quentin and Shreve develop an unconventional bond:

> They stared at one another ... their quiet regular breathing vaporizing faintly and steadily in the now tomblike air. There was something curious in the way they looked at one another, curious and quiet and profoundly intent, not at all as two young men might look at each other but almost as a youth and a very young girl might out of virginity itself—a sort of hushed and naked searching. (240)

Faulkner describes the naked searching of a sexual awakening as these two young men talk about love in a "happy marriage of speaking and hearing" (253).[8]

That Faulkner figures the language itself as a marriage further supports the reading of homoerotics in this text. The surface of the text clearly suggests the homosocial bonds of narrative itself. Men come together—first General Compson and Thomas Sutpen, then Mr. Compson and Quentin, then Quentin and Henry Sutpen, and finally, Quentin and Shreve—to tell this story to each other. Their individual relationships to the story differ, but in each case the telling of the story strengthens their bond to each other.[9] In the Harvard dorm room, the narration slides from the homosocial to the homoerotic. Alex Vernon suggests that Faulkner's use of the marriage trope to describe the young men's conversation is relevant to the characters' obsessions with genealogy and bloodline: "Quentin and Shreve cannot physically continue a family line, but oh how they can further a story" (162). Vernon elaborates, "The novel's evolving narrative line, particularly as furthered by Quentin and Shreve, invokes a direct correspondence with the evolutionary process whereby genetic transmission through sexual intercourse becomes narrative transmission through conversational intercourse" (170).

Their talk, however, is more than simply the transmission and reproduction of a story. In *The Literary Speech Act*, Shoshana Felman writes about the seductive power of speech: "Speech is the true realm of eroticism, and not simply a means of access to this realm. To seduce is to produce language that enjoys, language that takes pleasure in having 'no more to say.' To seduce is thus to prolong, within desiring speech, the pleasuretaking performance of the very production of speech" (28).

Quentin and Shreve seem to delight in the performance of speech, arousing themselves and each other as they enlarge the narrative by turns. As Shreve narrates, Quentin punctuates his additions to the tale with "yeses." At the end of chapter 6, as the tale appears to build to a climax, Quentin's final "yes" is followed by Shreve's breathless, "Wait then . . . For God's sake wait" (174–75), and the two prolong and postpone the culmination of desire. Later, when Shreve again takes the narrative lead saying, "Let me play a while now" (224), the storytelling becomes a seductive display designed to heighten ecstasy. Faulkner's italicized sentences, which encourage quick reading and overemphasis, resemble seething passions that can barely be controlled. David Minter points out that when Faulkner tells us the two young men's talk soon "overpass[es] to love" (253), the word choice is particularly apt "since it is not only love that Quentin and Shreve begin to discuss; it is love they begin to experience" (Minter 78). As Quentin and Shreve take turns as storyteller, they use the seductive power of language to penetrate their subject, Charles and Henry, and each other:

there was now not two of them but four, the two who breathed not individuals now yet something both more and less than twins.... not two of them there and then either but four of them riding the two horses through the iron darkness and that not mattering either: what faces and what names they called themselves and were called by so long as the blood coursed. (236–37)

Two becoming one (or four becoming two) echoes biblical language describing sex and marriage, and this male union centers on the erotic image of horseback riding. Words allow the two youths to understand, to identify with, even to merge with each other and with their long-dead counterparts, and Faulkner links their verbal and mental merger to the physical throb of the blood.

Quentin, however, is still a product of his culture. Quentin's and Shreve's awakening that the novel figures as a marriage in language, coupled with the repressed knowledge of the similar sexual desire of the past, induces a form of homosexual panic in Quentin similar to the panic displayed by Henry Sutpen. Quentin succumbs to the first manifestation of this panic after discovering the aged Henry lying in bed: "He was twenty years old; he was not afraid, because what he had seen out there could not harm him, yet he ran; even inside the dark familiar house ... he still ran" (297). If Quentin is not afraid, perhaps he runs from a recognition of himself in Henry Sutpen and the running is a hysterical response to his attempt to repress this knowledge. Quentin and Shreve project the screens of blackness and a heterosexual surrogate onto Charles's and Henry's relationship in order to make it less threatening. But these same screens are not available to Quentin in his interaction with Shreve; repression of forbidden desire is therefore even more important for the Quentin in the Harvard dorm room than it was for the Quentin living in the past, and this repression is marked by repeated references to whiteness. Faulkner emphasizes that Shreve is from Canada (208, 276, 289), an area far removed from the racial tensions of southern Mississippi in the late nineteenth and early twentieth centuries. Compared to Mississippi, Canada is further associated with whiteness through the snow that covers the landscape and the fact that relatively few blacks lived there. In New England, the frequent references to the color of his skin, referred to as pink (147, 176, 177, 220) or blond (141), and the white snow or ash emphasize Shreve's whiteness and symbolically underscore a continued repression: "There was snow on Shreve's arm now, no sleeve on his arm at all now: only the smooth cupid-fleshed forearm" (176), and a pipe "lay overturned, a scattering of white ashes fanning out from the bowl, onto the table before his crossed naked arms" (205). These references to snow and white ash occur in tandem with references to Shreve's naked flesh and to Cupid, or Eros, the god of love. The ash spills from an "overturned" phallic pipe, as if the snow and ash were meant to freeze or extinguish the desire engendered by this nakedness. Symbolically, white often represents purity and absence, marking a repression or closeting of desire.[10] Racially, identification with cultural definitions of whiteness—which, as discussed earlier, are coded as masculine and heterosexual—would be the antidote to a socially disgraceful desire that lies beneath the surface.

Such forbidden desires might elicit a fear of being labeled a race traitor, "someone who defies the rules of whiteness so flagrantly as to jeopardize his or her ability to draw upon the privileges of white skin" (Ignatiev 82). W. J. Cash, who in 1941 published the landmark critical study of southern history and culture called *The Mind of the South*, refers to this anxiety as the "savage ideal . . . that ideal whereunder dissent and variety are completely suppressed and [white] men become, in all their attitudes, professions, and actions, virtual replicas of one another" (90–91). Like Quentin Compson, Cash, shortly after "tell[ing] about the South" (Faulkner, *Absalom* 142) and betraying the bond that supposedly unites all white men, committed suicide (Hobson 247), thereby testifying to the power of the savage ideal and the shame of being labeled a "race traitor."

But as Quentin and Shreve discover more about the past and about each other in their "tomblike" room, their repression becomes harder to maintain: "Then the darkness seemed to breathe, to flow back; the window which Shreve had opened became visible against the faintly unearthly glow of the outer snow as, forced by the weight of the darkness, the blood surged and ran warmer and warmer" (288). Quentin's surging warm blood, forced by darkness, competes with the cold white snow on the threshold of the window Shreve has opened. The window's threshold represents the familiar boundaries between our culture's definitions of black and white, male and female, gay and straight, a liminal space that, as evidenced by the repeated references to it, obsesses Quentin (and Faulkner?) almost as much as the Sutpen tale. Presumably, this is the same window that launches Quentin's first conscious moment at the beginning of section 2 in *The Sound and the Fury*: "When the shadow of the sash appeared on the curtains it was between seven and eight oclock and then I was in time again, hearing the watch" (76).[11] If, as I suggest, the window represents the threshold between racial and sexual binaries, the fact that its shadow returns Quentin to temporality on the day of his suicide seems significant. It connects his suicide not only to feelings of displacement in his time and culture, but also to feelings of displacement regarding his position with respect to these binaries. This window is the figurative shadow hanging over him as well as the literal one. His suicide occurs in June, nearing the end of his term at Harvard, but for a time, at least, the distancing snow of New England provides the safety that enables Quentin to finish in his mind the tale begun back in Mississippi and to consign it to a safe cultural and temporal space: "Now he (Quentin) could read it [his father's letter], could finish it—the sloped whimsical ironic hand out of Mississippi attenuated, into the iron snow" (301). Whatever truth Quentin might glean from this sloping hand of Mississippi is attenuated, temporarily, by the cold, obscuring, distancing whiteness of the snow.

In this white world, miscegenation is the answer that the two young Harvard men impose on the tale near the very end, after generations and pages of struggle to explain what prevented the marriage between Charles and Judith and what prompted Henry's murder of Charles. But if, as Noel Polk suggests, we examine this conclusion critically, we encounter some significant flaws in their logic:

> First, you have to believe that Sutpen is far more race-conscious than he proves himself to be in any other place in the novel. Second, you have to believe that Bon at birth had physical characteristics—skin pigmentation, hair texture, lip thickness: something—that identified him as black, but which disappeared as he got older so that he could enroll at the University of Mississippi and pass as white all of his life. Third, if you believe that Supten was worried about dynasty, traditional problems of primogeniture, you have to overlook the Mississippi law that forbade a black son to inherit a father's estate. (20)

Though their conclusion does not add up on the literal level, symbolically it makes perfect sense. Thadious Davis points out that Faulkner's "white world must have its 'Negro,' because it cannot face itself without this scapegoat, this buffer which, even in its most ineffectual symbolic shape, can absorb the shock of self-confrontation" (Faulkner's "Negro" 237–38). That which these particular white men cannot face in themselves, that which they seek to buffer via the "Negro," is a recognition of their homoerotic desire. In the elite New England setting of Harvard, overwhelmingly white in landscape and population, Quentin must import his black-white scapegoat via the story. If, as Anne Goodwyn Jones suggests, "[white] southerners constructed their manhood on a daily basis of racial difference" ("The Work of Gender" 53), what better way for Quentin to reassure himself of his masculinity than to impose racial difference on the actions of Charles and Henry that might otherwise seem uncomfortably similar to his own?[12] Significantly, the novel's structure suggests that Quentin discovers the "truth" about Charles's racial heritage when he goes upstairs to find Henry in bed.[13]

In the approved tale, what prevents heterosexuality is not homosexuality but blackness. In Quentin's and Shreve's retelling, however, just after Henry learns of Charles's black blood, we encounter a scene in which it is impossible to ignore the homoerotic suggestion:

> Now it is Bon who watches Henry; he can see the whites of Henry's eyes again as he sits looking at Henry with that expression which might be called smiling. His hand vanishes beneath the blanket and reappears, holding his pistol by the barrel, the butt extended toward Henry.
> Then do it now, he says.
> Henry looks at the pistol; now he is not only panting, he is trembling. (285–86)

Charles's hand vanishes beneath the blanket and reappears holding a symbolic phallus; he then extends the butt toward Henry and invites him to "do it now."[14] Looking at Charles's symbolic phallus, Henry pants and trembles. Rather than acknowledge the homoerotic tension, Henry projects this taboo onto the more familiar one of miscegenation. Quentin trembles in a similar way as he lies in bed in the cold dorm room at the novel's end.

Because he is lying in bed, Quentin's panting and trembling conjures images of orgasmic ecstasy. Quentin's shaking, however, has often been interpreted as a hysterical symptom of repression, a hysteria that might also be labeled homosexual panic.[15]

Judith Butler suggests that passing engenders homosexual panic because, if the disguise is so easy, we may be misled by others or we may even mislead ourselves. By discovering the secret of miscegenation as the "truth" in *Absalom, Absalom!* Quentin and Shreve attempt to locate the Otherness of Charles and Henry in the antebellum past, thereby containing it. A homosexual Otherness might seem more frightening because it resonates more closely with Quentin's and Shreve's present. But as Shreve hints at the end, miscegenation is not contained in the past either: "in a few thousand years, I who regard you will also have sprung from the loins of African kings" (302). This blurring of category and distinction that Faulkner suggests through *Absalom, Absalom!*'s narrative structure, through the ambiguous desires of its characters, the racial amalgamation suggested at the novel's end, and the conflation of homosexual desire and miscegenation, even up to this last quotation, destabilizes the powerful cultural force of whiteness.

"A STRANGE NIGGER"
Faulkner and the Minstrel Performance of Whiteness

—JOHN N. DUVALL

Despite the assertions of many racist characters in Yoknapatawpha County, William Faulkner's fiction repeatedly illustrates that race is not a simple matter of essence or biology but is always mediated by performance. Faulkner particularly makes visible an opening between racial and cultural identity through certain reflections on the racist construct "nigger." During his year at Harvard, Quentin Compson comes to realize that "a nigger is not a person so much as a form of behavior" (Faulkner, *The Sound* 86). In *Go Down, Moses*, we see a trickster Lucas Beauchamp who, when the need arises, can manipulate threats from the white world by becoming "not Negro but nigger, not secret so much as impenetrable," who masks his intelligence "in an aura of timeless and stupid impassivity almost like a smell" (58). But if Faulkner opens a space between black performance and racial essence through the depiction of certain African American characters, he is equally aware that not all Caucasians are fully white in a South that wishes to absolutize all racial difference. What I wish to emphasize is the performativity of whiteness in Faulkner, deriving from his figurative use of two distinct but not unrelated theater traditions: not simply American blackface minstrelsy but an older European whiteface minstrelsy as well. The result is a fictional world in which one sees, by turns, a dizzying variety of masking: whites in blackface, blacks in blackface, whites in whiteface, and blacks in whiteface. Clearly, such multiple performative possibilities serve to unhinge the southern binary that would oppose whiteness to "the Negro."

My thinking in this essay is indebted to Toni Morrison's work on the Africanist presence (as well as the use of figurative blackness) in texts by canonical white American novelists and to Susan Gubar's work on "racechange," forms of racial metamorphosis in art, which she sees emerging in the twentieth century as a "crucial trope of high and low, elite and popular culture, one that allowed artists from widely divergent ideological backgrounds to meditate on racial privilege and privation as well as on the disequilibrium of race" (5). Despite drawing on Morrison and Gubar, I do see limitations to their projects inasmuch as they always identify white writers' engagements with blackness as a problem or a failure. Morrison typically identifies a failure in aesthetic design, while Gubar sees the failure more in ethical terms. For Gubar, in the last instance, every white appropriation of blackness can only be a net loss in the search for a more ethical understanding of race.[1] And of course Morrison and Gubar are correct: there are aesthetic and ethical shortcomings to be identified in a white writer's appropriation of blackness. But they may be only half right, because there is also something potentially productive in such appropriations. In Faulkner's case, there are in-between characters—Caucasians who instantiate blackness in ways that complicate the southern racial binarism. These presumptively white characters come to embody black culture, where "black" is not exactly race any longer, but (because it is the South) it is not exactly not race either.

I make this last assertion following E. Patrick Johnson's interrogation of what is at stake in, to invoke his book's title, "appropriating blackness." Blackness, as Johnson casts it, is not a racial essence but always involves performance. The questions he asks are germane to this essay:

> What happens when "blackness" is embodied? What are the cultural, social, and political consequences of that embodiment in a racist society? What is at stake when race or blackness is theorized discursively, and the material reality of the "black" subject is occluded? Indeed, what happens in those moments when blackness takes on corporeality? Or, alternatively, how are the stakes changed when a "white" body performs blackness? (2)

For Johnson, "'blackness' does not belong to any one individual or group. Rather, individuals or groups *appropriate* this complex and nuanced racial signifier in order to circumscribe its boundaries or to exclude other individuals or groups" (2–3). Johnson is fully aware of the dangers of stereotypes and fetishization that can accompany white appropriations of blackness, such as the linguistic appropriation of white rappers. What Johnson is willing to imagine (in ways that Gubar and Morrison seem less able to) is that "cross-cultural appropriation of blackness" need not result only in "colonization and subjugation" and may in fact "provide fertile ground on which to formulate new epistemologies of self and Other" (6).[2]

It is in Johnson's spirit of openness that I pursue the figurative blackness of a number of presumptively white characters in Faulkner's fiction. These characters suggest that Faulkner's appropriation of blackness is not simply a fetishistic gesture in service of white hegemony. By "not simply," I mean both "not only or exclusively" and "not in a simple fashion." In other words, even to the extent that these characters in some ways are implicated in fetishistic appropriation, both their constructions and their effects are complex, never simple. When I claim, then, that Faulkner's appropriation of blackness has a productive side, I do not mean at the level of mimesis. For the characters in his fiction, their relation to blackness is often confusing, painful, and occasionally fatal. Faulkner's use of figurative blackness is literally productive because it allows him a way to map imbricated relations between one form of otherness (racial) and other forms of otherness (gender/sexuality and class). More importantly, it allows Faulkner's readers to see that, whatever the residual racism of William Faulkner, his narratives negotiate racial struggle even when race seems absent from their field of vision; these narratives are, in other words, racialized in a way that enables a critical purchase on whiteness.

The two classes of Caucasians not granted full southern whiteness in Faulkner's world are 1) those characters who exhibit sexual or gender ambiguity and 2) poor whites. In short, sexual or class difference works to exclude certain Caucasians from the metaphysical privilege of whiteness. As an example of the first category, a metaphorically masked figure is strikingly present in Faulkner's second novel, *Mosquitoes*, where a young woman, Jenny, recalls meeting a funny little "black man" who she finally remembers is named Faulkner. Her friend is confused, since "black man" does not really signify in 1920s parlance, and asks if he was "a nigger" (144). Assuring her friend that he was white, she maintains that Faulkner's blackness is associated with his crazy performance of gender, one in which he stands ready to couple with either male or female partners on the dance floor. Fictional Faulkner's "blackness" models subsequent minstrel performances of masculinity in Faulkner's fiction; the excessive libidinality of "Faulkner," which opens nonheteronormative possibility, signals the way that the Caucasian loses white identity and shades toward blackness.

This figuration of a black "Faulkner" is anticipated in *The Marionettes*, Faulkner's hand-letter play with a series of pen and ink drawings. Working within the modernist Pierrot tradition, Faulkner imagines a psychologically divided figure: two of the main characters are Pierrot and Shade of Pierrot.[3] While Pierrot is a drunken dreamer, Shade of Pierrot is the successful seducer of Marietta. In Faulkner's drawings, Pierrot is a tall clown, but Shade of Pierrot, as he serenades Marietta with his lute, is (perspectively) a funny little black man. Faulkner's Pierrot is a minstrel figure. First developed in commedia dell'arte, Pierrot was reimagined in French pantomime by Jean-Gaspard Deburau in the early nineteenth century. The forerunner of the whiteface circus clown, Deburau's Pierrot established the character as the ineffectual lover, always represented on stage in baggy white clothes and whiteface makeup. And this is how Faulkner draws Pierrot: from his stylized cupid's bow lips to his caplike hair, Pierrot is not simply white; rather, he is in whiteface. Faulkner's male artists and sexually ambiguous characters, in this figurative space, therefore, present a white face to the world, but this whiteness masks a "black" identity. The limitation of Faulkner's portrayal of figurative blackness is that it draws on stereotypes of African American and primitive sexuality, but at the same time it significantly unhinges blackness as a form of unlicensed sexuality from a biological or essentialist notion of race: Caucasians as well as Negroes can perform blackness.

In *Mosquitoes*, the professional liar named Faulkner is not the only artist associated with blackness. Another young woman, Patricia, identifies the sculptor Gordon similarly when, after he refuses to give her a statue that resembles her, she asks him, "Why are you so black?" (25). She can't identify what makes him black but knows that something marks him in this fashion; the novel, however, links Gordon's blackness to his primitivism as artist, a primitivism that ultimately problematizes his heterosexual performance.

Such "black" Caucasians recur throughout Faulkner's major period: in *Sanctuary*, Temple Drake identifies the sexually ambiguous Popeye as that "black man" (42, 49); the sexually tortured, feminized Quentin Compson, always followed by his black shadow, is identified by the boys fishing by the bridge as enacting the linguistic performance of a "colored man" from the "minstrel shows" (Faulkner, *The Sound* 120); and Joe Christmas's sexual in-betweenness, aside from his unknowable racial identity, would be sufficient to mark him as black. Even Ike McCaslin, whose repudiation of his patrimony also terminates his performance of heterosexuality and leads to his retirement into the extreme homosociality of the hunter's world, is marked as his text's secret black man. Unlike his good-old-boy father and uncle, Uncle Buck and Uncle Buddy, who under the appropriate social circumstances can be Mr. Theophilus and Mr. Amodeus, Uncle Ike can never be a mister. Having repudiated his patrimony at the age of majority, Ike has also repudiated his proper white identity, and so tracks along the path of the pliant African American male, who is always "boy" until old age sometimes grants him the honorific "uncle."[4]

All of these characters are in a sense blacks in whiteface; they present a white face to the world, but their being (through primitivist art or sexuality) at some deeper level is marked as black, which leads to all sorts of social misrecognitions because this blackness usually goes unremarked (except by the occasional confused comments of a Temple, a Jenny, or a Patricia). This figurative blackness, as I have argued elsewhere, should be read in light of Havelock Ellis's work on sexual inversion. Ellis sees three groups with higher than average tendencies toward inversion—the primitive (read nonwhite) races, the lower classes, and artists and intellectuals.[5] For Faulkner's whiteface males, their association with blackness queers white identity.

The reader by now may well have questioned the gendered nature of my discussion of Faulkner's whiteface minstrelsy, which I have cast as a problem of white southern masculine performance. One might reasonably object that there are feminine examples as well. Aren't Caddy Compson and her daughter, Quentin, examples of women performing black sexuality in whiteface? While they certainly are implicated in black performance, it does not occur in whiteface and fundamentally differs from the way Faulkner's whiteface males experience blackness. If we listen to the male voices that censure female sexuality, we can begin to hear why. Caddy's brother Quentin asks, "*Why wont you bring him to the house, Caddy? Why must you do like nigger women do in the pasture the ditches and dark woods hot hidden furious in the dark woods*" (92). Jason complains about his niece in similar language: "I'm not going to have any member of my family going on *like a nigger wench*" (189; emphasis added).

There's a big difference between having one's behavior named through a simile (you're acting *like* a "nigger") and being identified as (or sensing that one's identity is) black. In the former, whiteness is not really problematized and in fact is confirmed. There is no social misrecognition: white is white and Negro is Negro. Telling these women that they are behaving "like niggers" merely polices the boundary of their whiteness; it's their behavior (which is correctable), not their being, that is linked to racial otherness. In the latter, however, the recovery of whiteness is quite problematic. Faulkner's whiteface male minstrels have crossed over: they're not *like* blacks; they *are* black. It is precisely this masked black being that creates social misrecognition. Jenny and Patricia may identify "Faulkner" and Gordon as "black" but neither the identifiers nor the identified understand exactly what that means.

Turning to the second category of Faulkner's racechanging Caucasians, poor whites, I wish to suggest that one of the ways we might begin to speak of the complexity that emerges when white southerners perform black subjectivity is in relation to the concept of diaspora. African Americans who migrated from the South are doubly diasporic. First, as the descendants of slaves forced to leave their homeland, they constitute an African diaspora. But after generations of living in the American South, those blacks who participated in the Great Migration also experienced a more immediate and personal relation to diaspora. At the beginning of the 1890s, the decade Faulkner was born, 90 percent of African Americans lived in the South; by the 1960s, the decade Faulkner died, only 10 percent of the African American population lived in the South. Forced by the threat of lynching and other violence to leave the only home they knew, these black migrants experienced a southern diasporic identity. The sense of home they carry with them to their new locations creates a second-order "historical rift between the locations of residence and the locations of belonging" (Gilroy 124).

It is precisely the southern diaspora constituted by the Great Migration that, in a profoundly ironic way, turns back on the very white racist culture responsible for the intolerable conditions that caused blacks to leave the South. One group to bear the brunt of black migration is the poor white. I am not suggesting that the construct "white trash" emerges at the time of the migration; the poor white as the socially abject was part of antebellum culture. Rather, the migration further blurs the boundary between "nigger" and "white trash." Even if they remain on the land as sharecroppers, Faulkner's poor whites become so alienated from home as to be in a sense homeless. Perversely, in a kind of mirrored fashion to black displacement, these homeless whites experience identity in diasporic fashion as locationless, hybrid, and uncomfortably mixed. This hybridity is most often represented through racechange in which their whiteness is simultaneously knowable and unhinged by a figurative relation to blackness.

My linkage of diaspora and whiteness may strike many readers as wrongheaded at best and at worst as openly blaspheming the work of postcolonial scholars. The concept of diaspora, quite simply, would seem to be usable only in relation to oppressed, displaced peoples. As Paul Gilroy notes, "Slavery, pogroms, indenture, genocide, and other unnameable terrors have all figured in the constitution of diasporas and the reproduction of diaspora consciousness in which identity is focused, less on the equalizing, predemocratic force of sovereign territory and more on the social dynamics of remembrance and commemoration defined by a strong sense of the dangers involved in forgetting the location of origin and the tearful process of dispersal" (123–24). How could whites, then, possibly participate in such consciousness?

If white identity knows itself in relation to the foil of blackness, what happened when African Americans migrated from the rural South to escape its violent racism? In terms of southern epistemology, there became a need for someone to stand in for the rural Negro who was migrating to urban areas or out of the South entirely. This need is doubled in the realm of economics. If during the violence of the post-Reconstruction South, rural black workers leave for Harlem, the Midwest, the Southwest, or even the urban South, what do large landowners need? As the number of black farm workers falls, there emerges the economic need (every bit as much as the epistemological one) for, to borrow the title of a famous Flannery O'Connor story, "artificial niggers."

The subject position of the sharecropper is perhaps the most obvious one in which black and white bodies inhabit an identical subject position. As John Egerton succinctly summarizes it:

> To be a sharecropper or tenant farmer in the South in 1932 was to be caught up in an existence that often was nothing more than peonage or forced labor—just one step removed from slavery. You rented the land from its owner, and made the crop for him with his furnish of seed and fertilizer and mules and tools; he sold you food and other necessities on credit at high interest in his commissary; he kept the books, handled the sales, and divided with you at harvest time. You were lucky if you broke even; some went in the hole, and not one in ten actually came away with a few dollars profit. (20–21)

Faulkner certainly knew about black and white tenant farmers, individuals he had seen since childhood shopping on Saturdays in Oxford, Mississippi. By 1910 approximately two-thirds of all farmers in Lafayette County worked in the tenant system: 80 percent of black farmers and 54 percent of white farmers (Doyle 307). Nevertheless, despite the shared conditions of existence, attempts to unionize tenant farmers met with limited success precisely because of the barrier of race.[6] This same barrier often prevents Faulkner's poor white characters from fully recognizing the ways in which they enact blackness.

In *Absalom, Absalom!* Thomas Sutpen begins his young life as a displaced person, a migrant from his mountain home in (West) Virginia, who comes to see that his being Caucasian is a necessary but insufficient condition to enjoying the status of southern whiteness. Although sharecropping emerges as a major form of African American farm labor after the Civil War, white tenant farmers did form part of the antebellum South's landscape, and while it is not clear that Sutpen's family were tenant farmers on the Pettibone plantation, Faulkner does make clear that his family served as the progenitors of future white sharecroppers. Insulted when a black servant turns him away from the front door of the plantation house, young Sutpen discovers his race as his class ceases to be transparent. Retreating into a cave, the young Sutpen begins to see how the plantation owner views poor whites such as his family:

> as cattle, creatures heavy and without grace, brutely evacuated into a world without hope or purpose for them, who would in turn spawn with brutish and vicious prolixity, populate, double treble and compound, fill space and earth with *a race* whose future would be a succession of cut-down and patched and made-over garments bought on exorbitant credit.... (Faulkner, *Absalom* 190; emphasis added)

When he emerges from this cave, Sutpen is reborn into a strange, newly raced world. Still "white," he is simultaneously not-white because he no longer enjoys the primary marker of whiteness, which is an experience of the self as unmarked by race. He now feels himself to be a member of a race apart, one that is subhuman and in that regard difficult to distinguish from the black slave. Both the poor white and the African American are denied humanity by southern whiteness; indeed both groups are identified as animals. Beginning as a Caucasian animal, Sutpen seeks nothing less than a specieschange (from subhuman to human).

As a result of this self-consciousness of himself as a member of an oppressed and displaced race, his subsequent southern whiteness is always performance. As Mr. Compson puts it:

> He was like John L. Sullivan having taught himself painfully and tediously to do the schottische, having drilled himself and drilled himself in secret until he now believed it no longer necessary to count the music's beat, say. He may have believed that your grandfather or Judge Benbow might have done it a little more effortlessly than he, but he would not have believed that anyone could have beat him in knowing when to do it or how. (34–35)

While it certainly makes sense to speak of Sutpen's performance of himself as a kind of class passing, class has been marked by (and indeed as) race, and as a result Sutpen has a heightened sense of the danger of racial mixing.

This marking of class as race is elsewhere represented by another more literal form of entertainment he provides when he himself owns a plantation, a performance that confuses other white men because they would not do what he does. Sutpen's fighting his slaves becomes a way of denying that he was ever a member of a subhuman race, even as his direct physical contact with blacks (a figurative mixing of the races) points to their metaphorical kinship as the Other of southern whiteness. The complexity of figurative racechange, however, becomes more explicit in "Barn Burning" (1939), where Faulkner imagines another poor white, Abner Snopes, who has a more developed understanding of the interchangeability of "white trash" and "nigger." Class analysis once again is so coded in relation to figurative blackness that it instantiates a kind of racechanged, minstrel performance of whiteness.

I'd like to juxtapose Faulkner's story with one by Richard Wright, another native Mississippian, because together they underscore the economic slavery experienced alike by black and white sharecroppers. Wright's "The Man Who Was Almost a Man" (1940) also helps us better recognize the performativity of Faulknerian racechange. In Wright's story, Dave Sanders, a seventeen-year-old black male, the son of a sharecropper, suffers at the outset from a sense that, despite performing the labor of a man, he is not acknowledged as one in his community. In an effort to gain respect, he buys a gun with which he accidentally shoots the white landowner's mule.[7] When the truth of the accident is revealed to the gathered crowd, Dave receives only ridicule, and the landowner demands fifty dollars for the mule, which Dave will be required to work off at the rate of two dollars a month (or 100 percent of his wages for the next two years). In thinking the gun will grant him respect, Dave fails to realize that manhood is simply not available to the African American male in his southern community. Throughout the story, Dave is addressed by every character as "boy," which points to the fact that any African American male of any age could be hailed by this demeaning designation, since the honorific "mister" was never used to address a black man. At the end of the story, Dave has a dawning, if unarticulated, moment of class consciousness in which he wishes he had another bullet so that he might take a shot at the landowner's big white house before he begins his personal migration to the North. But when the Daves of the South leave home, somebody still has to do the work.

Faulkner's "Barn Burning" might have been titled "The Boy Who Was Almost a White Boy." As both Richard Godden (126) and Matthew Lessig (82) argue, although this story is set in the 1890s, it in fact is informed by Faulkner's understanding of the struggles of sharecroppers in the 1930s. From the outset, the nomadic, sharecropping Snopes family embodies a kind of pastiche of the diaspora consciousness that one associates with African American experience. The class lesson that Abner Snopes tries to teach his son Sarty in Faulkner's "Barn Burning" is uncannily similar to the one Dave begins to learn. Like Dave, Abner is under a judgment—Dave, if he remains, must pay the landowner for a dead mule; Abner must pay the landowner, Major de Spain, for a rug he has intentionally ruined. Both choose flight, coupled with violence against the landowner. Dave's violence is unrealized for lack of another bullet, but Abner burns barns. If Dave's education begins by his attempt to advance an assertion: "Ahm gettin t be a man like anybody else!" (12), Abner similarly prefaces his lesson to his son: "You're getting to be a man. You got to learn. You got to learn to stick to your own blood or you ain't going to have any blood to stick to you" (8). Based on an essentialist notion of clan-based identity, Abner's bloodpride opposes the pride in lineage of the southern aristocracy, while also marking an absolute line that separates poor whites from black blood. The lessons Abner teaches are uncomfortable both to the boy and to the reader because, though they are correct in terms of class analysis, their articulation is virulently racist. Forced to move to a new tenant home, Abner requires his youngest son to accompany him to the big house, saying: "I reckon I'll have a word with the man that aims to begin to-morrow owning me body and soul for the next eight months" (9). This certainly articulates Abner's understanding that the sharecropper's marginalized existence is a form of economic slavery. After the visit in which Abner stains de Spain's rug with manure, he asks Sarty to turn and look at the plantation owner's house: "'Pretty and white, ain't it?' he said. 'That's sweat. Nigger sweat. Maybe it ain't white enough yet to suit him. Maybe he wants to mix some white sweat with it'" (12). In a fashion that anticipates Ralph Ellison's invisible man and his experience at the Liberty paint factory where ten black drops are the special ingredient that makes their white paint so very white, Abner's reading of the white house (in which appropriated African American labor figuratively is what coats the de Spain house) correctly sees that his own and other white sharecroppers' labor (sweat) is identical to exploited black labor. Clearly Abner's racism is the only thing that prevents him from fully recognizing that he in fact is an "artificial nigger." The sticking point, of course, is the label "nigger." It is the name Abner uses to address the elderly black servant who attempts to block his entrance into the big white house. But the servant has already marked Abner's status in saying "Wipe yo foots, white man, fo you come in here" (11). In the black man's eyes, Abner clearly falls beneath the necessity of addressing him as "sir" or "mister." In other words, Abner may be Caucasian, but falls short of whiteness. Interestingly, it is another unnamed African American who serves as the agent denying Abner his putative racial identity (just as the unnamed black servant, noted earlier, initiates young Sutpen's dawning awareness that he is not fully white by turning him away from the planter's front door).

As Godden has pointed out, everything about Abner is associated with blackness—his black hat and frockcoat, but most particularly his relationship with fire. Faulkner's repeated use of the term "niggard" to describe the fire that Abner burns for his family, serves as wordplay that both points toward, even as its etymological difference deflects attention away from, "nigger" (Godden 127–28).[8] To Godden's analysis I would add another possibility of Abner's blackness. In the initial courtroom scene in which Harris testifies against Abner, he tells the court that Abner sent a "strange nigger" with a dollar pound fee to collect the Snopeses' roaming hog, as well as with a warning that "wood and hay kin burn."[9] But what has become of this African American? This is certainly a question the judge wants to know:

> "Where is the nigger? Have you got him?"
> "He was a strange nigger, I tell you. I don't know what became of him." (4)

Too much of what is not stated about this individual who is identified as African American doesn't quite hold together. Is he a stranger or, as the locution seems to suggest, odd or unusual? The plaintiff, Harris, would likely know by sight most of the black people who lived and worked near him. African American males who were strangers would have been viewed suspiciously by the white community. And what African American would do a favor for Abner? Perhaps a local black man who feared Abner's retaliation, but Abner clearly does not socialize with blacks. How likely would Abner be to trust an African American with a dollar, especially one who might be simply passing through and therefore not be around to intimidate later?

I wish to suggest that the story's "strange nigger" is actually in the store where the hearing takes place and is the very figure of the man in black, Abner Snopes. Since almost the only person Abner would trust with a dollar is himself (or close kin), it seems plausible that Abner (or perhaps his eldest son) blackened up in order to collect his hog and deliver his warning in person without being recognized. Two objections might be raised to my suggestion of a blackface Abner, one logical and one textual. An immediate objection might be that surely Harris would recognize such a ruse and would be immediately able to distinguish an artificial from an authentic black. But as Eric Lott has pointed out, audiences of minstrel shows in the nineteenth century often were completely fooled by the racial masquerade and assumed that the white performers who entertained them were actually black (20). A more text-based objection might argue that my assertion is undercut by Sarty's question and comment when he realizes his father intends to burn de Spain's barn: "'Ain't you going to even send a nigger?' he cried. 'At least you sent a nigger before'" (21). However, the detail of the black man carrying a warning is one Sarty more likely learned about from Harris's testimony, since it is only after the trial that Abner begins to include his youngest son in his plans. Sarty effectively knows no more about the identity of the "strange" black than the reader, and his question in no way proves that he had firsthand knowledge about his father actually sending a racially black messenger to Harris.

If Abner is "black," what finally is Sarty? Following metaphorically the one-drop rule of southern race, Sarty too must be figuratively black. Whether or not one believes that the "strange nigger" is Abner in blackface, in the symbolic logic of the story's second instance of barn burning, Sarty effectively becomes the "strange nigger" who warns de Spain that barns can burn. This strange status is signaled by Sarty's full name, Colonel Sartoris Snopes. Abner may ironically name his son (the landowner class may appropriate my labor but I can appropriate their names and titles) but that doesn't keep Sarty's name from implying a form of miscegenation, much as the names of many of the African American characters in Faulkner's fiction bear the same names as those that circulate in the white families to which they're related. When Sarty escapes to warn de Spain, he does so in an attempt to reshape his filiation. He believes he is acting with the discernment of a white man in choosing honor and justice, but just as Dave (who sought a means of claiming manhood through the southern code of gun ownership) remains "boy" throughout Wright's story, Sarty is still only "boy" at the conclusion of Faulkner's story. Sarty's entire exchange with de Spain is rendered as follows:

> "Barn!" he cried. "Barn!"
> "What?" the white man said. "Barn?"
> "Yes!" the boy cried. "Barn!"
> "Catch him!" the white man shouted. (23)

What is striking in this twenty-word passage is the narrator's overt marking of Major de Spain's whiteness, not once but twice. Sarty and de Spain are racially Caucasian yet only one of them, the southern aristocrat, is fully white. From his privileged position of whiteness, de Spain fails to acknowledge or even register Sarty's commitment to the aristocracy's sense of itself as the embodiment of honor and noblesse oblige. Sarty is merely something to catch and hold accountable. Eennie meanie minee moe. But they can't catch this artificial black, and Sarty, much like the earlier "strange nigger," disappears from both his family's and de Spain's spheres of influence; in ways that anticipate O'Connor's poor whites (though without O'Connor's insistence on this racialized moment as an instance of grace), Sarty, utterly adrift at the story's conclusion, is a displaced person who makes clear that whiteness is not a racial essence but is linked to and limited by class. There is an important difference to register between Sarty's and Abner's relation to blackness. By literally blacking up, Abner appropriates blackness as a protective strategy; he is a kind of blackface minstrel. Sarty, however, is not conscious of becoming black. Instead, he is appropriated by blackness. To the extent that he represents the racechanged figure, Sarty becomes something more transgressive because his transformation is invisible both to himself and his culture: he performs cultural blackness in whiteface.

Faulkner's minstrelsy, both blackface and whiteface, complicates southern racial thinking by illustrating that whiteness is not so much a race but a metaphysics, a kind of structure or system of privilege. The differences between Negro and Caucasian are unknowable because they are always overwhelmed by a constellation of cultural values placed on blackness and whiteness. Faulkner's whiteface minstrelsy, however, uncouples blackness and the Negro, meaning that cultural blackness may reattach itself to racial whiteness. To make this claim is neither to cast William Faulkner as a forerunner of critical whiteness studies nor to see him as a traitor to whiteness. Faulkner the man was clearly of two minds, as his racist letter to the editor of 15 February 1931 on lynching that appeared in the Memphis *Commercial Appeal* so shockingly shows.[10] But if his fiction is populated by white characters that aren't exactly white, then it is a testament to an artistic imagination that recognized the contingency of racial identity. We can never know precisely how the man born (and who signed his lynching letter) Falkner experienced race, but the artist William, whose first fiction was merely one letter long, created the self-progenitive nom de plume Faulkner, a signifying difference that proleptically resonates with African American Lucas Beauchamp's recasting of his white name Lucius. As his early fictional portrait of "Faulkner" as a funny little black man suggests, white identity was never precisely a given for the Nobel laureate from Oxford, and "Faulkner," whether the artist or the character, always served as a mask enabling his performance of blackness through a minstrelsy of whiteness.

MOONSHINE AND MAGNOLIAS
The Story of Temple Drake and *The Birth of a Nation*

—DEBORAH E. BARKER

he Story of Temple Drake is well known today as a "scandalous" pre–Production Code film. However, before it was ever shown to a movie audience, the film was a sensation owing to the controversy surrounding its literary origin, William Faulkner's *Sanctuary* (1931).[1] Even in the pre-Code era, the Hayes Office demanded dramatic cuts in the film adaptation of *Sanctuary* and stipulated that it could not bear the name of Faulkner's (in)famous novel. The most lurid and horrific elements of *Sanctuary* include the rape by corncob of the southern belle, Temple Drake, and the fiery lynching of Lee Goodwin, the accused rapist, neither of which is actually shown in the film. Despite Hayes's interdiction, advertisements for the film flaunted the connection between Faulkner's *Sanctuary* and *The Story of Temple Drake*, referring to the adaptation as revealing the "flaming story" of the "year's most sensational novel" (fig. 1). Even those ads that did not refer specifically to *Sanctuary* frequently added "William Faulkner" to the list of credits (often above the name of the director, Stephen Roberts), signaling the film's connection to Faulkner and erroneously intimating that Faulkner had written the screenplay.[2]

Reviewers, assuming that the audience knew the literary origins of the film, repeatedly commended the film for not "sacrificing any of [the novel's] essential quality" (qtd. in Ramsey 20). Writing for the *Atlanta*

FIGURE 1 Advertisement for *The Story of Temple Drake*. The Story of Temple Drake *Press Book*. Paramount Pictures, 1933. Courtesy of the J. D. Williams Library Special Collections, University of Mississippi.

Constitution, Ralph Jones enthused that it was "quite a blessing" that the film "isn't deleted enough to spoil the story," and he assured all "[a]dmirers of WF and readers of his book about that peculiar gal, 'Temple Drake' (And aren't we all?)" that they "will jump at the opportunity to see their favorite story on the screen" (qtd. in Ramsey 20). The "essential quality" of the film that censorship could not spoil is not just a story of rape, but a story of white identity formation that is based on what W. J. Cash in the 1940s would refer to as the "Southern rape complex" (115), a story that is told through the body of Temple Drake and the historically shifting representations of the southern belle.

The southern rape complex has been one of the most devastating and far-reaching "stories" to come out of the South. In the southern rape complex, which assumes a black male rapist and white female victim, the victim is transformed into a symbol of a threatened white southern culture while the black male symbolizes the threat. Rape, in the cinematic southern context, carries with it a dramatic resonance associated with southern history and issues of war, Reconstruction, and racial conflict, and has taken on almost mythic proportions in its justification of violence against black men. Not only is the logic of the southern rape complex integrally linked to the lynching of innocent black men; its distorting lens has also made white female sexuality socially unacceptable and rendered sexual violence against black women socially invisible.

To understand the cultural significance of *The Story of Temple Drake*, it should be read not only in relation to Faulkner's novel but also in relation to cinematic representations of the southern rape complex, the most blatant of which is Griffith's *The Birth of a Nation*. As the most patently propagandistic employment and expansion of the southern rape complex, *The Birth of a Nation* depicts the black male as a threat to white America in general and to white American womanhood in particular, both northern and southern. It is not coincidental that *The Birth of a Nation* (based on Thomas Dixon, Jr.'s *The Clansman*), which is credited with the origin of the Hollywood style and the feature film, is also the first film to blatantly define (white) America through the threat of the southern rape complex. Griffith cinematically reunites the nation by constructing an image of besieged whiteness and employing a narrative of normative middle-class whiteness.[3] In *The Birth of a Nation*, Griffith combines the "racy" elements of the lower-class entertainment of the penny arcade (sensationalism, sex, and violence) with literary source material, a higher ticket price, longer viewing time, and an elaborate musical score (which includes classical pieces), in order to appeal to and to define a white American middle-class audience.[4]

The Clansman, *The Birth of a Nation*, *Sanctuary*, and *The Story of Temple Drake* all draw on sensational elements of the southern rape complex; however, *Sanctuary* and its film version, *The Story of Temple Drake*, also complicate and disrupt the categories of race, gender, and region that the myth implies. *Sanctuary* and *The Story of Temple Drake* redirect the focus of the southern rape complex from the image of the black male rapist to the figure of the decadent southern belle and the violent lower-class white man. While this move is progressive in that it undermines the racial justification of lynching, ultimately it merely narrows previous definitions of whiteness without dismantling white racial privilege. Like *The Birth of a Nation*, the happy ending in *The Story of Temple Drake* is based on a unification of normative middle-class whiteness.

In comparing *Sanctuary* and *The Story of Temple Drake* to *The Birth of a Nation* and its literary antecedent *The Clansman*, I focus on the rape scenes in each film and novel and the depictions of victims and perpetrators. In each scene I look at the threat to whiteness (as depicted by the white southern belle) and how the threat is modified from novel to film adaptation. Comparing these novels and movies allows us to see how southern rape narratives have contributed to the changing "story" of whiteness. Released in 1933, *The Story of Temple Drake* historically refigures the southern rape complex and the southern belle in the light of the Depression and Prohibition and then cinematically refigures them in the light of the emerging genres of the horror and gangster films.

THE CRACK IN THE BELLE

Even as Griffith's film adaptation of *The Clansman* promotes and exploits the narrative of the southern rape complex, it visually suggests the cracks in the foundation of the complex that would later be directly represented by Faulkner and others as they dismantle the pillars of the complex: the pure southern belle, the gallant gentleman, and the bestial black man. In characterizing the literary legacy of the southern rape complex and its relation to the southern woman, Kathryn Lee Seidel best describes Dixon's and Griffith's use of the narrative:

> Before the Civil War, the South had been an Eden, the southern lady its Eve. But evil entered the Garden in the form of northerners, and in the Civil War the North raped the South. Now these northern vultures, as they were often called, selected as their favorites the virile blacks, who would rape southern women as well. White blood would be tainted with colored blood; generations of unbroken patriarchal bloodlines would be lost. After the war, when a southern gentleman paid chivalrous homage to a woman, he was no longer addressing just an ideal homemaker but the chief character of the plantation myth and the sanctuary of values. Thus, in the years of Reconstruction, southerners were united by a desire to preserve white male superiority, to defend the symbol of that superiority, white woman, to keep blacks in their place in the hierarchy, and to punish those who violated the taboos. (14)

Ironically, although white supremacists like Dixon use essentialist arguments to promote their belief in white superiority as symbolized by the white woman, in Dixon's conception of white female purity it is not simply an essential quality, or even something defined by a woman's own actions: it is something that can be destroyed by outside forces, specifically by black men.[5]

In *The Clansman*, Dixon makes clear that Marion Lenoir—who is attacked in her own home and raped by Gus, a former slave—is not at fault; yet she is polluted and must die because her whiteness has been sullied. Marion, the former sweetheart of the hero Ben Cameron, is the kind of quintessential mythic white southern woman that Cash describes as "the shield-bearing Athena gleaming whitely in the clouds, the standard for [the South's] rallying, the mystic symbol of its nationality in the face of the foe" and "the lily-pure Maid of Astolat" (86). Marion reacts to the rape as the symbol of white southern womanhood and a member of a shame culture should—she dresses in her best white dress, a symbol of both virginity and racial purity, and kills herself.

Marion's death, of course, also eliminates the possibility of her bearing Gus's child, a child who would not be racially "pure." In a form of reverse heredity, the possibility of a racially mixed child negates Marion's status as racially pure herself. This reverse heredity, it seems, extends even to the previous generation. Fearing that her mother, who was forced to witness her daughter's violation, will betray her shame through her transparent face, Marion persuades her reluctant mother to jump off the cliff with her. Though her mother tries to come up with alternatives that allow them to live—move away, do not tell anyone—Marion is adamant that their only choice, the only way her name can remain "sweet and clean," is if they both die (305). Honor, therefore, can and should be maintained even at the expense of truth, and even if the innocent must die to protect this concept of purity.

In characterizing attitudes toward whiteness in Western culture, Richard Dyer asserts that "[b]lack people can be reduced (in white culture) to their bodies and thus to race, but white people are something else that is realized in and yet is not reducible to the corporeal, or racial.... At some point, the embodied something else of whiteness took on a dynamic relation to the physical world, something caught by the ambiguous word 'spirit'" (*White* 14–15). But, according to Dixon's conception of whiteness, the "spirit" does not transcend the body. Before her daughter's defilement, Mrs. Lenoir contemplates her husband's favorite saying: "Beauty is a sign of the soul—the body is the soul!" (301). The first part of Mr. Lenoir's assertion reflects the views of the Scottish Common Sense philosophers—popular with American intellectuals in the nineteenth century—who maintained that external beauty revealed an inner goodness.[6] Dixon, however, takes this idea a step further. In the second statement, the body moves from an indexical sign of the soul to the soul's equivalent. The body and soul are one and therefore pollution of the body means pollution of the soul, regardless of the guilt or innocence of the victim.

Despite Marion's total dedication to her purity and honor, her last name, Lenoir, seems to foreshadow her downfall at the hands of Gus and his band, or, even more radically incongruent with her role as standard bearer of white purity, to suggest a hereditary connection on her father's side with the darkness that is symbolized by Gus. The belle's possible connection to the "dark side," and therefore her own culpability, becomes increasingly overt as the southern rape myth is retold. Griffith's *The Birth of a Nation* includes the external threat to the belle's purity as in *The Clansman*, yet reconfigures the behavior of the southern belle (not just her name) in ways that implicate that she is tainted even before she is attacked. In the film, the character of Marion is conflated with Flora, the rape victim in Dixon's *The Leopard's Spots*, the young daughter of a poor ex-Confederate soldier who hates blacks. Flora in *The Birth of a Nation* is not Ben Cameron's former sweetheart, but his exuberant little sister. The cinematic Flora, however, is a more problematic figure than either of the novelistic victims; though young and innocent, she is not as young as Flora of *The Leopard's Spots*, who is attacked on the way home from school, and she is not the ideal of the grace and strength of southern womanhood, as is Marion.

Griffith differentiates between the "tainted" belle and the Southern Lady by contrasting Flora and her sister, Margaret, who is introduced as an example of southern gentility, "a daughter of the South, trained in the manners of the old school." The disparity between the sisters is highlighted in a crucial scene in which the "black guerrillas" invade the Cameron home. Margaret, though upset, remains calm in the face of danger and admonishes Flora for her hysterical behavior. As the mother and daughters hide in the tight confines of the cellar, Flora, giddy and near hysteria, puts the family in danger by almost giving away their hiding place with her laughter. Her hysterical behavior in the cellar mirrors the out-of-control behavior of the black troops overhead; both actions threaten the safety of the southern family.[7] Later, when Ben returns from the war, he warns Flora not to go out alone, but Flora insists on going to the spring to fetch water. Her childish and exuberant nature is manifest in her delight over seeing a squirrel, and instead of returning home to safety, she stays to play, allowing Gus, a former slave and a newly promoted captain in the army, to follow her to the woods.

Michael Rogin argues that, in the famous chase scene in which Ben pursues Gus as Gus pursues Flora, Ben's incestuous desire for Flora is actually mediated through Gus. Rogin maintains that in *The Birth of a Nation*, white "[p]aternal and fraternal desire is displaced onto the blacks who are punished for it. The displacement and punishment of that desire gives birth to the new nation" (280). What threaten the national family as depicted in *The Birth of a Nation* are the extreme forms of endogamy (marriage within southern "aristocratic" families, and its most extreme manifestation, incest) and exogamy (marriage between blacks and whites, miscegenation). Ben, as representative of the white South, must rid himself of the closed world of aristocratic southern intermarriage, as represented by the little sister as southern belle, in order to fully rejoin the Union and embrace the North as ally.

Rogin's argument assumes that Flora flees from Ben's incestuous desire and Gus's miscegenationist desire, but not from her own desires. Although Flora is clearly depicted as a victim, her hysterical reaction to Gus's advances puts her in further danger. Rather than running home to safety, she runs deeper into the woods and then to the top of a cliff. Through a series of crosscuts we see the brother and sister call to each other, and we know that Ben is not far away. Flora, however, does not wait to be rescued but kills herself instead. Her earlier response to the black soldiers' penetration of her house—her giddy laughter—denotes her own excitement at the transgressive breaking of boundaries between black and white. To be saved from Gus, she need only wait for her brother to rescue her, but to be saved from her own desire, she must leap to her death. In Griffith's version, as opposed to Dixon's, whiteness is threatened not just from external forces, but, perhaps even more significantly, it can be destroyed by the belle's own weakness, in the form of desires that lead to the possibility of both incest and miscegenation.

Griffith not only subtly transforms the belle, he alters the linchpin of the southern rape complex by altering the threat represented by the black male, Gus. In *The Clansman*, Dixon leaves the readers no doubt as to the guilt of the assailant, and he even has Dr. Cameron go to great lengths to prove Gus's guilt. Using the latest in pseudoscientific theories, Dr. Cameron examines Mrs. Lenoir's retina and finds the image of Gus imprinted on her eye, proving that he was the ultimate cause of her death and ironically confirming, even in death, Marion's fear that people would "read" the horror of her attack in her mother's eyes. To corroborate his forensic evidence and his own intellectual superiority, Dr. Cameron, at Gus's Klan trial, uses mesmerism to get a confession out of Gus. The film version circumvents such elaborate evidence by having the young Flora live long enough to whisper the name "Gus." The lynching scene was also severely edited and in the existing version, after the Klan declares Gus "guilty" in a "fair trial," his dead body is dumped on the porch of Silas Lynch. Flora's death allows Griffith to maintain the purity of the belle while condemning the threat of the black man, and brings home the concept that a belle would choose death over defilement. As presented by both Griffith and Dixon, there is no such thing (or there should be no such thing) as a rape survivor.

In his representation of Gus, Dixon also goes to great lengths, describing in elaborate detail Gus's African characteristics, even down to his "African" footprint. Griffith's Gus, however, as a white actor in blackface, does not have "African" features, nor is he a physically imposing figure. Writing in 1898, Alexander Manly, the editor of the *Wilmington Daily Record*, a black North Carolina newspaper, wrote a rebuttal to the pro-lynching speeches of Rebecca Latimer Felton. Manly maintained: "Every negro lynched is called a 'big, burly, black brute,' when in fact many of those who have thus been dealt with had white men for their fathers, and were not only not 'black' and 'burly,' but were sufficiently attractive for white girls of culture and refinement to fall in love with them, as is well known to all" (qtd. in Hodes 194). The anxiety and outrage produced by Manly's statements eventually led to the Wilmington riots, fictionally recorded in Charles Chesnutt's *The Marrow of Tradition* (1901), and in Dixon's *The Leopard's Spots* (1902), but the import of Manly's words lingers in Griffith's depiction of Gus. Although we do not have the "director's cut" of *The Birth of a Nation*, there are indications from reviews and personal comments that the "rape" scene of Flora in the original cut portrayed Gus in a harsher light and left no doubt that he intended to rape Flora. In response to criticism that the portrayal of Gus (as a generalization of blacks) was animalistic, it appears that Griffith cut the scene and added an intertitle in which Gus tells Flora he wants to marry her and, as she flees in horror, he pursues her, calling out, "Wait, missie, I won't hurt yeh" (Lenning 117–41). As depicted on the screen, Gus is more visually indicative of Manly's white-fathered black men than of Dixon's "burly black brute." In *The Birth of a Nation*, Gus is lynched not for raping Flora but for proposing to her, and, in turn, Flora must die because of the possibility of her own attraction to Gus. Rather than ameliorating the negative portrayal of African Americans in the film, Griffith's censored version of the chase actually lowers the bar for offenses that are represented as a justification for lynching.

FROM COTTON TO CORN

The rape complex, with its emphasis on white purity and superiority and its fear of miscegenation, serves at least two important functions: it obfuscates the South's dependence on a black male workforce and the more prevalent source of miscegenation—white male rape of black women. The economic mainstay of the pre- and post–Civil War South was cotton, which depended on an African American work force, particularly the labor of young black men. The southern rape complex downplays the South's dependence on black laborers by presenting these very same black men as a threat to the society, thus justifying laws that "controlled" the unruly black male, but that in effect attempted to force black workers to stay in the South and accept low wages.[8] Gus, who is presented as an actual rapist in *The Clansman*, and as a would-be rapist in *The Birth of a Nation*, is not only represented as a threat to southern white womanhood but, as a Union soldier, he is presented as a pawn of the North and not as a southern laborer. Although Reconstruction had ended long before the release of *The Birth of a Nation* in 1915, black labor, war, and the price of cotton were still divisive issues. From 1914 to 1915, the South experienced another economic crisis with the drop in the cotton market brought on by the start of World War I in Europe, weakening southern support for President Woodrow Wilson's military preparedness proposals and causing southern congressmen to urge Wilson to provide economic aid to bolster the falling cotton prices (Grantham 74–75).

While Wilson resisted what he characterized as the "preposterous and impossible schemes to valorize cotton and help the cotton planter out of the Reserve Banks" (qtd. in Grantham 74–75),[9] he was able to show his support and sympathy for the South symbolically through the White House showing of *The Birth of a Nation*. The film is ostensibly presented as antiwar through the epilogue in which the god of war is defeated by Christ, the Prince of Peace; however, the film's attempt to reunite white America through a shared sympathy for the defeated South was just the kind of political propaganda that could help to rally the southern states in support of a war in which Americans fought together against an external foe. It was also the kind of propaganda that helped to revive the Klan in 1915, a Klan that saw not only blacks but also immigrants as a threat to the "American" way of life.

By the 1931 release of *Sanctuary*, the Depression-era drop in cotton prices, exacerbated by overproduction, on top of the damage done by boll weevils in the twenties, accomplished what the Klan alone could not: it forced the foreclosure of many black-owned farms and sent even more southern blacks to the urban North in search of work.[10] In a time of massive unemployment and falling cotton prices, the South was not as dependent on black laborers as it once was. Unlike Dixon and Griffith, Faulkner does not present the threat to the South in the form of the black man. In *Sanctuary*, Faulkner rewrites the southern rape complex as a class conflict within the white community played out over the scarce resources of the Depression.[11] Low cotton prices and Prohibition made corn, not cotton, the South's new cash crop in the form of illegal bootleg whiskey, which was easier to transport and brought a higher price than cumbersome bales of cotton or bushels of corn. Because it was illegal, whiskey had the added advantage of being untaxed, but its illegal status also necessitated its clandestine production and distribution, making the hill country or backwoods the perfect location (rather than the working plantation) and the bootlegger/gangster the perfect distributor (rather than the elite planter class). As a result of this combination of circumstances, including the fact that over five million southerners moved into the cities from 1880 to 1910, the former plantation, now in ruins, ironically becomes the perfect secluded "hideout," the southern gentleman becomes the consumer (not producer), the belle becomes the degraded gangster's moll, and two threatening lower-class white stereotypes emerge: the urban gangster and the rural hillbilly moonshiner.[12]

Faulkner, like Griffith, calls into question the conventions of the southern belle, but while Griffith indirectly exposes the dangers of the southern belle's vanity and willfulness, Faulkner creates an overtly flirtatious and seductive belle in Temple Drake, who many would say is (as Rhett Butler says of Scarlett) "no lady." As Seidel explains, it was Faulkner's great-grandfather, Colonel W. C. Falkner, who first suggested that the threat to the belle's purity lies within. *The Little Brick Church* (1882) features the seduction of the belle by a northerner and the lynching of that same man because of his brutal and lascivious treatment of his female slave, which brings about her death. "Being seduced . . . because of an innate flaw was a new trait for the belle. Beginning with this novel, she can be seduced by her own sensuousness" (140). Colonel Falkner presents lynching as a necessary means of reining in the libidinous vices of the northern male and the sexual weakness of the white southern woman. Forty-nine years later, William Faulkner desecrates the temple of white southern womanhood with the brutal, "instrumental" rape of Temple. The nature of Faulkner's desecration of the belle at the hands of a white man, not a black man, points to the shift in the economic underpinning of the South as a result of the Depression.

As a symbol of the South and its vulnerability, the belle is also emblematic of a beleaguered southern economy. In both *The Birth of a Nation* and *The Story of Temple Drake*, the belle's disgrace is symbolically linked to the plantation system's collapse. In *The Birth of a Nation*, the "insult" of Gus's proposal to Flora is preceded by a scene that ties the degradation of the belle directly to the deflated post–Civil War image of cotton. Preparing for her brother's homecoming after the war, Flora attempts to use cotton to regain her status as belle and southern aristocrat. Attaching strips of raw cotton to her dress, she kneels down to use the soot from the fireplace to create the effect of ermine. The intertitle reads "'Southern ermine,' from raw cotton, for the grand occasion." In the manner of the belle, Flora rushes to the mirror to admire her handiwork, but the sooty raw cotton on the homespun dress creates a pathetic rather than a royal appearance, and her smiles turn to tears. Now that King Cotton is dethroned, it no longer has the power to ensure the social status of the southern aristocratic belle. Flora's dress is literally unrefined, in terms of both the raw and homespun cotton she wears, highlighting the fact that the antebellum South relied on cotton as an export to be processed in northern or British factories. The war has limited the South's ability not only to produce cotton but also to exchange it for costlier goods, like the silk that Flora wore before the war. In a film that is so self-conscious about preserving white purity, Flora's impulse to blacken the white cotton out of vanity suggests that the belle is "tainted" by her own desires before she encounters Gus. But Flora's actions also symbolically reveal the crucial role that blacks played in maintaining white southern economic and cultural privilege.

Temple's fall is, of course, linked through her name to the architectural analogy of the plantation house. The plantation house at the Old Frenchman place, a symbol of the centerpiece and foundation of the "aristocratic" southern planter lifestyle, like Temple's reputation, is in need of repairs, and (also like Temple) is now in the hands of poor whites, who tear it down bit by bit and use it as the headquarters for their bootlegging operation. Unlike that of the plantation house, however, Temple's fall is not directly related to the Civil War. Faulkner takes the belle out of the plantation and puts her in a college dorm, giving her education and independence, two important ingredients for the 1920s New Woman, but in 1931, over ten years after women gained the vote, feminism and the women's movement have stalled. Unlike the earlier image of the independent New Woman, Temple has no intellectual ambitions; she is not at college to pursue any lofty goals. As a college girl, she also has no chaperone to protect her or to enforce ladylike behavior but merely uses her freedom to sneak out of the dorm to go joy riding with the local townies. Temple more closely fits the image of the fun-loving flapper—drinking and smoking—but, before the rape, she draws the line at the sexual freedom associated with the flapper.[13] Even as she violates the propriety of the belle, when push comes to shove, Temple attempts to fall back on her privileged background to salvage, at least, an appearance of virtue.

Faulkner unmercifully demonstrates what happens to the belle as flapper in the wake of the Jazz Age when the social structures that guard and limit her behavior are removed. Just as the white moonshiners have taken over and destroyed the former plantation house, it is equally symbolic that Temple's scene of degradation occurs at the hands of the white bootlegger/gangster in a corncrib and with a corncob—the abject remains of the main ingredient in moonshine whiskey. Temple herself, like the hollow corn shucks that seem to follow her wherever she goes at the Old Frenchman place, represents the abject remains of the tradition of the aristocratic southern belle and of the New Woman/flapper of the Roaring Twenties.

In *Sanctuary* and *The Story of Temple Drake*, lower-class whites are directly connected to the fall of the belle: they are the source of illicit pleasure, of censure, and of the violation. Temple's fall at the hands of Popeye is preceded by her fallen reputation, which is linked to her tendency to "go slumming" with the white town boys because they, unlike the college boys, have cars and can take her away from campus. Similarly, Gowan Stevens is willing to "go slumming" at the Old Frenchman place to get more alcohol from Lee Goodwin. For Temple's contemporaries in New York, the source of excitement and alcohol was often associated with Harlem and therefore linked to race. In *Sanctuary*, Temple and Gowan fulfill their illicit desires through lower-class whites and their access to cars and alcohol, two key elements associated with the freedom of the Roaring Twenties.[14]

Another sign of Temple's fall is that those who are lower on the social hierarchy criticize her. Ironically, the characters in the novel condemn Temple not for being too "loose," but for not being loose enough. The town boys complain that she is a tease, but Temple's harshest critic is the white lower-class former prostitute, Ruby, who judges Temple's behavior from the perspective of class and economics. Ruby does not read Temple's virginity as a virtue, or as a sign of white female purity, but as proof that Temple is a tease and an upper-class hypocrite who deserves whatever she gets.[15] It is perhaps not surprising that a former prostitute would view sex as an economic commodity, but Ruby's critique reveals the economic basis of Temple's relationships as well (her need for a car).

Temple, however, even as she violates the standards of behavior for an upper-class woman, employs the privilege of her position, the prerogative of nonpayment. The sign of upper-class power is not the ability to pay, but the ability to define the exchange rate, or even to refuse payment altogether.

> "Oh, I know your sort," the woman said. "Honest women. Too good to have anything to do with common people. You'll slip out at night with the kids, but just let a man come along.... Take all you can get, and give nothing. 'I'm a pure girl; I dont do that.' You'll slip out with the kids and burn their gasoline and eat their food, but just let a man so much as look at you and you faint away because your father the judge and your four brothers might not like it. But just let you get into a jam, then who do you come crying to? To us, the ones that are not good enough to lace the judge's almighty shoes." (57–58)

Despite depicting the horrors Temple endures, which make her an object of pity, the novel also participates in a kind of vicarious pleasure in witnessing the belle get her comeuppance, which is also apparent in the movie version (fig. 2).[16]

In both film and novel, Temple combines the frivolous elements of the flapper and belle and is forced to "pay" for her frivolous behavior through sexual violence. As Hollywood censor Jack Vizzard explains, "With the

FIGURE 2 Advertisement for *The Story of Temple Drake*. The Story of Temple Drake *Press Book*. Paramount Pictures, 1933. Courtesy of the J. D. Williams Library Special Collections, University of Mississippi.

crash, the party was over. In the littered debris of confetti and tickertape, an enormous sense of guilt set in. . . . In a mood of sobriety, a chastened citizenry reacted against those symbols of its great debauch and began to punish them" (38–39). However, in the film, Temple attempts to take more control over her body and her sexuality. The advertisements for the movie, included in the press book distributed to local theaters, promote the idea of Temple as a manipulator, proclaiming that she is a girl who "thought she knew how to handle men" (fig. 1). The use of the past tense implies her downfall at the hands of a man she could not control.

The first scene of the movie presents Temple as just such a "girl who thought she knew how to handle men." In the opening shots we see only her hand on the doorknob and hear only her end of the conversation as she tells her beau goodnight. The first words we hear her speak are "Do I sho' nough? Just me? Men are funny." "Sho' nough," a phrase she repeats several times throughout the movie, is spoken with an extreme southern accent, and labels Temple not only as southern but as a belle, as she uses this phrase only on men and as part of her performance as a belle, i.e., as flirtatious but innocent. She drops the lilting southern drawl when her date does not take "no" for an answer as she barks, "I said no," and "Hey, you're too rough; let go." Once she has pushed her date safely on the other side of the door, she resumes her drawl as she smiles and says a lilting and multi-syllabic "good night." Her smile fades, as she looks upstairs as if she anticipates another battle. A similar performance is enacted moments later when her grandfather meets her on the stairs, scolding her for coming in too late: "Why is it late sho' nough? I didn't know," she croons and then distracts her grandfather by asking him to help unfasten her dress and assures him that her date is a "nice boy" (i.e., a gentleman) who went to her grandfather's college (i.e., he is one of us).

This opening scene is also important regarding the costuming and lighting and establishes the symbolic use of light and dark that is pervasive throughout the film and that signals Temple's dual nature and her "dark" secret. The white crinoline dress of the belle has given way to the sophisticated, shimmering lamé evening gown that clings to Temple's body, leaving nothing to the imagination. Even after Temple turns off the light to go upstairs, her luminous dress still highlights her figure. The muted lighting of the darkened hallway, however, literally foreshadows the even darker tonal palate of the Old Frenchman place, and in both worlds Temple's "whiteness"—as expressed by ability to reflect light—stands out.[17] Miriam Hopkins seems to have been chosen for this role because of the markers of whiteness she represents, from her nimbus of blonde hair to her white skin set off by her radiant clothing. In sharp contrast to Temple is the austere, dark-toned portrait that literally stands between Temple and her grandfather as they talk on the stairs. The portrait, done in the style of the Dutch Masters, is presumably a Drake ancestor, who appears to look down disapprovingly at Temple, and suggests an erosion of propriety in the family.

The symbolic contrast of light and dark is repeated when Temple tries to explain to the dashing lawyer, Stephen Benbow, why she cannot marry him. Alluding to her divided nature, she explains, "It's as if there are two me's. One of them says, 'Yes, yes, quick don't let him get away,' but the other, I won't tell you what it wants, does, or what'll happen to it. I don't know myself. All I know is I hate it." The pair are standing outside on the veranda and Stephen has his back to the brightly lit mansion where the dance is held; Temple is facing him and though there is no source of light behind her, she is backlit, creating the radiant blond hair as in the first scene, while her face is in shadow, suggesting her dual light and dark/good and bad character.

In the ads and press book used to promote the film, Temple's divided nature and her reputation as a good/bad girl are directly linked to an inherited "wild streak" in the Drake family. Like Flora, Temple is portrayed as a tainted belle even before the actual rape, and also like Flora, the threat to Temple's purity stems from both inside and outside. The ads contain several variations on the theme of the "Drake wild streak." Some ads simply state, "All the Drakes had a wild streak," or question the source of the corruption in the family—"What was this bad streak in the Drakes?"—while others indicate Temple's internal struggle: "I'm a half-good girl! I tried to be . . . longed to be respectable . . . and what? The other side of me . . . the wild Drake streak . . . it's too strong! . . . it's like there are two me's?" The line in the movie from which the ads were drawn is spoken by Stephen's Aunt Jenny, who actually says, "They're a stiff-necked lot, most of them—proud and all that—but there's a wild streak in them. Every now and then one of them comes along, like Temple, with something bad in them, something wrong. Maybe she'll get over it, but not one of them that's had it that didn't end in the gutter." The advertisements, however, extend the line to indicate that all the Drakes had a wild streak, and further speculate on the nature of the streak.

Stephen, who is in love with Temple, refuses to listen, but Aunt Jenny's comments are part of a montage of gossip about Temple, beginning with the Drakes' African American maid who, examining Temple's torn slip, laughs that Judge Drake would know more about his granddaughter if he did her laundry. Judge Drake assumes that Temple's whiteness is a sign of, and a guarantee of, her purity, but the maid is able to read Temple's "dirty laundry," and therefore her hidden sexuality. The gossip sequence ends with the image of a black cat, which Paula Degenfelder reads as a negative comment about the "catty" remarks against Temple. Rather than simply representing criticism of the gossipers, given the negative depictions of Temple as a "bad" girl, the black cat has a double meaning, which includes a crude slang allusion to Temple's "dark sexuality"—her "black pussy"—an image of Temple's racialized sexuality.[18]

White women's purity was so exaggerated in the southern rape complex that, even in the context of intraracial marriage, it was unacceptable to refer to or assume white women possessed sexual desire, and, therefore, female sexuality was projected onto black women.[19] Dyer notes the narrative ramifications of the impossibility of white female sexuality: "Whites must reproduce themselves, yet they must also control and transcend their bodies. Only by (impossibly) doing both can they be white. Thus are produced some of the great narrative dilemmas of whiteness, notably romance, adultery, rape and pornography" (*White* 30). An important element of the southern rape complex and the narratives it spawns is its obfuscation of the more common source of miscegenation in the South: white slave owners who violated their female slaves.

One of the arguments put forth by abolitionists was that slavery and the illicit relations between white masters and slave women corrupted the morals of the white family, including the daughters. But, as Harriet Jacobs explains in her narrative, white planters' daughters "know that the women slaves are subject to their father's authority in all things; and in some cases they exercise the same authority over the men slaves" (qtd. in Carby 20). Even Thomas Dixon's *The Sins of the Father: A Romance of the South* (1912) describes the corruption of the white race: "The fact that the negro race had for two hundred years been stirring the baser passions of her men—that this degradation of the higher race had been bred into the bone and sinew of succeeding generations—had never occurred to [Mrs. Norton's] childlike mind" (85). Dixon, keeping with his racist agenda, blames African American women for their own violation, but interestingly uses the language of biological inheritance to describe successive generations of whites who continued to be corrupted by "the sins of their fathers."

The visual connections among sexuality, darkness, and the Drakes' wild streak intimate that miscegenation is already part of the southern family tradition. This, I would argue, is precisely the unstated allusion in the ads' persistent question about the origin of that "wild streak."[20] The anxiety surrounding the southern rape complex included the need to limit and control the desires of both black men and white women. Unlike her forefathers' sexuality, Temple's is a threat to the Drake name. As was the case with Flora, the threat to Temple's purity as presented in the film's promotional materials comes from both within and without, and includes both miscegenation and incest.

The miscegenistic suggestion of the "dark" Drake hereditary wild streak in the press book is accompanied by a psychological analysis of the incestuous implications of the novel. As in the chase scene in *The Birth of a Nation*, the threat of incest follows close on the heels of the threat of miscegenation. Dr. Frank Payne, a "consulting psychologist," in an article featured in *The Story of Temple Drake* press book, analyzes Temple according to his reading of *Sanctuary*. Dr. Payne declares that "[u]ndoubtedly we have an Oedipus Complex situation between 'Temple Drake' and her father, the great and learned judge." Temple is, according to Dr. Payne, the "typical psychopathic personality which has been molded and forced into being by the repressions of our civilization, the repressions of religion, coupled with eugenic inbreeding of our so-called fine families and fine stock, which have been inbred so much that they cannot stand the pressure and tension of our civilization." In relation to Temple, Payne's comments seem to allude to the closed world of the southern aristocrat, but he maintains that this "psychopathic personality" can be seen in New York as well as the Deep South, suggesting that class exclusiveness—inbreeding—whether it be at the lower or the upper levels, weakens the white race. Given the climate of segregation in the 1930s, it is unlikely that Payne was advocating interracial marriage, yet, like Griffith and Dixon, he does seem to promote intermarriages across class and religious lines as a way to strengthen white "civilization."

Payne's comments refer to Temple's relationship to her father in the novel. Although the father is noticeably absent in the movie and Judge Drake becomes Temple's grandfather, the incestuous overtones remain. In the opening scene on the staircase, we see Temple using her sexual charm to seek her grandfather's indulgence, suggesting that even Judge Drake, who turns a blind eye to his granddaughter's indiscretions, is taken in by her seductiveness. As her grandfather unzips her dress, Temple reassures him that her staying out late is not a threat to her purity because her date, Toddy Gowan, went to the judge's alma mater. Just as the judge assumes that Temple's whiteness is a sign of her purity, he assumes that Toddy's connections to the judge, through class and education, are guarantees of his honor and his status as a gentleman—or at least that as a gentleman he will marry Temple if he gets her pregnant, maintaining the "eugenic inbreeding of our so-called fine families" to which Dr. Payne alludes.

THAT BLACK MAN

Just as in the film Temple's sexuality is coded through the image of the black cat and the contrast of light and dark shadows, in the novel, as critics have pointed out, Popeye, the rapist, though white, is also coded as "black."[21] Because of the tradition of slavery and Jim Crow in the South, at one level when we talk about race in a southern context, especially a small-town southern context, there is still the lingering myth of racial identity—that on a practical, everyday level we know who is black and who is white, and that these identifications still have a strong bearing on where you go to church or whom you marry. But as Michael Omi and Howard Winant explain: "The effort must be made to understand race as an unstable and 'decentered' complex of social meanings.... Race is a concept which signifies and symbolizes social conflict and interests by referring to different types of human bodies" (55). Because "race" is also signified by speech, dress, behaviors, etc., a character can be coded as one race while visually signifying another. Though Popeye is directly referred to as a white man, the narrator describes Popeye's skin as having a "dead, dark pallor" (4). Horace Benbow comments that "[h]e smells black" (7), and Temple refers to him as "[t]hat black man" (49). His connection to "blackness" is exposed even when he is being directly referred to as white. Commenting on Popeye's skittishness, Tommy asserts, "I be dog if he aint the skeeriest durn *white* man I ever see" (19). The implication of Tommy's comment is that blacks are naturally scared, but Popeye's fear is unusual for a white man, i.e., it is more typical of a black man.

What does it mean, then, that Popeye is coded "black," yet inhabits a white subject position? What happens in the slippage between black and white? Joel Williamson in "How Black Was Rhett Butler?" argues that in addition to *Gone With the Wind*'s black-coded references to Rhett Butler's "swarthy face" and his "springy stride of a savage," Rhett is also created as a "hipster-trickster": "independent, cocky, and insufferably yet subtly insolent" (99). Rhett's association with blackness enhances his sexuality, but his position in (and his return to) polite Charleston society ultimately marks him as "a 'true' gentleman." Rhett is the good/bad boy. In *Sanctuary*, which predates *Gone With the Wind* both as book and movie, Popeye's link to blackness and the lower classes only makes him a more ominous character. His connection to whiteness is not enough to redeem him fully, yet it does allow the white reader to plug into cultural and racial fantasies and stereotypes, while still having the safety net of whiteness to alleviate (even more) frightening images of the black rapist (which would be offensive to the African American community and which would have the added stigma of causing racial controversy as it did in *The Birth of a Nation*).

Popeye's ambiguous racial coding allows Faulkner to debunk the myth of the black male rapist on more than one level. Popeye must use a corncob, an instrument, to accomplish his crime against southern womanhood. In this reading, by analogy, the myth of the black male rapist is, like the corncob, just an instrument in the hands of an impotent white culture. On the other hand, if we read Popeye as coded "black," *Sanctuary* creates a countermyth that the black man, even in the position of the rapist, is impotent. Therefore, even if he were to attack a white woman, there is no fear of miscegenation from a corncob. Popeye's black/white status thus allows Faulkner to invoke all the sensationalism associated with the myth of the black male rapist, discredit the myth as an instrument used by whites, and allay white fears about the "real" power of the black male.

Faulkner's use of the black-coded white man does not necessarily exonerate the black man, but does shift the focus of the threat to the

South to the southern whites themselves, especially lower-class whites. As a critic in the *American Mercury* describes it, "The thesis of this book, to the native southerner, is horrifying but undeniable: it is that the low-down southerner, with his talent for the dirt, as he calls it, is probably the most depraved of white Americans" (qtd. in Ramsey 12). The qualifying use of the word "white," as in Tommy's statement, establishes the possibility of even more depraved nonwhite Americans, suggesting that Popeye—the most depraved of white Americans—is more nonwhite than white. The connection between the rural lower-class hillbilly and the black man is not new, but *Sanctuary* marks a reconfiguration of urban and rural lower-class whites as a new and threatening figure, in terms of both violence and sexuality. Popeye's race and impotence doubly dispel the threat of miscegenation, but not the actuality of sexual violence and murder. J. W. Williamson, who traces the history of the hillbilly in American culture, maintains that "[o]ur secret dread is that the dark, drunken hillbilly is not other, but us" (6).[22]

The historical source material that seems to have inspired *Sanctuary* further links the novel to bootlegging, rape, and lynching (Williamson, *William Faulkner* 157–58). The event that precipitated *Sanctuary* was the story of Popeye Pumphrey, a Memphis bootlegger who was reported to be impotent, but who was also rumored to have raped a woman with an object.[23] The subsequent lynching of Goodwin and Faulkner's description of the murder committed by Goodwin's black jailmate both include details from the 1908 lynching of Nelse Patton that occurred in Oxford when Faulkner was a boy. Patton, also a well-known bootlegger, had been convicted on five counts of selling alcohol. While serving as a "trusty," Patton went to the home of a white convict to deliver a message to his wife, Mattie McMillan. A fight ensued, Mattie McMillan drew a gun, and Patton slit her throat, almost severing her head, though she still managed to run into the front yard.

Joel Williamson suggests that Patton was probably acquainted with both Mr. and Mrs. McMillan in connection to his bootlegging operation, and that Mattie was not necessarily protecting her "honor" when she drew the gun, though this was how she was portrayed after the fact: "Somehow in the Patton case the community found itself confronting the alarming results of a commingling of race and sex with the disinhibiting effects of alcohol," resulting in a mob of reportedly two thousand men who worked for hours to break into the jail and kill Patton (161). Senator William Sullivan, the ringleader, unabashedly admitted to instigating the lynching: "Cut a white woman's throat and a negro? Of course I wanted him lynched. I led the mob which lynched Nelse Patton and I am proud of it" (161). In the novel, the same grisly details of the murder, including the nearly headless woman running into the yard, are incorporated, but the interracial element is left out. The black jailmate has murdered his wife, not a white woman, by slitting her throat, and though he waits to die for his crime, there is no impetus from the white community to lynch him.[24]

Griffith and Dixon project all dark desires onto the black man and portray the Klan as upstanding citizens who value truth and law, despite their role as vigilantes. In *Sanctuary*, lower-class white men take on the sins attributed to the black man in the southern rape complex, but equally important, they, not a senator or other upper-class member of the town, also take on the violent specter of the vigilante. Even the middle-class lawyer Horace Benbow is not safe when the white mob threatens to lynch him for representing a rapist. The depiction of the Klan as a lower-class phenomenon increasingly distances the middle-class southerners from the cinematic Klan as it is played out in future Faulkner film adaptations, including *Intruder in the Dust* (1949) and *The Long Hot Summer* (1958).[25]

THE SOUTHERN GOTHIC MONSTER AS THE "GANGSTER OF THE ID"

Conflating the fear of the black man—as presented in the southern rape complex and promoted by Griffith and the revived Klan—with the image of the lower-class man (especially the dark-skinned immigrant), Popeye in *Sanctuary*, the "low down southerner," impotent, syphilitic, and voyeuristic, becomes Trigger in *The Story of Temple Drake*, a brutal but virile immigrant gangster. Previously, in the 1920s, the gangster and bootlegger were often portrayed as successful businessmen or even as heroes, who supplied a willing public with what many deemed a harmless commodity.[26] Al Capone maintained, "I make my money by supplying a public demand. If I break the law, my customers, who number hundreds of the best people in

Chicago, are as guilty as I am. The only difference between us is that I sell and they buy" (qtd. in Rosow 95).

For early Depression-era audiences, during the peak of the classical gangster film, 1930–32, the gangster presented an alternative model of social mobility and rags to riches in a time of limited opportunity (Shadoian 29). His determination and bravado appealed to audiences. Popeye/Trigger, however, represents the darker side of the gangster, whose determination also incorporated the sadistic violence and authoritarianism of the protofascist dictator (Rosow 175–79; Atkinson 118–19). Ted Atkinson explains that after 1932 gangsters were

> depicted more often than not as insidious figures intent on disrupting the rule of law. Simply put, the gangsters of post-1932 Hollywood were more like Faulkner's Popeye Pumphrey than Edward G. Robinson's Rico Bandello or James Cagney's Tommy Powers. In place of the gangster, representations of an unruly public now simultaneously reflected the longing for decisive action in the vacuum of ineffectual leadership as well as the need for civil restraint to prevent revolution. (141)

The Story of Temple Drake was able to take advantage of the popularity of both the gangster and the horror film and the fears that fed them during the Depression era, presenting Trigger as a combination of the dark ravisher, violent gangster, and gothic monster.[27] As David Skal explains in his analysis of the cultural significance of the horror and gangster genres:

> The wreckage of the jazz age was a forbidding new landscape. Millions waited for a scapegoat or a deliverer. A new and controversial kind of entertainment—the gangster picture—served as a lightning rod for public anger and cynicism; audiences vicariously took part in adventures outside the law and standards of fair play that now seemed utterly irrelevant. The popular interest in gangsters wasn't an entirely vicarious identification: Prohibition, after all, had literally turned millions of otherwise law-abiding citizens into criminals.... But the most lasting and influential invention of 1931 would be the modern horror film. Monster movies opened up the possibil-

ity of psychic lawlessness; a monster, for Hollywood, was a gangster of the id and unconscious. (114)

The conflation of the horror film and the gritty realism of the gangster film is already suggested in the reviews of *Sanctuary*: "The horrors of any ghost story pale beside the ghastly realism of this chronicle" (qtd. in Ramsey 12). The movie, capitalizing on the connections, is split geographically between the dark Gothic world of the rural, dilapidated plantation house, complete with "monsters," and the hard-edged realism of the urban boardinghouse/ house of prostitution.

In the opening credits, *The Story of Temple Drake* takes advantage of the novel's horrific rape and the image of the decaying plantation house to create a scene of southern Gothic horror. *The Story of Temple Drake* features numerous elements of the horror film, including the dark and decaying castle/mansion as the visual sign of the entrance into the Gothic world of monsters. In the novel, Temple and Gowan Stevens approach the house in daylight; in the film, however, the car accident, which strands the pair, occurs in the dark so that Temple and Toddy Gowan advance toward the house in the darkness of a stormy night. But even before we see the couple approach the house, the opening credits are juxtaposed with the image of the darkened plantation house intermittently illuminated by flashes of lightning. The ominous scene of the plantation house is interrupted with insert shots of the actors as they appear in the movie, beginning, of course, with Hopkins as the eponymous star Temple Drake. Hopkins is shown before her fall in the opening shots, illuminated with backlights that make her blond hair glow and which bring out the lustrous quality of her evening gown. Another important change from novel to film is Temple's hair color, which in the novel is red, but in the film is blond.

Miriam Hopkins is the perfect choice for the good/bad girl. Even the "whiteness" of this initial view of her links her visually to both sex and violence and to both horror and gangster films. In her most important role to date, Paramount's first horror film, *Dr. Jekyll and Mr. Hyde* (1931), Hopkins plays a dancehall girl, Ivy, who (unlike Temple) does not play hard to get. In her first scene in the movie, the gentlemanly Dr. Jekyll rescues her and, to show her appreciation, she performs a striptease for him.

Although the censors insisted that Ivy be a dancehall girl and not a prostitute, amazingly they allowed this scene to remain in the film. The scene is filmed with high key lighting accentuating the whiteness of Ivy's dress, skin, and bedspread. As she removes her garters, playfully zinging them at Jekyll, we see plenty of leg, although the camera coyly averts our gaze with cross shots of Jekyll's amused reaction. As Ivy takes off the rest of her outfit, the camera returns to Ivy before she has covered herself with the white bedspread, clearly revealing that she has nothing on and exposing a good deal of her back, part of her breast, and her dangling leg that beckons Jekyll to join her.

Despite his gentlemanly refusal, the dangling leg, superimposed on the screen, follows Dr. Jekyll as he leaves the room and walks down the street. Later, of course, the same setting of seduction will be the scene of Ivy's murder at the hands of Jekyll's lascivious alter ego Mr. Hyde. The horror movie had an added benefit for Hollywood of circumventing censorship because, as Skal points out, the Production Code did not mention monsters (117). The early horror films were typically set in Europe, with monsters that originate there, but *The Story of Temple Drake* brings the setting closer to home, complete with monsters of our own making.[28]

In 1932, moving from the horror to the gangster film, Hopkins again plays a dancehall girl (a taxi dancer), Gloria Bishop. And again she is the cynosure of the male gaze, as she excites the interest of a naïve trumpet player, a bandleader, and a gangster, Louie Brooks, played by George Raft. Brooks is taken with Gloria's spectacular and sensuous rendition of "St. Louis Blues," and his fascination with the song eventually contributes to his death. Predating *The Story of Temple Drake*, the advertisements for *Dancers in the Dark* also label Hopkins as a "Half good girl . . . half bad girl," declaring that "Dark secrets from her past should not matter—but they do!" As with *The Story of Temple Drake*, Hopkins's "dark secrets" and her sex appeal are racially coded. Writing about Hollywood's use of "St. Louis Blues" from 1929 to 1937, Peter Stanfield argues that the song was repeatedly and consistently used "as a means to articulate racial instability in the characterization of women who represented problems in terms of their sexuality, their morality, and their (lower) class status" (84). Gloria Bishop represents all three of these things, and her performance of "St. Louis Blues" presents her as a sexual siren who lures men to their death, even if that is not her intent.

Paramount capitalized on Hopkins's previous roles as lower-class temptresses in creating the racial and class ambiguity of Temple Drake as a fallen belle, another "half good girl . . . half bad girl."

In a similar vein, Trigger's role as monster is superimposed on his role as black-coded villain. The insert shot of Trigger in the opening credits links him back to Gus in *The Birth of a Nation*. Griffith marks Gus's sinister nature several times in the film in framing shots, but particularly through the use of the iris. Before the zoom lens, Griffith uses the iris shot to highlight aspects of a shot and to create the effect of a "close-up." Gus's dangerously lascivious nature is highlighted by the use of the framing iris, which captures him leering at the innocent heroines, Elsie and Flora, and which precedes his fatal pursuit of Flora. Though an actual iris is not used in *The Story of Temple Drake*, Trigger is lit in such a way as to illuminate his face in an oval of light, leaving the rest of the shot in darkness, similar to the effect created by the iris shot.

From the initial shots of Trigger in the opening credits leading up to the rape scene, his status as monster, "gangster of the id," is created through the use of light and darkness. Many scenes at the plantation house have only one source of illumination, a candle or a kerosene lamp, and the use of low-angle lights creates looming shadows, particularly in relation to Trigger (fig. 3).[29] In the absolute blackness of the night after the car accident, Trigger's flashlight is the only source of light, which he uses to perpetrate his first violation of Temple. As she lies prostrate on the ground, Trigger focuses the light on Temple's exposed legs. When Temple stands up, he again uses the light to move slowly over her body from her feet up to her face. This scene forms a visual link to Miriam Hopkins's strip tease as Ivy in *Dr. Jekyll and Mr. Hyde*, but Trigger is not the gentlemanly Dr. Jekyll, who averts his eyes; he is already the monstrous Mr. Hyde.

Throughout the film Trigger's shadow looms ominously between Temple and freedom. As Temple goes downstairs, leaving her room for the supposed safety of the barn, we see Trigger's shadow and the balustrade—with its broken and tilted spindles—projected twice their size against the staircase wall.[30] This scene is eerily similar to the famous scene in *Nosferatu* in which the vampire's exaggerated shadow with its long fingernails reaches for the innocent traveler's doorknob, as the lines of the staircase form black bars on the wall. When Temple steps outside the plantation house to seek

134 DEBORAH E. BARKER

"The Story of Temple Drake", filmed from a novel by William Faulkner and opening............at the...........Theatre, brings Miriam Hopkins a new emotional role. Jack LaRue, playing the role of "Trigger", is seen as the menace, with Miss Hopkins, in the Paramount picture.

FIGURE 3 Advertisement for *The Story of Temple Drake*. The Story of Temple Drake *Press Book*. Paramount Pictures, 1933. Courtesy of the J. D. Williams Library Special Collections, University of Mississippi.

sanctuary, we see Trigger from an oblique angle, backlit, and in silhouette against the decaying house.

Later, when Trigger menacingly approaches the unguarded Temple in the barn, the lighting mirrors that of Dracula's dilapidated castle with slits of sunlight highlighting the gloom, cobwebs, and decay, and projecting bars onto the unsuspecting victim. In *Dracula*, however, there are parts of the castle that have been refurbished and in which a roaring fire and a series of candelabras provide a warm glow. There is no such lighting in the plantation house; it is a world of darkness and decay shrouded in shadows. In addition to the visual similarities between Trigger and his vampire precursor, David Skal's analysis of Dracula sounds uncannily similar to Trigger/Popeye and his effect on Temple:

> Dracula, after all, is the ultimate charlatan and con man. He is a "castrated" seducer who cannot penetrate in the conventional way; all sex energy is displaced to his mouth. Instead of providing stimulation, repeated encounters only drain and depress his lovers, who can barely recall his visits. Unconsummated in normal terms their passion soon becomes undead as well. (126)

The lighting techniques that create Temple as the good/bad girl and Trigger as a monster of the id are the work of Karl Struss, a cinematographer who began his career as an art photographer and was well known for his artistic and technical innovations, especially in working with black and white. Struss worked with Griffith, as well as with F. W. Murnau (the director of *Nosferatu* [1922]), Rouben Mamoulian (who directed Hopkins in *Dr. Jekyll and Mr. Hyde*), and with Hopkins on several other films.[31] Explaining his lighting technique in *The Story of Temple Drake*, Struss commented:

> For the dramatic effects such as those achieved in *The Story of Temple Drake*, we'd sort of make the actors look screwy or gruesome by having low lights hidden on the floor, behind chairs or tables, and casting them up. Large shadows would be on the wall in the back of the actors depending, of course, on how much was there and the size of the shot. And there would be variety. Sometimes we'd just have a full light directly at a 90-degree angle from one side or the other

so you couldn't see anything of the opposite side of the face—there would just be half a face illuminated. Sometimes under the shadow side of the face we'd have a kicker light to outline the face. (qtd. in Harvith 16)

Struss believed in creating deep blacks for night shots, as in the accident scene with Temple and Toddy.[32] Struss was also willing to use total darkness for dramatic effect, as in the scene when Ruby puts out the only source of light in the room and we, like Temple, hear rather than see Trigger come into the room. When Trigger attacks Temple in the corncrib, the scene again fades to black, and we hear her scream. This use of darkness, unlike the others, is not diegetic; Temple sees her attacker, but, as in the novel, she never fully narrates the rape scene. The audience, however, that has either read or heard of the novel and knows that Popeye/Trigger rapes Temple with a corncob, can fill in the censored material. The fade-to-black is part of the grammar of the scene, which highlights what is omitted, so that the scene, but not the audience, is left in the dark.

After the rape scene Temple is transformed from the monster's innocent victim into the gangster's moll as the film shifts from the rural plantation house to the urban underworld and takes on the trappings of the gangster film. In the novel—in a speech similar to Ruby's earlier condemnation of Temple—Minnie, the African American maid at Miss Reba's, rebukes Temple for staying drunk and for not being grateful to Popeye: "What you want to treat him this-a-way, fer? Way he spend his money on you, you ought to be ashamed. He a right pretty little man, even if he aint no John Gilbert, and way he spending his money" (227). Minnie contrasts Popeye with the matinee idol of the silent screen John Gilbert, who starred opposite Lillian Gish, Greta Garbo, and Mary Pickford: Popeye is not the hero, but rather represents the antihero of the Depression, the gangster who has money to burn.

As discussed earlier, Popeye is coded as black, but Trigger as gangster is coded as dark, both ethnically and racially. Though the studio could not get George Raft—who played opposite Hopkins in *Dancer in the Dark*—to play Trigger, Jack Le Rue, who was finally cast, had appeared in several gangster films, and his dark hair, complexion, and dark tailored suit mark him as a member of the ethnically defined gangster underworld. In early storyboard depictions of the rape scene, Trigger was referred to as "Mex," further indicating the interest in creating Trigger as ethnically Other.[33] While Trigger's name links him to the phallic image of the gun and the violence associated with the gangster (and he is also the trigger that precipitates the events of the movie beginning with Temple's rape), and rhymes with a racial slur, given the small size of a trigger and its propensity to fire with only slight pressure (hair trigger), or to go off "half-cocked" (characteristics that are also associated with Popeye/Trigger), it still suggests sexual inadequacies. Even Trigger as gangster-rapist—though cruel and violent—does not quite measure up to the myth of black male sexuality.

The ambiguous status of Popeye/Trigger and Temple in many ways makes them a greater danger to a hierarchical system based on race, class, and gender superiority than Gus and Flora. Like the mulatto characters in Dixon's works, Popeye/Trigger and Temple undermine a system based on difference by their very existence. Faulkner's revision of the southern rape complex does not resolve the ambiguities; although the status quo reasserts itself in the end, Faulkner highlights the hypocrisy upon which the myth is based. In Faulkner's ending, the belle is drawn back into the patriarchal society by her father and brothers, who convince her to lie about who committed the rape and therefore allow an innocent man to die. Temple gains nothing from lying and her testimony seems to be another form of male (incestuous) violation in which in "rapt abasement" she responds to her father and is surrounded by her four "stiffly erect" brothers who "in a close body ... passed through the door and disappeared" (289–90).

The Story of Temple Drake redeems the southern belle by drawing her into a "national" story of justice. The film, in opposition to the novel, has the violated belle punish her attacker and restore justice at the end of the film. Temple first lies to protect Stephen, then kills Trigger, and finally agrees to testify to defend Lee Goodwin. Because of her good/bad girl position in the movie, Temple can act as both gangster's moll and victim and takes the law (the gun) into her own hands. Significantly, the death of Tommy, the lower class "feeb," and Temple's own violation are not incentive enough for Temple to act; it is only after Trigger threatens Stephen (the law) that she is spurred into action. She rewrites the southern rape complex because, in her degradation, she fails to personify the purity of the threatened South. Instead of dying, killing herself, or allowing herself to be rescued (as a "proper" belle should do), she stays with her attacker until she finally kills him, further circumventing the justification for the Klan to act.

In comparing the novel and movie, Degenfelder maintains that in the film version "[n]ot only did good triumph over evil, but Temple, wavering genteelly between these polarities, was, in the end, restored to her shrine" (546). While I agree that Temple is identified with good in the end, she is not restored to the shrine/pedestal of the southern belle. *The Birth of a Nation* jettisons the tainted southern belle and reinscribes and softens the northern New Woman as American belle. *The Story of Temple Drake*, on the other hand, recasts the belle as a male-defined New "American" Woman and redefines honor as based on truth and law, not purity and social reputation. Chivalry and the Drake "wild streak" have let Temple down, but American justice will redeem her.

REUNITING NORTH AND SOUTH

The Story of Temple Drake begins and ends with a courtroom scene that signals the shift from a "southern" code of honor based on white supremacy to an "American" code of justice that assumes an unproblematic, classless, normative whiteness. Whereas *The Birth of a Nation* begins with scenes that associate the Old South and racial hierarchy with harmony, peace, and family, the opening scenes of *The Story of Temple Drake* set up a series of signifiers of southern decadence—the flirtatious belle, the drunken, effete gentleman, the racially prejudiced judge—that indict white upper-class racism and elitism. In *The Birth of a Nation* the final "victory" of the whites, both southern and northern, cannot restore the Old South, but does suggest that the harmony equated with racial hierarchy in the beginning of the film is the key to a new post-Reconstruction national identity. Griffith was able to portray the racial model of the South as the national model for the future. In *The Story of Temple Drake*, on the other hand, the South is associated with racial prejudice, decadent belles, and "white trash" bootleggers. The film's final disavowal of all things southern, therefore, serves as the solution to the "negro problem," the "woman problem," the "class problem," and the "crime problem." The South is presented as the locus of the problems, and not as a model for the solutions for Depression-era America, a move that will be especially appealing and used with greater frequency in movies that deal with the civil rights era.

In turning to a "national" legal solution to the southern rape complex, rather than a local illegal solution, the film distances itself from *The Birth of a Nation*'s white supremacist vigilantism, but also from *Sanctuary*'s southern decadence and cynicism. To accomplish this, the movie rewrites Horace Benbow's failure as a lawyer to serve his client or justice. Just as the impotent Popeye of the novel is changed to the more virile Trigger of the film, the ineffectual Horace Benbow becomes the determined Stephen Benbow, who wins the case and the girl.[34] In the novel Horace naïvely tells Lee Goodwin, "You've got the law, justice, civilization" (132) and reassures Ruby, "You may know more about whiskey or love than I do, but I know more about criminal procedure remember" (270). Unfortunately, he actually knows less about all three, and his faith in the justice system does not take into account the reality of vigilante justice and the legacy of lynching to which his client succumbs.

The initial establishing shot of the movie indicates what Stephen is up against in fighting for American justice by referencing the fictional world of Dixon's *The Clansman*. The courthouse is not in Faulkner's Yoknapatawpha County, but in *Dixon County*, and, as if the audience might miss the significance of the setting, using a crane shot, the camera pulls into an extreme close-up of the words "Dixon County." Inside the courthouse, the silhouette of justice is displayed on the wall, but when the judge speaks we realize that justice in this courtroom is not blind. The judge advises the jury not to blame Stephen for taking the case because the court appointed him. Stephen vociferously objects that the judge's comments are "prejudicial to the interests of my client," maintaining that he willingly took the case. The viewer must infer the judge's meaning, but presumably Stephen is the court-appointed lawyer of the working-class black man who sits behind him, and the judge, assuming the defendant's guilt because of his race, is defending not justice but the white lawyer for taking the case in the first place. Stephen's partner comments that they will never win the case now, but Stephen concludes that they "never had a chance."

The southern courtroom in "Dixon County" is a place where justice is not served. As Seidel explains,

> Authors of the 1930s who indicted southern traditions often used the metaphor of the courtroom trial.... Moreover, most of the belles in these novels are portrayed as the daughters of judges, who represent the traditions that are on trial.... [I]n books before 1900 her father was a planter-squire. The modern belle's father lives in town and works as a lawyer judge whose task is to preserve legal traditions—hence the easy analogy with his role as a faded inheritor of the southern past. (157)

Stephen is distanced from the southern courtroom not only because of his objection to the judge's statement but also because, although he is part of the southern upper class, he does not speak with a southern accent. Unlike Temple, Stephen does not "sound" southern either in what he says or how he says it. This is reinforced in the next scene in which Stephen visits Judge Drake. The judge, who is the epitome of the southern gentlemen, tells Stephen that he must accept the laws, which Stephen maintains are "obsolete" and "totally out of key with our times." The juxtaposition of Stephen's defense of his black client and his attack on outdated laws suggests that he condemns laws that are unfair to African Americans. Ironically, even as the judge is chiding Stephen to follow the laws regardless of how he feels about them, the judge produces a bottle of whiskey from his desk and proceeds to pour a drink, an act of hypocrisy that surely would not be lost on a Prohibition-era audience. The whiskey also negatively reinforces the earlier link between the judge, Todd Gowan, and the image of the southern gentleman. The judge assumes that Toddy is a gentleman because they went to the same college, and Toddy insists that, as a gentleman, he was taught how to drink, but it is Toddy's never-ending search for more alcohol that takes Temple to the Old Frenchman place. And, in his drunken stupor, Toddy is unable to perform the function of the gentleman, to defend Temple's honor.[35]

In the final trial scene in the film, Stephen's cross examination of Temple reconstitutes the novel's rendering of the rape, turning Temple's hallucinatory account told to Horace Benbow into a male-identified call for truth and justice. In the novel, Temple never actually explains what happens to her; instead she recounts to Horace—in an almost trance-like state, and with the ubiquitous sound of the corn shucks in her mind—her delusional attempts to avoid the rape by transforming into a man and magically acquiring a penis: "That was when I got to thinking a funny thing. You know how you do when you're scared. I was looking at my legs and I'd try to make like I was a boy. I was thinking about if I just was a boy and then I tried to make myself one by thinking" (216).[36]

Temple's story about Popeye's assault and his murder of Tommy should be the key to freeing Horace's client. Yet, instead of empowering him as a lawyer, Horace's role as witness to Temple's degradation implicates him in her abjection. Ironically, although Temple was not able to turn herself into a boy, her story does have the effect of emasculating Horace, as he is transformed in the text into a victimized woman—after running to the bathroom to throw up in a delayed reaction to Temple's story—through a shifting of pronouns and point of view:[37]

> [H]e gave over and plunged forward and struck the lavatory and leaned upon his braced arms while the shucks set up a terrific uproar beneath her thighs. Lying with her head lifted slightly, her chin depressed like a figure lifted down from a crucifix, she watched something black and furious go roaring out of her pale body. She was bound naked on her back on a flat car moving at speed through a back tunnel, the blackness streaming in rigid threads overhead, a roar of iron wheels in her ears.... Far beneath her she could hear the faint, furious uproar of the shucks. (223)

Horace's transformation begins and ends with the sound of corn shucks, a symbol of abjection, the leftovers from the production of moonshine, made by people who themselves are referred to as "white trash," stored in the barn, which also serves as an outhouse and the scene of Temple's rape.

The sound of the corn shucks signals Horace's hallucinatory descent into a place that corresponds to Julia Kristeva's description of abjection as "the place where meaning collapses" and boundaries dissolve (2). Abjection, the primary repression of the maternal body, though a necessary step in the formation of the self, returns to threaten identity. Corresponding to Horace's nightmare image, abjection is a "weight of meaninglessness, about which there is nothing insignificant, and which mashes me. On the edge of nonexistence and hallucination, or a reality that, if I acknowledge it, annihilates me" (2). It is not simply a "lack of cleanliness or health that causes abjection"; it, like Popeye, is "what disturbs identity, system, order. What does not respect borders, positions, rules. The in-between, the ambiguous, the composite. The traitor, the liar, the criminal with the good conscience, the shameless rapist" (4). Kristeva's theory explains Popeye's role as the agent of abjection and his ability to annihilate all that he touches.

Popeye, because he is the most brutal character in the novel and the one who rapes and kidnaps Temple, is the most obvious source of the "logical pattern of evil" that Benbow discovers after hearing Temple's story, but as the novel's ending indicates, Popeye is just the sad product of syphilis, poverty, and ignorance. The calculating "logical pattern of evil" lies not with Popeye or with Temple as the flirtatious shallow belle, but with the respectable southern belle, Narcissa, Benbow's sister—"the criminal with the good conscience"—who would allow a man to be killed to prevent even an indirect taint upon her reputation. Or, as Faulkner would depict her in the short story "There Was a Queen" (1932), Narcissa is the belle who would actually have sex to protect the public appearance of innocence. As her name implies, Narcissa is the shallow, self-centered belle at the heart of the novel.[38]

Faulkner totally deflates the high drama of the Southern rape complex and condemns white middle-class morality by depicting Narcissa, the representative of a stuffy, white middle-class hypocrisy, as the prime mover of the rape and the lynching. It is her callous rejection of Gowan that drives him to drink and to turn to Temple for consolation, and that sets the events in motion that lead to Temple's rape and abduction. But even more important, it is her desire to protect her name that leads her to sabotage Horace's case by revealing information about his surprise witness to the District Attorney in order to bring the trial to a speedy conclusion and conviction. Like Marion of *The Clansman*, Narcissa wants her name to remain "sweet and clean," and she is willing to let innocent people die to accomplish her goal. Rather than kill herself in the process, however, she is willing to sacrifice Temple and Lee Goodwin. Or, what is even more callous, Narcissa does not know or care about the nature of the information that she gives the D.A. Temple's rape, Goodwin's guilt or innocence, and her brother's sense of honor are all totally irrelevant to her. The only thing she cares about is that her brother is being gossiped about, and that this, in turn, may besmirch her family name by linking her to the disreputable acts of "white trash" bootleggers. Narcissa fights to preserve her racial and class status, even if it means emasculating her own brother.

In the film, in order to celebrate white middle-class American values, Narcissa disappears and Horace's filmic counterpart Stephen is able to do what Horace cannot: he extracts Temple's confession on the stand in service of his client, the law, and justice. Rather than being overcome by the abjection he encounters, Stephen restores "borders, positions, rules" and white identity. He does so by compelling Temple "to be a man," to metaphorically acquire the phallus, the name of the father, and to tell the truth in order to "destroy the evil streak" in her: to overcome the effects of the rape, reclaim her sense of honor, free an innocent man, and restore order. What finally induces Temple to tell her story to the jury is Stephen's impassioned speech that she live up to the Drake sense of family honor: their "courage, their willingness to make sacrifices, their love of truth." Stephen goes down the list of Temple's male relatives who have died for honor in battle, including not only the Civil War but also the "World War," a war in which North and South fought together against a foreign foe. He concludes, "You're a woman, but you're still a Drake. You want to act like one, don't you?" In his speech Stephen counteracts Aunt Jenny's earlier assertions about the hereditary Drake wild streak, with its implications of miscegenation, by asking Temple to live up to her "American" family lineage of sacrifice and duty. He banishes the flirtatious belle/flapper not with an ambitious or self-defining New Woman but with a male-identified woman willing to take her place in the patriarchal order and expose her "darkest secrets" in the name of justice.

Judge Drake, as the representative of the southern gentleman, is, of course, outraged that Stephen would suggest that Temple testify, and he will not even entertain the thought that she could be involved in the case at all. One of the justifications for lynching in the South was the need to protect the woman's honor not only by seeking revenge (which could easily be carried out by a trial) but also by preventing her from the shame of having to describe the rape in open court. In urging Temple to testify in order to free Goodwin, Stephen abandons the notion of southern chivalry by asking her to forget about her "honor," i.e., her reputation as pure, and to redefine honor as based on truthfulness and justice.

The final reversal of the courtroom scene occurs when Temple faints after giving her testimony, and Stephen, carrying her in his arms out of the courtroom, says to Judge Drake, "You should be proud of her. I am." This image is significant in many ways. First it indicates that Temple's transformation into a "man" was only temporary. It allows her to reassume the role of the innocent, fragile woman and the film to present Stephen as her protector. This is an important move because, before the courtroom scene, Temple has already taken the phallus (gun) into her own hands to kill Trigger and to protect Stephen. But this image also reinscribes a scene from *The Birth of a Nation*, in which Elsie is confronted by the threat of miscegenation by Silas Lynch, her father's mulatto protégé who wants to force her into marriage.

Elsie, like Temple, assumes that she can control the situation by refusing Lynch, but when he locks her in and grabs her, her initial hysterical reaction mirrors that of Flora and Temple. Elsie, however, has the presence of mind to rush to the window, break it, and call out to two Klan spies, who eventually bring the Klan to rescue her. Lest she be seen as too independent and resourceful to be a proper lady, after she calls for help, she faints, and Lynch holds the unconscious body of Elsie in his arms. Griffith's decision to use Lillian Gish to play Elise was validated when, in rehearsing the attack on Elsie by Lynch, Gish's blond hair came undone as Lynch held her in his arms; this scene apparently appealed to Griffith as an emblem of white womanhood in the hand of the dark ravisher (Rogin 267). Also, according to Rogin, Gish as American belle replaced not only the southern belle, but also the more threatening image of the New Woman, whom Griffith had earlier presented through the actress Blanche Sweet (260–68).

At the end of *The Birth of a Nation*, Flora's dramatic exit from the film leaves Elsie, though a northern woman, to take on the visual signs of the southern belle and to replace Flora as a more appropriate partner for Ben.[39] Elsie's transformation to northern belle is made apparent in the movie's climax as Ben and Elsie are on their honeymoon. Elsie is wearing a tulle shawl, which surrounds her in a gossamer cloud, and she now has on the white, ruffled dress of the belle. The next intertitle reads, "Dare we dream of a golden day when the bestial War shall rule no more. But instead—the gentle Prince in the Hall of brotherly love in the City of Peace." Griffith then depicts the god of war wielding his sword and Christ superimposed over a crowd in the "hall of brotherly love." The members of the heavenly throng, like Elsie, are covered in tulle veils and shawls. In a split screen, Ben and Elsie, on a hill overlooking the sea, seem to look out at the Celestial City as "The Star-Spangled Banner" plays. Elsie's apotheosis as northern belle is complete in her ultrafeminine and "heavenly" costume. The final intertitle reads, "Liberty and union, one and inseparable, now and forever!" Ostensibly, the intertitle refers to the newly united states, but also to the marriage. Purged of the weakness and willfulness associated with the belle, Elsie is fit to preside over not just the new nation but also the Celestial City.

The Story of Temple Drake reverses this process. In the courtroom scene Temple no longer dresses in the frivolous fashion of flapper/belle, but instead wears a more sober gray suit, whereas in the novel she wears black satin with a "shoulder knot of purple" (284). In the film, the disparity between rich and poor whites is neutralized in the courtroom. The sartorial class differences between Temple and Ruby that were so evident at the Old Frenchman place are no longer so pronounced; now both are modestly and neatly dressed. Ruby is transformed into the picture of motherhood, holding her child rather than leaving it in a box on the woodpile to keep it away from the rats. Even Goodwin, the lower-class bootlegger, though not wearing a tie, is transformed into the jacket-clad father/husband presiding over his nuclear family (not the dysfunctional "family" at the old plantation), an innocent man returned to the loving arms of his "wife."

In the final scene in *The Story of Temple Drake*, Stephen, like Rhett carrying Scarlett up the stairs, reasserts his masculinity; he literally assumes the position of the dark ravisher—an image also linked to the horror film, in which the monster carries away the prostrate heroine—but, unlike Rhett's or Lynch's, Stephen's actions are in support of the law. Temple's faint is not the feigned swoon of the belle; rather, it acts out Ruby's earlier statement that if a "'real man' touched her she'd faint." Stephen is the "real man," not the southern gentleman, and Temple now is a "real woman," not a southern belle. Originally, the movie version of *Sanctuary* was to be named *The Shame of Temple Drake*, but the Hollywood version has taken Temple out of a shame culture; her story is a story of whiteness preserved through the courts, not through lynching.

Walter Benn Michaels asserts that "for Dixon, racism was crucial to the reinvention of the American state; only by freeing themselves from slavery, destroying their familial bonds to blacks, and intermarrying with their racial kinsmen from across the Mason-Dixon line could whites become Americans" (34). In *The Story of Temple Drake*, the perpetuation of the "American state" is based not only on the erasure of slavery and miscegenation, but also on the erasure of the South as the focus of racial problems. The courtroom has miraculously been freed of racial prejudice simply by creating an ostensibly all-white space, where race is no longer addressed. Temple frees herself from the dangerous threat of her incestuous and miscegenistic lineage by becoming a typical white middle-class American, rather than a southern upper-class belle, and by destroying the malevolent and racially ambiguous lower-class white male. Unlike Flora, whose "dark desires" lead to her death, or Marion, whose honor and "whiteness" could be corrupted by a black man, Temple's "whiteness" is no longer an issue, and her honor—even in the face of violation by a white/black man, and her own degrading behavior—can be renewed, not through "spirit" or religion, but through upholding the principle of truth, justice, and the American way.

INSIDE AND OUTSIDE SOUTHERN WHITENESS

Film Viewing, the Frame, and the Racing of Space in Yoknapatawpha

—PETER LURIE

Cash Bundren is a lover of music. At the end of *As I Lay Dying*, hearing sound coming from the new Mrs. Bundren's house in Jefferson, Cash comments that "[it] was playing in the house. It was one of them graphophones. It was natural as a music band" (235). Later he muses, "It's a comfortable thing, music is" (235); and, in *As I Lay Dying*'s last chapter, "I reckon it's a good thing we aint got ere a one of them. I reckon I wouldn't never get no work done a-tall for listening to it. I dont know if a little music aint about the nicest thing a fellow can have" (259). As these remarks imply, Cash's "graphophone" is also a product, one that, like Anse's false teeth, Vardaman's electric train, and Dewey Dell's bananas, offsets his trip to Jefferson and the Bundrens' burial of their wife and mother.

Cash's gramophone, though, is unlike these objects in that it furnishes a pleasure that is at once technological and aesthetic. Due to its portable nature, particularly, as well as to the fact that it is a machine, the gramophone allows Cash to enjoy music as a reproduction and in the comfort of his home. Listening to music on the gramophone would seem a simple enough activity (if it is not also "as natural as a music band"). Especially because, as Cash describes it, such relaxation can newly be enjoyed in what was, before the advent of this particular entertainment technology, the isolated countryside. For one of the historical and cultural shifts that *As I Lay Dying* reveals is the role of modern commodities and their availability to formerly rural families like the Bundrens.[1]

I say "formerly" with a deliberate eye on the Bundrens' journeying. Coming to Jefferson, they do not quite become "town people"—despite Dewey Dell's efforts to the contrary, evident when she puts on her Sunday dress as the family reaches Jefferson's outskirts. Yet as the end of the novel and events within it suggest, their trip does afford them certain changes. In addition to acquiring the "new" Mrs. Bundren (an acquisition that seems troublingly like another product), they are initiated into a world of commerce and modernity that differs from their former, more purely rustic way of life. This introduction, though, comes with a cost: in addition to burying Addie, the family consigns brother Darl to the care of the state.

It is interesting in this light that in his close Faulkner does not return the Bundrens to their family spread. Rather he leaves them in the streets of Jefferson, having complied with the local police's demand that they bury their putrefying mother. This lack of clear resolution concerning location implies at least a potential extension into aspects of modernity, including the Bundrens' lingering within, if not urban space, then a domain of commerce, legality, and exchange that in the period of the novel's events was also becoming increasingly racialized.[2]

That location is suggestive. Anse may complain early in the book about the incursion into his private farming life of taxes and the road ("Durn that road" [35]). And with the book's close, it would appear that he was right to suspect that this new tie to town or even metropolitan life and public space would deny him one of his farmhands. Important to my considerations, though, is this curious induction into civic life as well as into modern consumer pleasures like Cash's gramophone and the possibilities they offered families like the Bundrens. For if we consider other then-new cultural forms in relation to families like Anse's, we would see that they bear an affinity with what Cash considers his own "indulgence" in music. And this is true in ways that have to do as much with social history as with developing aesthetic technologies and tastes.

One of those new forms was the cinema. Though neither film nor film viewing is ever named in *As I Lay Dying*, both the apparatus of cinema and what we might term its sociohistorical effects are evoked powerfully by and in the novel. These include the passing before the reader's "gaze" of the discrete, separate "frames" of the various characters' monologues, as well as, in particular sections, a fascination with watching machinery that resembled the interest of early film viewers in the cinematic apparatus (see Doane 108). It may seem unlikely that we would find a similar fascination with machinery per se in Faulkner's South. Yet at the river Darl evinces what we might call an urban-filmic sensibility. Watching Jewel and Vernon Tull in the water searching for Cash's lost tools, Darl muses, "From here they do not appear to violate the surface at all; it is as though [the river] had severed them both at a single blow, the two torsos moving with infinitesimal and ludicrous care upon the surface. It looks peaceful, like machinery does after you have watched it and listened to it for a long time" (163). We might consider too, as have others, the jolting, montage-like shifting across the novels' chapters.[3]

If Vardaman and his family are not explicitly depicted as film viewers, they nevertheless show signs of what has been theorized as a modern and cinematic optics or perception. The importance of the novel's references to consumer culture, though, or of its potential filmic overtones is not simply a historical and perceptual congruence. Rather, they allow us to see the Bundrens' transformation into, not only a different family, but arguably a new identity of both race and class.

Such a shift was occasioned outside the novel by an odd configuration: the empowering effects of two "modern" phenomena that shared a reliance on spectacle and an attendant framing as well as segregating of space: film viewing and lynching. Neither appears in *As I Lay Dying*. Both phenomena, however, play significant roles in "Dry September" and *Light in August* and, as the following discussion avers, in connection with one another. For this as well as other reasons, *As I Lay Dying*'s links to cinema operate differently than do those in later Yoknapatawpha works. Its perhaps subtle evoking of modernity and film, however, set terms for a process across Faulkner's fiction that increasingly related film viewing to modern demands for a white, national identity, one that was also marked by class and which, over the period of his life and writing, became increasingly violent. As such all three cases offer ways to consider the impact of early film viewing in its connections to racial identity and social power—the link between southern whiteness and what Richard Dyer calls cinema's "culture of light."[4]

Before we turn back to Faulkner's fiction, it is useful to note that moviegoing changed considerably in the early twentieth century. Exhibited publically for the first time in 1895, two years prior to Faulkner's birth, film was originally considered a somewhat tawdry activity, enjoyed by working-class and immigrant laborers in industrial cities. By the late nineteen teens and, certainly, the twenties, though, it had become a far more respectable activity. This change in status was due to specific efforts on the part of both particular directors such as D. W. Griffith and the burgeoning film industry to incorporate members of the middle class into the viewing public. As Lary May has shown, the efforts in the early 1900s of social reformers, film distributors and producers, and the National Board of Review combined to "create the beginnings of a truly mass entertainment" (30). Part of this change depended on the close monitoring of narrative content: all of these parties called for newly "moral" films, ones that included story lines as opposed to an earlier cinema's reliance on burlesque or bawdy, nonnarrative "attractions."[5] Additionally, the National Board of Review worked hard after 1908, when half of the films shown in nickelodeons were foreign (with their own supposedly ribald imagery), to enforce a reduction in imports by 1913 to 10 percent (May 30). Lastly and importantly, these new films, understood as more suitable for a nonimmigrant, middle-class audience, were appearing in theaters that held more than a thousand viewers. (This was a dramatic change from the crowded, often unclean nickelodeons, which couldn't seat more than three hundred.)[6]

In the South especially, this increase in film audience was also subtended by a particularly racial manner of organizing spaces like the cinema. For the class transformation in film's audiences did not cut across lines of race. The importance of whiteness to this development is clear if we consider the kinds of films that viewers of the period would have seen. May surveys the prominence of pictures by D. W. Griffith, the so-called "grandfather of film," including but not limited to his infamous epic *The Birth of a Nation*, in the first two decades of the twentieth century. During the cinema's silent era, and in the period when Griffith's enormous popularity incorporated both middle- and working-class viewers, audiences were shown "warnings" about the risks of mixing with immigrant groups who, Griffith believed, did not share his embrace of conservative, Victorian mores (May 41–42). Michael Rogin similarly traces the impact that Griffith's magnum opus had on race relations, not in Faulkner's South, but in the North. He describes how, with the waves of immigration that spread into northern cities (and that fueled bitter debates in the 1920s about nativism), northerners became sympathetic to *Birth of a Nation*'s story about a "beleaguered" white population in the South.[7] Film viewing in this period, that is, and irrespective of class, became a purview of belonging to a new "nation" while it contributed to the entrenching of a newly national (and increasingly nationalist) white identity.

This new class and national collective and its racial cast would be especially important for a family like the Bundrens. For as moments from *As I Lay Dying* make clear, this family of poor whites has a hard time distinguishing itself from southern African Americans. On the outskirts of Jefferson, they pass through what Darl describes as a "negro" district. We will remember that, at the start of this chapter, Darl refers to the fact that the back of Jewel's shirt is "stain[ed] . . . black with grease" (227) that covers his burns, suffered while rescuing Addie's coffin the night before. Darl notes that Jewel's skin later darkens, taking on a "deeper tone of furious red" (229), just before he turns on the group of African Americans who have inadvertently insulted him by reacting negatively to the smell of Addie's body on the wagon. Like other southern laborers, Jewel and the Bundrens may appear "black" in other ways as well: unlettered, rural, defined by their status as indentured laborers. In his angry encounter with the group of black travelers as well as, moments later, a "goddamn town fellow" (230) on the road, Jewel seeks to establish a higher class and, particularly, racial identity for the family.

Yet as events from the novel and the period in which it is set suggest, such social "whitening" has already begun for the novel's characters. As we've seen, their movement to Jefferson allows them to enjoy some of the same consumer pleasures as other middle-class whites. Other details further suggest that a transformation in economic life is underfoot. Cash's name clearly evinces the move to a wage system, as opposed to the South's use of tenant farming. Similarly, Cora Tull's cakes and her calculations about "saving out" eggs (6) suggests her preparedness to engage the market. Once the Bundrens arrive in Jefferson, and extrapolating from electric trains, bananas, and the gramophone, I'd speculate that, time permitting, the family may have taken in a picture show. If so, such an experience would have added to the Bundrens' increasing whiteness in town.

While the Bundrens' potential as consumers in the novel is clear, as Cash's gramophone and other commodities reveal, their visit to the movie house remains speculative. But as other Yoknapatawpha works like "Dry September" and *Light in August* show more directly, Faulkner's characters do frequent the movies, as Faulkner did himself.[8] What these works share with the Bundrens' story is an emphasis on the spatial dynamic of modern southern racial identity, the at times lethal play of "inside and outside" a white public realm that the cinema both facilitated and enforced.

As the history of film viewing during Jim Crow reveals, the question of access to the space of the cinema, like other public spaces, pivoted on questions of exclusion, on who, in other words, enjoyed the privilege of being "interior" to the workings of the state. Darl may be consigned to a wandering position "outside" the law, as Patrick O'Donnell has suggested (91). But by implication, the Bundrens secure a position inside the law and civic space—one that resembles that of the (white) audiences for film. Robert C. Allen has written about what he calls the "racing of [southern] space" during Jim Crow, particularly around public areas such as cinemas. He points out that owing to the legal status of most exhibition spaces as private enterprises, movie theaters were particularly well-guarded areas of white privilege. "Unlike streetcars, railroad cars and station waiting rooms, movie theaters in the South were regarded and treated, not as public businesses but as private spaces. This crucial legal distinction gave racial exclusion the force of law" ("Relocating" 75). As one piece of crucial historical evidence, Allen notes the near-concurrence of the *Plessy v. Ferguson* decision, which was handed down on May 16, 1896, and the debut three weeks earlier of Thomas Edison's Vitascope at Koster and Bial's Music Hall in New York City (71). As a result, he claims, "For nearly 70 years … the history of moviegoing and the history of racial segregation in the US, particularly in the South, are not only co-terminous but conjoined." Cedric J. Robinson writes about such spatial exclusion as well, noting the conjunction of legal segregation and the advent of film. "Moving pictures appear at that juncture when a new racial regime was being stitched together . . . accommodating the disposal of immigrants, colonial subjects, and insurgencies among the native poor. With the first attempts at composing a national identity in disarray, a new whiteness became the basis for the reintegration of American society. And monopolizing the refabrication of a public sphere, with a reach and immediacy not obtained by previous apparatuses (museums, theaters, fairs, the press, etc.), motion pictures insinuated themselves into public life" (xiv–xv).[9] As Allen elsewhere puts it succinctly, "Race is not just a part of the story of the history of moviegoing in the South; that story cannot be understood except in its relation to race. And once race is placed at the center of that story (where it belongs), it changes from an account of who saw movies where to an investigation of how the movies functioned as an instrument of social power" ("Decentering" 28).

The role of the cinema in the exercise of social power is evident in Faulkner's work. In both *Light in August* and in "Dry September," that exercise pivots on a southern definition of whiteness, but one that, as both works show, was also becoming national in the modern period. As these examples from Yoknapatawpha as well as particular film texts and theoretical works show, such a conflation depended on an association of whiteness with an abstract, "pure" conception of racial identity in which were subsumed actual markers of corporeal being. Yet importantly, both narratives also show Faulkner "re-embodying" southern and U.S. whiteness in an effort to cast it into relief, so to speak—showing whiteness more starkly, and thus dismantling its presumption of power through invisibility.

"Dry September" offers perhaps the clearest example in Faulkner of the nexus of film, whiteness, and southern social space. Published in *Scribner's Magazine* in 1931, it illustrates the reach of racial policing in connection with film that we will also find detailed in *Light in August*. Like the novel, Faulkner's story also returns to whiteness its own conspicuousness and visibility, in large part because of the affinities between film viewing and racial violence that both narratives reveal.

"Dry September" includes a crucial scene that draws readers as well as characters into the interior space of the cinema. Faulkner's description of this visit to the movies is notable, though, for how closely it relates the effects of both cinema and lynching on spaces that the story reveals are contiguous as well as similarly "raced." As Minnie Cooper approaches the movie house in Jefferson with her friends, she crosses a town square which, as one of the women with her notes, is emptied of African Americans. "'There's not a Negro on the square,'" she declares. "'Not one'" (181). The reason for this absence, we know, is the fact of Will Mayes's lynching, the event that preceded Minnie's reentry into what we might call the "sexual economy" of the town. Yet the episode of Minnie's visit to the cinema is significant, both within the story and within Faulkner's corpus and its attention to film and southern patterns of exclusion. Unlike the segregation or prohibition of blacks in southern movie houses outside the story, the withdrawing of African Americans from the town square here is performed voluntarily. The fact that there's not a single "Negro" on the town square appears to be an anomaly to Minnie's friends. But as Allen and others indicate, southern moviegoing was rigidly segregated from its beginnings until the civil rights movement. As a result, once Minnie and her friends enter the movie house and partake of its "silver dream" (181), the absence of African Americans would be in no way notable.

"Dry September" turns on this kind of social and racial exclusion, of inside and outside, as Minnie and her friends' journey to the space of the town square and the adjoining cinema makes clear. Allen refers to the fact that "Jim Crow laws and practices were a reaction against the increased visibility of blacks in the urban public space as well as their increased economic and spatial mobility within that sphere" ("Relocating" 73). Here we will recall the absence or *in*visibility of African Americans on the town square as Minnie and her friends approach the movie house following Will Mayes's lynching. Minnie's supposed rape by Will mobilizes the "need" to protect white women like her and the evacuation of the town square, a securing of white space or a racing of public space that finds a clear fulfillment in the cinema.

In addition to newly enjoying this space, what Minnie comes to (re)possess in the story is both her own status as commodity and what legal scholarship has described as her "property" in her racial identity. In connection with his observations about southern moviegoing, Allen cites work by the legal scholar Cheryl Harris in which she describes whiteness as a "form of property" based on the right of exclusion of the sort that defined cinematic viewing. As Harris puts it, "The possessors of whiteness were granted the legal right to exclude others from the privileges inhering in whiteness; whiteness became an exclusive club whose membership was closely and grudgingly guarded" (quoted in R. Allen, "Relocating" 78). Tellingly, it is Minnie's earlier exclusion from that white club that leads in part to her fabrication of the rape story. We learn early in the story that, at a point in her youth, Minnie had been the subject of gossip and, after losing her quality of being "unclassconscious" (174), no longer attended parties or social events with the town's elite. Like Joanna Burden in *Light in August*, in other words, who goes through an even more extreme transformation (from pariah to paragon of white southern womanhood), Minnie runs a circuit from being a neglected, almost nonwhite (or invisible) citizen of the town to being one of its prominent—and prominently visible—members. Such newly objectified status is evident when, crossing the square, "even the young men lounging in the doorways tipped their hats and followed with their eyes the motion of [Minnie's] hips and legs when she passed" (181). As the ending of "Dry September" shows, part of that reinsertion derives from her entrance into the extended space of the cinema and how it allows a "reclaiming" of her racial as well as class property. As Robert Allen puts it of Southern moviegoing, "Whether it was purposive in this respect or even rose to the level of consciousness ... the very act of moviegoing was for white Southerners an exercise of their property right to whiteness" ("Relocating" 79). It is Minnie's moviegoing that, along with the rape story, allows her to reclaim her property.

In addition to relaying Minnie's shift in social position, her access to an "inside" realm that is explicitly white, "Dry September" also shows the men of the community anxiously negotiating the social forces that assign positions inside and outside whiteness. As with other examples in Faulkner's fiction and in southern social reality, one of the obvious ways in which the men define themselves as white is in their violent opposition to what they perceive as black threat. An important effect of this opposition is the link between the mob mentality that subtends vigilante violence, both in the story and outside it, and the securing of exclusively white enclaves like the cinema. We will turn to the lynching episode in *Light in August* shortly, noting its own associations with the phenomenon of moviegoing. White men in both *Light in August* and "Dry September," as well as white viewers—both as they appear in these works and are evoked by them—fashion whiteness as an exclusionary identity against African Americans and other, less "pure" (or purely racist) whites.

This intrawhite dynamic is in play from the very beginning of "Dry September." In relaying it, Faulkner deliberately evokes film viewing and draws on readers' encounters with the cinema. The story opens on a conversation in a barbershop in which appear fault lines in racial solidarity. A visitor to the town, a "drummer" who is getting a shave from the shop's proprietor, sides with the other men present who believe Minnie Cooper's rape accusation—or who believe that, irrespective of what Minnie claims Will to have done, he deserves violent punishing. When Hawkshaw offers one of the only voices of reason in the room, pointing to his own familiarity with Mayes and his conviction that Will would not have accosted Minnie, the drummer responds by challenging him in explicitly racial terms. "'You're a fine white man,' the client said. 'Aint you?'" (170). The narrator's description of the drummer that follows is notable. "In his frothy beard he looked like a desert rat in the moving pictures. 'You tell them, Jack,' he said to [Butch]. 'If there aint any white men in this town, you can count on me, even if I aint only a drummer and a stranger.'"

As the narrator's reference makes clear, the drummer's outsider status is overcome, first, by his willingness to close ranks with other men from Jefferson when he distinguishes his capacity for racial violence from that of the local barber, Hawkshaw. In this way, he more fully identifies himself as white. Secondly, and suggestively, the drummer's strangeness is overcome by his donning what might appear by way of the narrator's reference to cinema as a racial *mask*, a version of "whiteface" in his "frothy beard" that parallels in function if not in form the practice of blackface, which reinforced whiteness for actors and audiences of early cinema alike.[10]

It is significant that the drummer's whiteness is compared here to an image from the movies. Crucially, Faulkner understands that his narrator's reference to the cinema will operate meaningfully for his readers, revealing subtly how film viewing in the period could function to unify consumers of mass culture generally as well as movie audiences in particular. "Dry September" was originally published in *Scribner's*, at a point in Faulkner's career when he badly needed the income that such mass-circulation publications offered.[11] Readers of the story, then, are drawn into the space of the cinema by way of this reference to an encounter with mass culture they would have been expected to have had. Yet, as Allen's remarks about southern moviegoing make clear, such an imagined as well as actual social space was deliberately constructed as white in the period of the story's events and its writing. As a result, at moments such as this readers come to occupy the same socially exclusive, "whitened" space claimed by Butch, McLendon, and the drummer.

Such complicity occurred outside the story as well. For a similar extension of the kind of racial violence that occurs in "Dry September"—and an implied inclusion in the realm of whiteness—was also enforced in other representations of southern vigilantism. Here I refer to the common practice in the Jim Crow South of photographing and retailing images of lynching on postcards. Such images became intensely popular in the 1910s, and their "success" at enforcing white rule owed much to their capacity to incorporate viewers through formal strategies like perspective. The cultural work performed by lynching photos has been commented on extensively by both Shawn Michelle Smith (118–22) and Grace Elizabeth Hale (228–30), who trace the troubling if tacit complicity of photographers, local police, markets, retail businesses, and institutions such as the United States Post Office in purveying these images as commercial products.

Such photos also included a key formal element that links them to Faulkner's story. And that is the way in which, like the passage from "Dry September" cited above, they include viewers in a textual space "inside" the represented event—irrespective of our wish to be so included. This is why looking upon the photographs of southern lynching in the photography collection *Without Sanctuary: Lynching Photography in America* is so disturbing. In a photo of the lynching of Thomas Shipp and Abram Smith, for example, viewers find themselves included, despite themselves, in a scenario and a (framed) space that has been defined violently as white (fig. 1). As the unnamed man in the foreground indicates *for the viewers* the direction of their gaze, we are drawn with him into a visual and social dynamic of looking upon a spectacle of violence that, by virtue of our positioning, affords us a power we have not asked for. The collection's title, *Without Sanctuary*, may reveal our own unwitting participation in the same prerogative as the whites who appear in the photos and our incapacity to separate ourselves from such events. Referring to these dual spectacles "under the

FIGURE 1 Photograph taken by Lawrence Beitler of the bodies of Thomas Shipp and Abram Smith, Marion, Indiana, August 7, 1930. Image reproduced courtesy of *Without Sanctuary: Lynching Photography in America*, ed. James Allen, Twin Palms Press.

visual regime of Jim Crow," Susan Donaldson writes, "[T]he rituals and the photographs also endeavored to situate the viewers as solidly and impregnably white, a visual rendering of the color line" (120).[12] As photographs such as these and Faulkner's story alike attest, membership in a mob is not only limited to those who participate in lynching directly.

Readers of "Dry September" do not participate in lynching, nor look upon one; significantly, Will's lynching is never in fact depicted. Yet as we have seen, the story's narrator nonetheless reproduces a position of privilege based on assumptions of racial power that social and cultural exercises of whiteness (such as lynching and the cinema) supported. Bringing them together as the story does affords readers a position inside such whiteness and its narrative framing that we may not have desired or anticipated. This is not to say that "Dry September" elicits readers' involvement in its events in the manner that actual lynchings or photos of them did. It is, though, the case that Faulkner fashions a readerly space and position defined by whiteness and white privilege—in other words, by whiteness as "social power."

Importantly, though, and despite these aspects, Faulkner's story also furnishes readers a critical space apart from its troubling racial operations. And it does so precisely with the story's ending(s). Minnie's laughter in the cinema reveals a meaningful gap between her understanding of events, including the fact of her reinsertion into Jefferson's sociosexual economy, and the townspeople's awareness of southern social and racial rituals. Robert Allen's point about moviegoing and its racial aspect not "[rising] to the level of consciousness" ("Relocating" 79) offers a useful way to understand Minnie's hysterical laughing at the end of the story. Like Darl's at the end of *As I Lay Dying*, Minnie's laughter appears prompted by a recognition of the absurdity of her circumstances. Darl mocks the Bundrens' insistence on "honoring" their dead mother by dragging her rotting corpse through the public byways; in "Dry September," Minnie responds to the "silver dream" (we might say "white dream") of cinema and the town's collective attitudes, enhanced by the culture industry and Jim Crow, toward various economies of sexuality, race, and power. Though Minnie may not be consciously aware of such attitudes, her unsettling laughter suggests an incipient awareness of the fragility around whiteness and southern racial identity. As such it allows readers a stance vis-à-vis this nexus that is different from that of other moviegoers, like Minnie's friends, or from our own position "with" McLendon and other white men in the story's early and, as we will see, closing scenes. Moments such as these, in other words, allow us a simultaneous position inside and outside southern whiteness and its legal, visual, and narrative frames.

To clarify this observation, it will help to make an important turn to other Yoknapatawpha fiction. Like "Dry September," *Light in August* is one of a handful of Faulkner's works that in fact makes direct reference to the cinema. In the context of the novel, the social and racial "meanings" of film viewing are clear: they relate directly to the book's culminating action and to Jefferson's treatment of Joe Christmas. On the Saturday before Christmas is captured, the people of Jefferson go to the movies. They leave the town square, we're told very simply, "as the picture show emptied" (456)—only to return in full on Monday in a "throng of people thick as on Fair Day" (458).

This reference to moviegoing seems innocuous enough. Yet, if we consider the changing demographics of film viewing in the period that novels like *Light in August* depict, we may draw some important conclusions about it. The audience for the picture show, importantly and newly in the 1920s, was multiclassed. As several critics have shown, the culture of Jim Crow and segregation served in forging what Jay Watson, in his introduction to this volume, calls a "post-Confederate cross-class regional (and eventually national) sensibility" (xi), a process that was facilitated by the experience of film viewing. Working-class or poor whites may well have been among the viewers of whatever movie was playing in Jefferson that night, along with more supposedly "respectable," middle-class inhabitants of the town. As cultural historians have shown, this was a new development in the early twentieth century following the rising cultural status of movies.

What happens in the hours after Jefferson's "picture show emptied" tells us something important about the effects of those changes. While we do not see this crowd directly, its presence is felt throughout the section of the novel that relays Joe's capture and his later execution by Percy Grimm. It is important in this light to reemphasize that going to the pictures in Faulkner's South was not a fully integrated activity. While white viewers of different classes may have enjoyed the different spaces of the film together (the imaginative space of the movie's narrative as well as the actual social space of the movie house), African Americans did not. If they were allowed access to the films, it was only in the segregated sections of the balcony, what was referred to variously as "nigger heaven," the "buzzard's roost," or the "crow's nest." It is this version of a (false) collective that Christmas is aware of throughout *Light in August* and which, along with Grimm, stalks and monitors his movements leading to his murder. This gathering, "collective" experience and identity defines small communities like Jefferson throughout the Yoknapatawpha works. What Faulkner also shows, however, here and throughout his fiction, is that whiteness in such towns was as much a function of exclusion as of inclusivity.[13]

While Grimm's pretext for imposing a martial presence on the square and his own vigilante justice is to maintain civic order, it is the mob's collective power, its "Fair Day" atmosphere, that in fact propels him. And this is a power and an energy that the movie house helps deliver. There is a homology, in other words, between the racing of space that occurs in the movie house and Grimm's policing of race in his pursuit of Christmas. The line I am drawing, then, is not a tenuous one, and it runs straight from the exiting movie crowd (in its class heterogeneity) to Grimm's stalking and his race-baited fellow citizens.[14] The narrator's mention of the picture show in the same chapter in which he introduces Grimm and the Mississippi National Guard thus seems more than incidental.

In his essay for this collection, Chuck Jackson examines the role of the National Guard in what he calls "emergency narratives" of the sort that inform works like *Light in August* and "Dry September." The mob mentality that is often on display in southern history and in Faulkner's fiction, which Jackson claims is extremely close to the makeup of a civilian military body like the National Guard, has also been seen as a step removed from the mass audiences for cinema.[15] What work like Jackson's and others' attests to is the way in which various institutions of American cultural and political life sought to galvanize the country's "impure" elements into a white hegemony that transcended differences of class and region. He describes whiteness "as tied to the horror of state-based violence that is predicated on the imagination of a pure 'America,' a national signifier that stands apart from the body and its imperfect borders" (191). The body to which Jackson refers is both geopolitical and physical, and his essay pays interesting attention to the ways in which the National Guard encouraged a disavowal of bodily, class, or regional identity in states like Mississippi in favor of a process in which individual men imagined themselves as part of an abstract, idealized (and white) collective (192–94). "The National Guard grooms the animalistic, rural bodies of white men, refining their rituals and habits so that each will fit into a more respectable, civilized national culture" (196). That the picture show in *Light in August* empties just before Faulkner turns to his account of the Mississippi National Guard suggests a link between the abstract "whitening" promoted by institutions like the military and the practice of film viewing in the rural South.[16]

Strikingly, Jackson's approach to state power and policing notes the same refining into a disembodied, "white, abstract personhood" (226 n5) that others have pointed to in film studies. Robert Allen, for example, takes issue with psychoanalytic and feminist approaches to film viewing that find in both film texts and viewers a "disembodied," idealized aspect, resulting in an implicitly universalist, white identity ("Relocating" 49–54). Like

Allen, James Hay advocates for a historicist film studies that incorporates more than "an internal dynamic of cinema and [. . .] theories of subject positioning" and calls for "a way of discussing film as a social practice that begins by considering how social relations are spatially organized" (216). It is this relation to both screen and narrative space that attends works like "Dry September" and events in both it and *Light in August*. Percy Grimm, for example, occupies a central role in the novel and in Jefferson due to historical developments like the National Guard and the cinema, as well as their way of conjoining both national and southern modes of whiteness.[17]

The work of "abstracting" whiteness in and through film viewing has been taken up extensively by Richard Dyer. In his meditations on this practice in Western visual culture, including painting, film, and television, Dyer points to pictorial elements and technological strategies that "naturally" accommodate white skin toward an ideal of abstractness or even spirituality. He describes how whiteness has operated in visual media for centuries to fashion a peculiarly disembodied quality, one that allows whites to fall back upon a presumed, pervasive presence that is, at the same time, an absence of physicality or demarcation. This sense of being "everything and nothing" (*White* 39) lends to whiteness its putative lack of corporeality and its affinity with both a spiritual realm "beyond" race and a baseline, common definition of humanity.

Dyer's thinking refers extensively to film and, in one essay ("Into the Light"), to an emergency narrative of the sort Jackson describes. Appearing well before Faulkner's Yoknapatawpha narratives, *Birth of a Nation* has much in common with them, including the affinities it develops between whiteness and purity, citizenship, and nationhood—as well as violence and death. The figuratively white militia of *Light in August* and the "cinematic" white men of "Dry September" and their connections to mob violence had their prototype, that is, in Griffith's and in southern history's Ku Klux Klan. In them all we find a literalized version of Dyer's "culture of light," the absorption of class and regional difference into a supposedly raceless, self-styled "pure" presence and identity. As several critics have described, the film revolves specifically around whiteness in both its ideological and aesthetic aspect.[18] *Birth* offers a singular example of whiteness due to effects unique to cinema. As Dyer puts it, "All film takes place on a white background (the screen); to fill the screen with white costume is to increase the radiation of light reflected off the screen. To have it swirl, as the Klan costumes [in *Birth*] do, especially when riding and rearing up on horseback, heightens the primary spectacle of film as light. This is the moment at which white men are whitest—but of course we cannot see their flesh" ("Into the Light" 173).[19]

The arguments surrounding the role of whiteness, the Klan, and Griffith's vision of a pure "nation" founded on the expunging of blackness would be difficult to summarize here. What is most salient to my discussion is *Birth*'s logic of nationhood in connection with a specifically southern vision of race, one that informs the so-called "emergency narratives" of *Light in August* and "Dry September." In this context, Percy Grimm in *Light in August* and Butch and McLendon in "Dry September" find their precursor in Ben Cameron, the southern hero at the center of Griffith's film who mobilizes his white neighbors in response to his younger sister having been propositioned by a former slave, Gus.[20] In the movie's famous ending, which follows the re-disenfranchisement of African Americans during Reconstruction—as well as Gus's lynching—Ben appears with his northern beloved as harbingers of a new nation united in opposition to blackness. As a movie that more than any in history contributed to a national film culture, a "new nation" founded on film viewing, *Birth* offered viewers a remarkable and racialized conflation of screen space, narrative violence, and imagined community, both within the film's vision of the new nation and in the actual experience of viewers in the cinema.[21]

Above all what Faulkner seems to have learned from the movies is the phantasmatic nature of whiteness, particularly in its southern conception. Film offers a useful model for this racial category precisely because of properties inherent in the medium itself. Film images, that is, like southern conceptions of whiteness, are chimeras, which rely for their existence not on any material presence or concrete fact such as "white" blood or even skin (or robes), nor on abstract ideals of national and racial purity, but on viewers' willing belief in them. As Doane puts it of *Birth*, "It is as though it were crucial to dissociate racial difference from the epidermal scheme [...] and to transform it into a floating signifier of itself" (228). As promulgated by early cinema, notions of whiteness such as those on display in Yoknapatawpha, as well as in Faulkner's lived world, likewise drew their force from southerners' need to believe in their meaning and unimpugnable "truth" as a floating, "transcendental signified."²² Faulkner's works thus reveal a link between southern notions of race and cinematic versions of whiteness that share an imaginative dimension that is *structural*. Drawing together the "silver dream" of cinema with the powerfully imaginary nature of Southern whiteness and its links to racial violence, as he does in both "Dry September" and *Light in August*, Faulkner reveals more than a casual link between the phenomena of film and lynching.

If we return to the story, we find this link manifested powerfully. It is crucial that in the barbershop scene Faulkner stresses that few of the men present know or actually believe that Will Mayes has assaulted Minnie. This gap between actuality and apprehension is figured in the story's opening paragraph. In the third sentence, the object of the men's "knowledge" (and of the sentence's predicate) appears at a remove of several clauses from the statement's beginning and in a particularly belabored syntax: "Attacked, insulted, frightened: none of them, gathered in the barbershop on that Saturday evening where the ceiling fan stirred, without freshening it, the vitiated air, sending back upon them, in recurrent surges of stale pomade and lotion, their own stale breath and odors, knew exactly what had happened" (169). As in the cinema, Faulkner's narrative apparatus posits a clear gap between belief and factuality. Hawkshaw's repeated statements of disbelief that anything happened between Will and Minnie are met with accusations of "niggerlover!" and sarcastic claims that Hawkshaw himself is "a hell of a white man" (170). White identity in such cases is predicated specifically on a suspension of disbelief, a capacity to embrace fantasy in a manner that gives the lie to truth but that commands its own veracity or verisimilitude (and is followed by a willingness to convert fantasy to violent action).²³

McLendon offers the final rhetorical fiat that both silences the other men's resistance and establishes the imaginary, conjured—and therefore, unshakable—nature of Will's "wrong" when in answer to a question about what happened, he shouts, "Happen? What the hell difference does it make? Are you going to let the black sons get away with it until one of them really does it?" (171–72). Factual wrongdoing, as Hale and others have noted, was rarely if ever the crucial animating motive in lynching activities. Rather, the impetus toward violence was the need to assert the communal identity of whiteness, one that, as in the segregated cinemas, "made race dependent on space" (Hale 228).²⁴ Like the various images of the cinema that Faulkner invokes in "Dry September," southern notions of whiteness are as flickering and as insubstantial as the shafts of light projected at the movie screen. Grasping at them powerfully, as McLendon, Percy Grimm, and the viewers of the picture show that empties into Jefferson's town square in *Light in August* all do, produces a capacity for violence as lethal and unsettling as the screen images are "beautiful and passionate and sad," accumulating, like Griffith's vision of a white futurity, "inevitably on and on" (Faulkner, "Dry September" 181).

Fortunately for readers, what works like *Light in August* and "Dry September" do is slow the tempo of those fast-accumulating narrative passions offered by film and of the perceived emergencies that prompt them, allowing a response that is slower and that arrests the forward momentum for which *Birth* was famous. Crucially, Faulkner's Yoknapatawpha narratives also reverse the terms of visibility on which whiteness has historically relied. In addition to its supposed universality, and predicated upon it, whiteness in Faulkner and in the South was often defined by way of visuality. The segregation of film viewing, the depiction of whiteness on screen, the spectacles of lynching and the circulation of lynching postcards—all relied on the capacity to *see* in ways that accrued to whites but conferred on whiteness its own lack of visibility.[25] Shawn Michelle Smith has written powerfully about this pattern and its attendant problems. Among them, as this discussion of Faulkner's emergency narratives has shown, is the fact of the viewer/reader's positioning vis-à-vis the spectacle of white violence. Smith avers that such a dynamic can, in fact, work to reinscribe black suffering in its visual and spectacular aspect, "in which the representation and reproduction of the violated black body can function as a kind of fetish" (118). Conversely, Smith stresses the crucial dimension of *in*visibility attributed to whiteness, a feature that allows whiteness to function as a presumed basis for subjecthood—but also to shield whiteness (and whites) from critical and scrutinizing view. Drawing on Dyer's account of whiteness as nontraceable, Smith points out that if "whiteness has historically secured its representational power through invisibility, by being that which is *not seen*, then *looking* at whiteness, making white bodies bear the burden of the gaze, can become an important critical task."

In closing, it will help to see how Faulkner pursues that task precisely. As with other examples cited above, he does so by way of "screening" whiteness and thus rendering it visible. What Faulkner shows at the end of "Dry September"—and in much of the Yoknapatawpha material—is a version of what W. E. B. Du Bois sought in his essay "The Souls of White Folk": the critical task of seeing whiteness clearly and "from unusual points of vantage" that reveal white "souls undressed and from the back and side" (quoted in Smith 116–17). As Du Bois put it of his own racial vision, "I am singularly clairvoyant.... I see the working of their entrails. I know their thoughts and they know that I know." We end Faulkner's story with McLendon, witness both to his violent abuse of his wife—ironically after "defending" white womanhood by lynching Will Mayes—and to his particularly "embodied" aspect. Denying McLendon the invisibility of abstraction that (white) viewers of the cinema enjoyed and that lynch mobs and militias like the state National Guard enabled, Faulkner forces us to see the story's racial antagonist in all his sweaty, singular, weighty mass.

> He went on through the house, ripping off his shirt, and on the dark, screened porch at the rear he stood and mopped his head and shoulders with the shirt and flung it away. He took the pistol from his hip and laid it on the table beside the bed, and sat on the bed and removed his shoes, and rose and took his trousers off. He was sweating again already, and he stooped and hunted furiously for his shirt. At last he found it and wiped his body again, and with his body pressed against the dusty screen, he stood panting. There was no movement, no sound, not even an insect. The dark world seemed to lie stricken beneath the cold moon and lidless stars. (183)

In the dark scene at the story's close, with the world lying "stricken" beneath the unending gaze of the "lidless stars," McLendon's embodied whiteness forcefully emerges under our readerly, critical, and, according to the prose's figuration, unending view. As does a grotesquely literalized version of the Du Boisian view of white "souls undressed." References to McLendon's body and to a "screen" are each repeated, enabling both to be strongly embodied and starkly *seen*. While the screen against which he leans is not that of the cinema, it nevertheless (as did the spaces of film and film viewing in Faulkner's South) sustains such notions of white identity as McLendon and others claimed. It also appears in this passage in a suggestive aspect as a specifically rectangular "frame" against which, as on the film screen, the image of the white body stands out. From our perspective "outside the inside" of McLendon's world and of the photographic as well as the literary frame, we see both the literal darkness of the cinema and the figurative darkness of Yoknapatawpha County, as well as a whiteness that, against such spaces and screens, emerges in its physical particularly.

Light in August includes its own evocation of film viewing that functions to expose the violent effects of a social and cultural practice defined by whiteness. We have seen the novel's reference to Jefferson's picture house and its audience, members of which also attend Percy Grimm's vigil in the town square. Additionally, some of these moviegoers also "view" Joe Christmas's mutilation and murder. That they do so is clear in the language that surrounds his scene of dying.

> For a long moment he looked up at them with peaceful and unfathomable and unbearable eyes. Then his face, body, all, seemed to collapse, to fall in upon itself, and from out the slashed garments about his hips and loins the pent black blood seemed to rush like a released breath. It seemed to rush out of his pale body like the rush of sparks from a rising rocket; upon that black blast the man seemed to rise soaring into their memories forever and ever. They are not to lose it, in whatever peaceful valleys ... in the mirroring faces of whatever children they will contemplate old disasters and newer hopes. It will be there, musing, quiet, steadfast[.] (464–65)

Several critics have described the notable separation between Joe and his antagonists here, one enforced by their detached and decidedly visual manner of perceiving. (We might say detached *because* visual.) Concomitant with that "spectatorial" separation is a marked difference from Joe's own visual capacity. With his open, "unfathomable and unbearable eyes," Joe clearly sees more than his onlookers. In addition to seeing all of the South's bias and race hatred, he regards his killers in their individual, "secret" and deeply threatened autonomy. (As Du Bois put it about seeing whites in their whiteness, "I know their thoughts and they know that I know.") And Faulkner makes evident that, while they look upon Joe's suffering and his final epiphany, Joe's is a reckoning his attackers do not share. As audience to

Joe's dying, they nevertheless—like the film viewer—lack the comprehensive and profound racial vision he displays.

Faulkner's evocations of film here are also more pointed than in "Dry September." For while we may relate the scenario of dispassionately watching Joe die to the townspeople's quite recent experience of moviegoing, Faulkner's depiction of lynching also, and perhaps deliberately, recalls an infamous scene of lynching from film. Prior to its protest by the NAACP, *Birth of a Nation* included an extended scene of Gus's castration and murder. Due to vigorous protest over this particular sequence from the NAACP, Griffith cut the scene from the film following its initial screenings. He did so, however, as much for reasons of marketability as for any moral concern over the film's potential to alienate black viewers. (More precisely, he cut the scene to placate censors from the National Board of Review, whose imprimatur he needed in order to distribute the film [Rogin, "Sword" 277].) For with the lynching scene, as with the rest of the film, Griffith fully expected his audience's sympathy for its account of a "beleaguered" white South that took such violent measures against the "threat" of newly freed black sexuality. With the scene excised, *Birth* became even more palatable to white viewers, presenting them with a vision of (their) whiteness that was "softer" than Griffith's own virulent racism and thus more flattering to northern or "reconstructed" audiences.[26]

Faulkner's version of lynching offers readers no such comfortable tempering. *Restoring* to his own scenario of lynching its basis in white violent efforts at social control, Faulkner more fully exposes readers to the kinds of machinations that Griffith's cinematic spectacle of lynching first relied on, but then muted. Like his treatment of McLendon at the end of "Dry September," Faulkner's attention to the onlookers at Joe's death presents them in their whitened aspect and links them to the phenomenon as well as the ideological effects of film viewing. Moreover, and unlike Griffith, Faulkner does not seek to mobilize sympathy for the white, vigilante violence that Grimm, like Griffith's Ben Cameron and his fellow Klansmen, visits on African Americans. Rather, he displaces that sympathy and subject position onto Joe. It is Joe whom readers know and through whose perspective we encounter the effects of racial violence. Pitting Joe's depth of vision, his encompassing, "unfathomable" gaze, against his persecutors' shallow, white, and filmic form of viewing along with their capacity for truly horrific violence, Faulkner reveals much more directly and critically what remains absent from Griffith's film. Like McLendon pinioned against the screen of his back porch, exposed fully to our readerly view, Joe's murderers stand revealed in their filmic but also all too real mode of violent discipline. That the terms of that violence and the meting out of such discipline draw on a cinematic construction of whiteness demonstrates Faulkner's awareness of the medium and its painful, often distorting manner of framing. As a result, Faulkner's readers, while not endowed with such clairvoyance as Du Bois or the vision of Joe Christmas, are nonetheless compelled to see the "unwhite" and impure souls of men like McLendon, Percy Grimm, and Griffith's berobed Klan, and thus to peer—or even dwell—inside a frame of whiteness outside of which we might prefer to remain.

WHITE DISAVOWAL, BLACK ENFRANCHISEMENT, AND THE HOMOEROTIC IN WILLIAM FAULKNER'S *LIGHT IN AUGUST*

—ALIYYAH I. ABDUR-RAHMAN

*L*ight in August was originally about white people: Lena Grove, Gail Hightower, and Byron Bunch were at the center of William Faulkner's initial conception of the novel. The murder and near decapitation of Joanna Burden was to be the event that tied these three characters together. Joe Christmas became the central character of the novel when it became evident to Faulkner that another element, an embodied racial signifier, was necessary to get at the heart of southern history. In Faulkner's text, the brutal murder of a white woman, followed by the quick capture and lynching of a (reputed) black man, exemplifies and encapsulates the ideological and cultural crisis of black-white relations in the post-Reconstruction era, as inflected by gender, class, and the then recent history of slavery in the South. In her article "Persons in Pieces," Nell Sullivan asserts, "Christmas became so compelling that Faulkner kept adding episodes to his early life in the flashback[s]. The shift of dramatic emphasis from Lena, Byron, and Hightower to Joe Christmas reveals Faulkner's recognition of the Negrophobe myth at the heart of the (white) Southern consciousness" (498). In writing Joe Christmas, Faulkner introduced a preoccupation he would continue to work out in such novels as *Absalom, Absalom!* and *Go Down, Moses*: miscegenation and its relation to history, to slavery, and to American genealogies. For Faulkner, miscegenation serves, as Krister Friday remarks, as a "metonym for the tragic aftermath of slavery, the Civil War, and Reconstruction" (41). The fact of miscegenation—of mixed-race bodies that could evade or straddle the color line and in their very embodiment recall the intimate and violent history of institutional slavery—provided Faulkner with a viable, living metaphor for the gruesome history, tumultuous present, and uncertain future of black-white relations in the postemancipation South.

Many critics have analyzed miscegenation in *Light in August* in terms of Faulkner's rendering of slavery and southern history. This paper diverges from such standard readings to argue that miscegenation is not simply a metaphor for the messy, entangled racial history of the South; miscegenation is also the principal means by which Faulkner contemplates and represents the imperiled state of white masculinity in the post-Reconstruction era and the homoerotic desire and dread underpinning the white male obsession with black manhood. Generally sexualized, degraded, and debased, the black figures in *Light in August* are placed in close proximity to white characters and spaces in order to demonstrate that, in the post-slavery South, black and white communities are dependent on and, in some ways, mutually constitutive of each other. Joe Christmas, however, is not simply someone whose racially inscrutable body reveals uncertain but possibly mixed-race origins; he is Faulkner's definitive (albeit white) "nigger." Like many of the black characters in *Light in August*, Joe Christmas has little interiority and even less discernable motivation for doing what he does. Like the flat surface of a painting, he is a drawn figure. However, unlike the caricatured, illiterate black men who appear for mere seconds in the novel and abruptly leave, or the sexualized black females who are connected to Joe, or the mammy figures who raise other characters in the novel, Joe Christmas represents Faulkner's meditation on the civic equality of black men in the post-Reconstruction era and its effect on the psyche of whites. Christmas acts out his historical moment and anticipates, if not precipitates, crises in the established economic, gender, and racial systems of that historical moment. This paper principally aims to understand the way in which Faulkner's mixed-race figure in *Light in August* emblematizes the crisis of the post-Reconstruction racial order. I attend specifically to Faulkner's linking of racial ambiguity and homoeroticism in the figure of Joe Christmas, arguing that Faulkner uses the historical fact of miscegenation and the perceived failure of white masculinity to critique southern culture and history and to offer ways of revamping and reconstituting whiteness in the modern—meaning postslavery—moment.

I.

As is the case with other early-twentieth-century American fictions, depictions of African Americans in *Light in August* provide William Faulkner with the means to critique fluctuations in racial, sexual, spatial, and other social arrangements in American culture and to ponder the effects of those fluctuations on white psychology. In their introduction to *Prehistories of the Future*, Barkan and Bush usefully describe the rac(ial)ist concept of "primitive irrationality" as "attractive to ... [the] modern, alienated intellectual because it provided the means by which to represent the individual unconscious" (6).[1] Marianna Torgovnick suggests that "primitives" were believed to be the "untamed selves [and] id forces—libidinal, irrational, violent, dangerous" of Europeans (8). The commodity nature and circulation of images of blackness in the early twentieth century furnished American authors of that historical moment with a repertoire of images associated with "primitivity" through which to conjure and explore the condition of psychic fracture for the dislocated white subject under the pressure of modernity in an increasingly multiracial urbanized sphere.

At the historical moment of *Light in August*'s emergence, blackness was highly visible and widely commodified in the culture at large. As Grace Elizabeth Hale has argued, new modes of production within capitalism enabled racial stereotypes to become firmly entrenched in the popular imagination. The railroad, photography, the cinema, and the advertising industry provided the means of disseminating quickly and nationally negative images of African Americans. Photographs of lynched black bodies that appeared in national newspapers and that circulated as postcards verified and provided a visual corollary for the belief that black Americans were less than human, unqualified for full citizenship, and unworthy of complete integration into the body politic. Minstrel performances helped to preserve derogatory characterizations of African Americans as dependent slaves even as they struggled to advance socially and politically beyond that former status. Furthermore, the plantation types depicted in minstrel shows helped to create enduring beliefs about black people that lasted well into the twentieth century. As Eric Lott elucidates, the minstrel show was "highly responsive to the emotional demands and troubled fantasies of its audiences" (6).

Blackface minstrelsy—including textual blackface—provided, moreover, a "space of fun and license" specifically to white artists (Lott 51). In his discussion of the important influence of African American dialect and African art on American modernist aesthetics in the early twentieth century, Michael North argues that representations of blackness were used by the "moderns" to disrupt conventional aesthetic forms. He posits that "in painting and in literature, the step away from conventional verisimilitude into abstraction is accomplished by a figurative change of race" (61). Artists and writers who sought to distort, to experiment, to transform, and to invent wholly new ways of writing and painting did so by importing and infusing elements of racial blackness into their artistic creations. Because blackness was itself believed to be the very condition of fracture, radical uncertainty, and resultant chaos both within oneself and in one's relation to the culture at large, textual blackface operated as a literary trope and practice that enabled meditations on and representations of the fragmented self in early-twentieth-century American culture. Representations of African Americans in white American–authored texts of this era have not tended overall to reflect African American people, their inner or cultural life; these representations have, instead, marked crucial moments in the development of white American culture and consciousness.[2]

II.

The mulatto—the putatively black but ultimately racially ambiguous figure—is one complicated and subtle manifestation of blackness. The performative quality of Joe Christmas's blackness is evident not only in his iteration of certain behavioral norms of blackness but also in his susceptibility to the violence generally reserved for black people—i.e., lynching and castration. Christmas is, furthermore, a compelling case study of how the status of a mixed-race person can be extended to represent African American people in the post-Reconstruction era in general. In *Faulkner's Negro*, Thadious Davis argues that Faulkner "provide[s] details which link Joe to the black side of Jefferson life.... [Christmas] enters Joanna's house like a nigger invading in the night, and he eats coarse food set for the nigger.... Even before he tells Joanna that he believes he is a Negro, he sees himself as the 'nigger' in her bed" (135–36). Davis contends ultimately that "Joe Christmas is both black and white" (135). Of course, what this means according to the one-drop rule is that Christmas is legally, if not completely culturally, black. To my mind, African Americans may be taken in general as a miscegenated group not only because of their mixed racial genealogies resulting from rampant interracial rape during and after slavery but also because of the inevitable cultural admixture resulting from African American presence in America since its founding. Race is not, nor has it ever been, completely corporeal. What determined white manhood in the nineteenth century was not simply white skin but access to the vote, access to the bodies of women, the right to defend one's country in war, the right to hold arms or property, the right to acquire capital, and, especially, the right and ability to dominate black people. What determined blackness was susceptibility to violence, a so-called inability to fend off or control primal urges, and an ultimate negation of the aforementioned rights and privileges. In the post-Reconstruction era when black men were enfranchised—after hundreds of thousands had participated in the Civil War and helped to bring about the defeat of the South, after some had even gained the wealth and education to fare better than some of their white neighbors—racial blackness in the U.S. itself underwent a cultural miscegenation: it became infused with some of the rights and properties of white manhood.

It is the position of black people in the aftermath of generational slavery that determines their abjectness and makes Joe Christmas a viable representation of postemancipation blackness in *Light in August*. My use of the word "abject" follows that of Julia Kristeva, who in *Powers of Horror* describes the abject as one who "disturbs identity, system, order. What does not respect borders, positions, rules. The in-between, the ambiguous, the composite" (4). In other words, indeterminate ontology creates the position of the abject, the specter who haunts social order. Joe Christmas is abject first and foremost because his paternal lineage and, by extension, racial origins are unknown—as traceable genealogies were unknown by the overwhelming number of emancipated African Americans. Christmas cannot be located in the strict racial economy of white over black that was inaugurated in slavery and that continues under Jim Crow legislation. He, therefore, remains a shadowy, haunting presence in the town of Jefferson. Described as carrying with him "his own inescapable warning, like a flower its scent or a rattlesnake its rattle" (33), Christmas is said to look like "a phantom, a spirit, strayed from its own world, and lost" (114). Furthermore, his white body is described as "slow and lascivious in a whispering gutter filth like a drowned corpse in a thick still black pool of more than water" (107). Despite his corporeal whiteness, Christmas's identity is associated with blackness, with filth, with fluidity. He is reputed to live "behind the veil," the Du Boisian term for life within black communities or beneath the dividing line of race. The narrator describes, "None of them [the townspeople] knew then where Christmas lived and what he was actually doing behind the veil, the screen, of his negro's job at the mill" (36). As has been noted almost to the point of consensus among contemporary literary critics, the difficulty *and potency* of the mixed-race person is her epistemic uncertainty, her ability to confound and render incoherent the signifying structures of race. Krister Friday suggests that "Joe's indeterminate parentage allows him to pass as both white and black but to 'be' or have 'been' neither. Without the anchor of an origin, Joe's past and present become open, unfinished possibilities rather than certainties, making Joe's 'presence' in the novel assume a spectrality" (49). Friday's observations are useful for understanding the threat of the mixed-race person to the racial schema in general. What I want to emphasize here, however, is the condition of blackness as abject itself, as indeterminate and in-between, once it is no longer contained in slavery, or once black people have been released from the fetters of a fixed definition and status as enslaved thing. My focus, then, is the similarity of the threat that Christmas's white skin poses to white manhood—as it masks the so-called blackness of his "black blood" and thereby allows him white masculine privilege—and the threat that all black men posed to the racial order in the post-Reconstruction period after they had been given the vote and the legal position as head of their families.

The acquisition of citizenship rights challenged and redeemed the prior enslaved status of black manhood in the same way that Joe Christmas's white skin challenges and redeems his own purported blackness. Enfranchisement masculinized black men because it established both their humanity and their U. S. citizenship; furthermore, black men's legal right to marriage and to function as fathers granted them a recognizable position within the (implicitly patriarchal) symbolic order.³ Taken together, the status of black men in the postemancipation South made them akin to white men. Robyn Wiegman describes deftly: "[T]he [black man's] threat to masculine power arises not simply from a perceived racial difference, but from the potential for a masculine sameness" (90). Black men in the postbellum era were the same as white men, but with a difference—they were (un)desirable, uncanny, a threat. Put another way, emancipation converted African Americans from captive African slaves to U.S. citizens who spoke the same language, benefited from *and believed in* the principles that underwrite American democracy; like Joe Christmas's racially indeterminable self, African Americans in the postbellum era delineated difference contained within, and undermined by, similarity.

The position of African Americans after slavery posed a threat not only to the established social schema but also to the very symbolic order that gave whiteness coherence. The end of slavery disrupted the oppositional relation between black slaves and white master-citizens. Following Saussure's formulation about signifying structures of languages and applying them to Faulkner's literature, Doreen Fowler writes, "Identity and meaning come about only as a result of difference, only by exclusion" (9); in other words, all meaning derives from and depends on difference because the meaning of a sign is ascertained only by its difference from, or the exclusion of, other signs. The same holds for subjective development, wherein a subject begins to emerge at the precise moment that she ascertains her separateness, her distinction, from those upon whom her existence has depended. Extended to the logic of racial formation in the U.S., blackness may be understood as the chaotic, debased, and negated part of the racial dyad that defines and delimits whiteness, giving shape to its enabling boundaries.

The dialectic of race, the contingency of racial definitions, is emblematized in the figure of Joe Christmas. In a pivotal scene in the text, "[Christmas] stood with his hands on his hips, naked, thighdeep in the dusty weeds, while the car came over the hill and approached, the lights full upon him. He watched his body grow white out of the darkness like a Kodak print emerging from the liquid" (108). This scene exposes blackness as the frame and backdrop for the emergence of whiteness. Surrounded by the darkness of night, Joe's corporeal whiteness is contoured and given center stage. This is imaged here despite the fact that in this very scene Joe is most concerned about his blackness, his nakedness, and its effect on the screaming white woman in the passing car. This scene reveals the epistemological uncertainty attending all racial differentiation, as race is shown to confound the visual technologies that have been put in the service of reifying it. Neither the bright light of the passing car nor the gaze of the imaginary camera exposes Christmas's reputed blackness. Instead, what racializes Christmas in this scene is his relation to the people in the car. Calling them "white bastards," he establishes his blackness relative to their whiteness (108).

Although Faulkner reveals aspects of Joe Christmas's interiority through flashback material about his childhood, his internalized racism, his sexual development, and his relationship with Joanna Burden, the main focus of Faulkner's depiction of Joe Christmas is the awe and rage he inspires in white men. Not only does Christmas exemplify the status of black men in the post-Reconstruction era; he also exposes the imperiled state of white masculinity as wrought by the legal abolition of slavery. Faulkner's meditation on the state of white masculinity in the postbellum era is accomplished through his pairing of Joe Christmas and a doppelganger in the figure of Lucas Burch, who goes by the alias Joe Brown. When Byron Bunch describes the recent arrival of two strangers to Jefferson, who now occupy the "Negro" cabin on Joanna Burden's property, he informs Lena, "Two fellows named Joe live out that way somewhere. Joe Christmas and Joe Brown" (53). The two Joes are linked first and foremost by their shared first name, Joe, and further by their outsiderness, their liquor selling, their similar economic status, their cohabitation. It is Christmas's grandparents who attend the birth of Lena and Joe Brown's son, and Lena mistakenly thinks that Joe Christmas, and not Joe Brown, has fathered her child (409). Though both men are taken for white, Christmas and Brown are described as having dark complexions. Brown's name references his color, and he is described as "[t]all, young. Dark complected" (55). Christmas is described as having a "dark, insufferable" face (32). What ultimately enables Lena to distinguish between the two Joes upon hearing about them from Byron Bunch and to determine which has fathered her child is the white scar near Brown's mouth. Brown's white scar separates him from Christmas in that, despite his dark complexion, it designates and literalizes his racial whiteness. While Brown's dark skin might gesture toward his own potential racial ambiguity, it functions more significantly as the "black" backdrop that surrounds and, thus, makes visible/emergent his whiteness.[4] Because racial whiteness is generally unmarked and unremarked on, to become visible, determinable even, whiteness requires a marking, its own bodily inscription. In locating Joe Brown's whiteness in a scar, Faulkner makes legible and literal the racial specificity of the white body. Regardless of Joe Brown's abandonment of Lena, his refusal of patriarchal responsibility, his "negro's job at the mill," and his shacking up with Joe Christmas, Joe Brown has a more stable identity than Joe Christmas—a definitive (white) racial ontology—which determines his social desirability, justifies Lena's continued pursuit of him, and keeps him present in the novel after Joe Christmas has been lynched.

III.

Though handsome and spirited, Joe Brown symbolizes all that has gone awry in southern manhood. He is unmarried; he's an alcoholic and a gambler. He resists both patriarchal and heterosexual imperatives. Instead of exemplifying the honor and chivalry of the old South, he exemplifies the decline and degeneracy of southern manhood. David Minter explains that in the postbellum era southern white men were "burdened . . . not only with indelible memories of a costly as well as humiliating defeat but also with the double burden of guilt—one born of having defended and one of having failed to defend an institution and practice that, in fact, could not be defended" (*Faulkner's* 7). Brown's abdication of his familial responsibilities, his low-class status, and the frequency with which he is manipulated, dominated, and beaten by other men reveal a masculinity assailed by all manner of defeat.

Nonetheless, it is the doubling and the interracial, homoerotic desire between Joe Brown and Joe Christmas that speaks most glaringly to the failure of white southern manhood and to the challenges posed by postemancipation black manhood to white identity and authority in the South. To make this point cogently, I must first illuminate the ways in which Christmas's racial indeterminacy is engendered and haunted by both same-sex desire and its policing in the town of Jefferson. In the same way that Brown and Christmas function as each other's doubles, Christmas functions in the novel as the double, the shadow, and the darker half of the white men in town. In *Doubling and Incest/Repetition and Revenge*, John T. Irwin explains: "The ego's towering self-love and consequent over-estimation of its own worth lead to the guilty rejection of all instincts and desires that don't fit its idealized image of itself. The rejected instincts are cast out of the self, repressed internally only to return externally personified in the double, where they can be at once vicariously satisfied and punished" (33). As I have discussed above, Joe Christmas embodies the black male threat to white masculinity even as he appears as the mirror image of white manhood. He is, thus, an incarnation of the unspoken desires and hidden dread white men had for black men who were no longer their legal property.

Joe Christmas's power as a racially inscrutable figure is not simply that he resists and negotiates the identity politics that govern race and race relations in the post-Reconstruction South but also that he calls into question endogamous heterosexuality as the reigning social and sexual paradigm in early-twentieth-century American culture.[5] Christmas's ability to engender a racial pass, or to escape definitive racial inscription, carries the distinct possibility of transgressing all sexual boundaries, first and foremost, because it allows him access to the bodies of white women. The product of a reputed black man's criminal engagement with white womanhood, Joe Christmas, in his sexual relationships with Bobbie, other white prostitutes, and Joanna Burden, violates the brutally enforced restrictions on black male sexuality. The predominant belief in black men's predilection for desiring across racial lines was itself essential to developing theories of homosexuality, as both interracial sexuality and homosexuality were believed to be characterized by an inappropriate choice of sexual object.

Heteronormative qualification at the turn of the twentieth century did not require simple heterosexuality but endogamy as well; as customary and judicial prohibitions on interracial *and* same-sex coupling made clear, the proper sexual object choice under the regime of compulsive heterosexuality was a person of the opposite sex *and* the same racial group.[6]

As did black men's status generally in the postbellum period, Joe Christmas dislodges both normative racial and sexual categories, transgressing their historically enforced boundaries. As Christmas's blackness is unhinged from legible racial demarcation and, further, as his sexual exchanges are patently nonreproductive, Joe Christmas is a figure who evades, if not defies, all manner of social and sexual regulation. In his analysis of Christmas's sexuality, Jay Watson notes that "Joe's identity is so radically uncertain, making it difficult if not impossible to ascertain and fix what is sexually permissible and sexually illicit where he is concerned" (161). Christmas is an unbound and unmanageable sexual agent/signifier whose racial ambiguity *itself* obfuscates (hetero)sexual identity and precludes for him any claim to heteronormative qualification. According to Watson, Christmas's unbound racial and sexual identity both engenders and reflects a hypermasculinity that "amounts to simultaneously [an] overdoing and undoing of masculinity, one that spells gender trouble because its excesses ... threaten the 'law and order' of Southern manhood itself" (161). It is important to note that Watson's definition of hypermasculinity extends beyond the predictable paradigm of a brutish and overly dominant maleness to convey, instead, a masculinity that is both excessive *and* (historically, internally) fractured. Although Watson's discussion of Joe Christmas does not explicitly link hypermasculinity to embodied black manhood in general, I want to emphasize precisely that connection here. Postemancipation black masculinity *was* both empowered and besieged. It, furthermore, had the ability to confound the racial schema and render conventional, racially inflected, masculine hierarchies unintelligible. Watson's characterization of Christmas as "something more like conventionally defined masculinity *and* its other" speaks finally to Christmas's status both as racially indeterminable figure and enfranchised black man.

The doubling of Joe Christmas and Joe Brown, with its insinuation of homoerotic desire, makes clear not only the extent to which black male identity has been freed from some of its traditional markers but also the extent to which white masculinity has depended on these exact markers of black male inferiority to secure its own ascendancy and legitimacy. When Brown reports to the sheriff that Christmas has murdered Joanna Burden, he is described by Bunch as speaking "louder and louder and faster and faster, like he was trying to hide Joe Brown behind what he was telling on Christmas" (96). In other words, the Joes' identities are so imbricated that Joe Brown's narration of Joe Christmas risks his own self-erasure. Moreover, Brown's disclosure of Christmas's putative black racial ancestry "outs" Christmas not only as a black man passing for white but also, as a result of his erotic entanglements with white women and men, as a sexual deviant. Speaking of Christmas's and Brown's relation to one another, Byron Bunch postulates:

> I reckon the only thing folks ever wondered about was why Christmas ever took up with Brown. Maybe it was because like not only finds like; it cant escape from being found by its like. Even when it's just like in one thing, because even them two with the same like was different. (87)

In his description of their (uncanny) relationship, of Christmas's "taking up" with Brown, Bunch intimates that a sexual relation undergirds the two Joes' attachment.

Rooted in narcissism, a felt desire for the self with a difference, the double—by which I mean both the reflected image and/or the shadow—engenders and exposes homoerotic desire. Siobhan Somerville suggests that a common sexual fantasy that accompanied racial thinking in the post-Reconstruction era was that "black was to white as masculine was to feminine" (35). In other words, race supplies the difference—imagined in terms of gender—that masks *and* marks same-sex eroticism while exposing and emphasizing the alleged perversity of interracial desire. Somerville posits further:

> In turn-of-the-[twentieth-]century culture, where Jim Crow culture erected a structure of taboos against any kind of (non-work-related) interracial relationship, racial difference visually marked [sexual] alliances . . . . In effect, the institution of racial segregation and its

cultural fiction of "black" and "white" produced a framework in which ... interracial romances became legible as "perverse." (35)

Because interactions across racial borders were so rigorously prohibited and policed in the postslavery South, any interracial contact outside of black labor and service to whites was believed to be criminally sexual.[7] When the sheriff hears about Brown's abandonment of Lena, he claims to have no interest in the "wives [Brown] left in Alabama, or anywhere else" (321). The sheriff insists that his concern is only with "the husband he seems to have had since he come to Jefferson" (321). In designating Christmas Joe Brown's husband, the sheriff acknowledges the eroticism informing the Joes' liaison. Byron Bunch describes Brown and Christmas as "set[ting] up together" in the "old nigger cabin in the back" (79). When Christmas moves Brown into his cabin with him, he hopes both to stave off Joanna's desires for him and to make her jealous. The "nigger cabin" is the former home of slaves that will become ultimately the birthplace of Joe Brown's illegitimate child. Throughout *Light in August*, the "nigger cabin" is the liminal, transitional space where unaccepted sexual urges—extramarital, interracial, homoerotic, violent—are explored and where character transformations are wrought. The homoeroticism framing the Joes' liaison signifies the vulnerability of white masculinity to penetration by black men in the social, economic, and political realms. Although the intimation of a sexual relationship between Joe Christmas and Joe Brown indicates a potential for equality in an interracial alliance between white and black men, it is depicted by Faulkner as carrying with it the threat of white racial subordination. Christmas is clearly the dominant of the two Joes—Christmas is described as the "master" and Brown as his "disciple" (45). Brown imitates Christmas's mannerisms and participates in his business. One evening after beating Brown, Christmas undresses, goes outside, and when he returns, goes naked to his cot. Christmas's beating of Joe Brown coupled with his nakedness implies that the nature of Christmas's and Brown's alliance is not only homoerotic and interracial; it is also sadomasochistic because both Joes willingly participate in a relationship of practiced physical domination and submission.

Brown is able to assert dominance over Christmas only by accusing him of having black blood, of passing for white.[8] In the period after slavery, there was growing anxiety within the white community around the fixity of racial categories. Rather than allow former slaves full citizenship rights, southern whites established a system of cultural superiority and racial segregation. The rise of Jim Crow, antimiscegenation laws, and the institution of legal segregation not only mandated who could participate in government and to what extent but also divided public and private spaces along racial lines. African American bodies were literally forbidden contact with white bodies. This anxiety around interracial contact must be understood first and foremost as anxiety around an integrated body politic and the refusal of postbellum America to grant to former slaves full membership in U.S. society. The 1896 ruling in *Plessy v. Ferguson* authorized white townspeople to determine the racial category of others and to publicize it to maintain segregation. Rumor and innuendo were essential to this project, and, thus, the accusation of "black blood" was sufficient evidence for one to be taken for, and convicted of being, African-descended. Brown's disclosure to the sheriff that Christmas had once confessed to having black ancestry sets in motion the events that lead to Christmas's ultimate demise. In other words, by accusing Christmas of being black *and* of raping and murdering Joanna Burden, Brown, in effect, causes Christmas to be lynched. Not only does Brown's revelation of Christmas's blackness become the means by which he gains an advantage over Christmas, it also becomes the means by which he disavows his prior subordination, particularly in his erotic relation, to Christmas.

Joe Brown is not the first character in *Light in August* to allege Christmas's black racial ancestry in order to conceal sexual transgressions and to effect his social removal. In what is often seen as the inaugural moment of Christmas's sexual development, a five-year-old Christmas hides in the closet of the dietitian who works in the orphanage in which he lives. While swallowing toothpaste and hiding amidst her garments, he witnesses a sexual exchange between the dietitian and a white male intern. The sexual exchange falls beyond the requisites of proper sexuality in two regards: it is extramarital and it is violent. The intern disregards the dietitian's repeated cries, "No! No! ... No, Charley! Please!" and aggressively continues his sexual advances (121). Readers are not given the specific details of the sexual violation that ensues, as the scene shifts into a narrative of Christmas's sensory—oral and aural—perceptions while witnessing it. Christmas's ingestion and eventual regurgitation of the toothpaste dramatizes and mirrors the dietitian's experience of sexual assault by the intern:

> [Christmas] saw by feel alone now the ruined, once cylindrical tube. By taste and not seeing he contemplated the cool invisible worm as it coiled onto his finger and smeared sharp, automatonlike and sweet, into his mouth.... He seemed to be turned in upon himself, watching himself sweating, watching himself smear another worm of paste into his mouth which his stomach did not want. Sure enough, it refused to go down.... He didn't have to wait long. At once the paste which he had already swallowed lifted inside him, trying to get back out into the air where it was cool. It was no longer sweet. (121–22)

While much critical attention has been paid to the association of the toothpaste with the "pinkwomansmelling" dietitian and, therefore, with femininity, I want to underscore its masculine features here. Described as a worm that coils and that issues forth from a cylindrical tube, the toothpaste operates as a phallic replacement. Christmas's initiatory sexual experience, then, simulates nauseating fellatio as he internalizes the victimized sexual position of the dietitian. When the dietitian, ravaged and "surrounded now by wild and dishevelled hair," peers into the closet and discovers Christmas, "limp, looking with slack-jawed and glassy idiocy," she projects onto him the image of her assailant, presumably now "limp" with the satisfaction of an accomplished sexual act. This is evidenced foremost in the racial epithet she calls Christmas in that a "nigger bastard!" hiding in her closet insinuates the black male rapist (122). Later, the traumatized dietitian fixates more on Christmas than on the intern who has actually assaulted her. "She lay most of the night now tense, teeth and hands clenched, panting with fury and terror.... The young doctor was now, even less than the child.... She could not have said which she hated most" (123). The dietitian displaces her outrage and terror onto Christmas. As his identity is radically unstable, both racially and sexually ambiguous, he alternately inhabits the position of violated (white) womanhood and of (now racialized) violating manhood. Foreshadowing Joe Brown's method of effecting Christmas's removal from the town of Jefferson, the dietitian relieves the shame and horror of the intern's sexual assault by alleging Christmas's black ancestry to secure his expulsion from the orphanage.

IV.

Under assault in the late nineteenth century, white masculinity asserted itself through physicality—through resemblance to and finally dominance over—black manhood. In severing the penis from the black male body and taking it into their literal possession, white men who participated in lynching rituals appropriated the symbolic and sexual power they themselves had previously ascribed to black masculinity. In *Manliness and Civilization*, Gail Bederman explains that white manhood was constructed in the late nineteenth century as both civilized and linked to the "'savagery' and 'primitivism' of dark-skinned races, whose masculinity [white men] claimed to share" (22). White men in *Light in August* are said to have more physical prowess and to be better suited for "negro jobs"—those that require maximum physical exertion—than black men (44). The revelation of Christmas's reputed blackness, which generally occurs after he has engaged in sexual activity with white women—Bobbie, the numerous prostitutes and other white women Christmas takes to bed between the ages of twenty and thirty-three, as well as Joanna Burden—is followed by a savage beating by the white men nearby. In the end, Joe Christmas is lynched in a communal spectacle.

In the climactic lynching scene, Joe Brown's desire for Joe Christmas, as well as its disavowal, is extended to the other white men in Jefferson.[9] Lynching's mechanized violence enacts and covers up the awe and the lust that black manhood engenders in some white men. After the ejaculatory gesture of firing a round of shots into Christmas's body, Percy Grimm stoops over and castrates him:

> "Now you'll let white women alone, even in hell," [Grimm] said. But the man on the floor [Christmas] had not moved. He just lay there, with his eyes open and empty of everything save consciousness, and with something, a shadow, about his mouth.... [H]is face, body, all

seemed to collapse, to fall upon itself, and from out of the slashed garments about his hips and loins the pent black blood seemed to rush like a released breath. (464–65)

As Trudier Harris has so usefully summarized, lynching functions as a "communal rape" of black manhood (23). By castrating him, Grimm inscribes onto Christmas's body the phallic lack of the feminine and, under the regime of slavery, of the black masculine. The shadow around Christmas's mouth is the specter of homosexuality and race. The black blood that rushes from his body like a released breath, or new life, signifies that murder and mutilation have finally situated Christmas firmly within a proper—that is, victimized and subordinate—black racial identity. Lynching's bloody rituals function to abate the threat of black masculine similarity/parity with white men in the post-Reconstruction era by feminizing the black male body and by simultaneously reracializing it. As Robyn Wiegman argues, lynching enacts a gruesome, racially motivated, homoerotic encounter:

> In the image of white men embracing—with hate, fear, and a chilling form of empowered delight—the same penis they were so overdeterminedly driven to destroy, one encounters a sadistic enactment of the homoerotic at the very moment of its most extreme disavowal. . . . [T]he lynching scenario and its obsession with the sexual dismemberment of black men to mark the limit of the homosexual/heterosexual—that point at which the oppositional relation reveals its inherent and mutual dependence—and the heterosexuality of the black male "rapist" is transformed into a violently homoerotic exchange. (99)

Grimm's final statement to Christmas bespeaks the challenge that Christmas represents to white manhood in the areas of sexual prowess and civic access, as symbolized in the figure of the white woman's body. Like McEachern's sexually charged and sadistic ritual beatings of Christmas as a child, Grimm's actions not only feminize Joe Christmas—concretizing what was believed in the early twentieth century to be a queer subjectivity—but also confirm and constrain his racial blackness. In other words, castration transfigures Christmas's hypermasculinity into the docile, emasculated, asexuality of the eunuch—or of the black male slave.[10] As lynching is the brutal enactment of homoeroticism and its panicked repudiation, lynching is also a strategy for the containment of racial difference in the post-Reconstruction era. The lynching of Joe Christmas functions, then, both as an expression and disavowal of same-sex desire *and* as a violent rejection of an egalitarian, racially integrated social sphere.

Emblematic of the crisis of race hatred in America at the turn of the century, lynching exemplified the problematic and interlocking constructions of racial, gender, and sexual identity in U. S. culture, as Winthrop Jordan, Angela Davis, Trudier Harris, and Judith Stephens have all argued. Most African Americans understood lynching to be an act of racial terrorism aimed at preventing their social, economic, and political advancement. It had more to do with the effect of black cultural encroachment on white manhood, and by extension on white community, than black male ravishing of white womanhood. Judith Stephens assesses, "For nearly a century, lynching was a highly visible and concrete expression of institutionalized white supremacy and symbol of the existing power relations between the black and white 'races' in the United States" (655). While I share Stephens's estimation that lynching was a highly visible manifestation of white supremacy, I do not believe that it reflected "existing power relations" as much as desperately sought-after ones. In other words, we might best understand white racial violence as a *will to whiteness*. The routinized, ritualized violence of the lynching act and the widespread white communal participation in it reveal a profound need on the part of whites (during Reconstruction and throughout much of the twentieth century) for some evidence that the racial order of slavery still governed black and white relations despite the legal abolition of slavery. Lynching, then, reflects a profound insecurity around the stability and supremacy of whiteness in the post-Reconstruction era.[11] Percy Grimm functions in *Light in August* as the white phallic authority that attempts to rejuvenate and restore white racial hegemony. Lynching functions in the absence of slavery's racial organization and operational logic to fix racial categories in the postemancipation period and to annihilate the threat that African American male enfranchisement posed to the desired (racist) social order.

Throughout *Light in August* narratives about slavery are depicted in the fragmented memories of key characters—namely Joanna Burden and

Gail Hightower. Discernible in those narrated flashbacks is nostalgia for the ease and heroism of an earlier time, particularly around the figure of the white patriarch. Although neither the characters nor the novel itself displays an overt longing for the reinstallment of institutional slavery, slavery does represent a neat social order in its rigid hierarchy of the races. All manner of miscegenation and diversity could be contained in slavery because the messiness of human contact—in the form of interracial sexual unions, mutually affectionate and dependent relations, violent confrontation—that inevitably erupted and to some extent undergirded the relations between blacks and whites on the plantation did not disturb the fixed, naturalized order of things that race-based slavery forcefully proscribed, policed, and preserved. It was only in its aftermath that the heinous practices and traumatic legacies of American slavery had to be confronted.

Light in August ends with a wish for the reconstructed white family: the redeemed, maternal white woman, the weathered but hardworking and upstanding white man, and the "manchild," upon whom the future of the white race depends. In those decades following the formal abolition of slavery, beliefs about the deviant and excessive sexuality of black people led to the myth of the black male rapist and to Jim Crow legislation and to lynching as the punishment for black men who supposedly raped white women. Sanctions against interracial marriage, as well as prohibitions on homosexuality, supported the ascendancy of whiteness and the unimpeded formation and multiplication of white families at the precise moment of the nation's reunification after the Civil War, westward expansion, the enfranchisement of former slaves, and the increased immigration of nonwhite peoples into the U.S. As did compulsory heterosexuality generally in the late nineteenth century, the intact straight white family with which *Light in August* concludes is offered as a buffer to white masculinity and a safeguard against the increased presence of nonwhite peoples in the national polis who demanded—and now qualified for—civic equality.

AMERICAN EMERGENCIES

Whiteness, the National Guard, and *Light in August*

—CHUCK JACKSON

WHITE BLOOD

Right before the National Guard emerges in William Faulkner's *Light in August* (1932) as a bicycle-riding, uniformed Grim Reaper who packs a pistol and wields a butcher knife, the novel flashes forward so that the reader can meet Gavin Stevens, Jefferson's "District Attorney, [who is] a Harvard graduate [and] a Phi Beta Kappa" (444). Stevens's character serves two functions in the novel: to escort the exhausted Mrs. Hines and her delirious husband, the raving white supremacist old Doc Hines, to Jefferson's train station, and to rehearse the story of Joe Christmas's death in order to prepare the reader for its direct narration in the pages that follow. Faulkner supplies Stevens with a ready listener, a nameless college professor and friend, who, coincidentally, disembarks from the train to pay the D. A. a surprise visit at the exact moment in which Stevens delivers the Hineses to their train car. As they travel from the train station back to Stevens's home, Stevens spins a classically Gothic tale about the last moments of Christmas's life as a panicky, interior struggle of blood against blood, fetishizing and racializing his liquid interiors by repeating the terms "black blood" and "white blood" (448–49).[1] Christmas's white blood, Stevens explains, provides him with moral reasoning, but his black blood rises against it, pushing him to pistol-whip Reverend Hightower and, ultimately, sweeping him into an ecstatic state in which "death is desire and fulfillment" (449).

The District Attorney relies upon a Gothic encoding of what he understands to be the divide between black and white, speaking the language of early-American writers for whom blackness, for the most part, signifies evil and the Devil's work, and whiteness, usually, signifies purity and religious illumination.[2] The lawyer's re-presentation of early-American Gothic rhetoric as a modern discourse of blood not only conflates the moral with the racial, but also, as spoken by the voice of law and education, authorizes such a discourse as learned, reasoned, and natural. Staged as a one-sided conversation between two Ivy League–educated white men, Stevens's monologue represents how the Gothic infiltrates modern racial thought, so much so that even Faulkner's Harvard-educated, state-representative lawman speaks of mixed-race in terms of a mythic—one might say eugenic—battle between good and evil blood pools. The silence of the emergent professor, who never interrupts, signals that he accepts, or at least remains mesmerized by, Stevens's fantastic narrative as a truth.

Stevens's interpretation of whiteness as the moral and racial force that drives Christmas away from the darkness of blackness emerges near the end of a novel that has already implicated whiteness in its Gothic structure. As Faulkner's readers are already aware, and as I will explore later in this essay, Joe Christmas's racial ambiguity colors the way that Jefferson's townspeople understand themselves as occupying a normative whiteness that differs from the whiteness of those ostracized by the community, especially Joanna Burden. Stevens's focus on the activity of white blood, as it resists and struggles against the blackness inside Christmas's body, distinctly ignores the other presence of whiteness in the scene he narrates—the whiteness of the force that ultimately destroys Christmas, not his "blood," but the National Guard, embodied by Percy Grimm. Unlike Stevens, who pictures racial antagonism as a Gothic horror of embattled bodily interiors, this essay redirects the (white) intellectual's gaze to see the Gothic materiality of racial whiteness—the novel's simultaneous articulation of and collapse between the National Guard and the southern lynch mob, a representation of whiteness as a racialized force of history and terror.[3]

GOTHIC WHITENESS

The contemporary turn in Gothic criticism to account for the particularities of race, gender, class, nation, and sexuality "posts" the classic interpretations of Gothic representations of darkness and light, especially as Gothic studies intersects with what has become known as whiteness studies in the academy.[4] This essay will articulate a theory of Gothic whiteness that examines the connection between Faulkner's southern Gothic and national history, once Faulkner's novel is understood as a national emergency narrative. Whereas Stevens's monologue explains the Gothic undoing of Joe Christmas as the result of an archetypal struggle between dark and light, this essay will demonstrate how, at the novel's close, the narrative disentangles "whiteness" from Stevens's understanding of it as a morally infused, blood-based racial category, and reimagines whiteness as tied to the horror of state-based violence that is predicated on the imagination of a pure "America," a national signifier that stands apart from the body and its imperfect borders. Gothic whiteness, I argue, is not only the besmirchment of what otherwise gets marked as supremely whitened, but also the haunting of white, abstract personhood by the white body it so desperately seeks to repress.[5] Such a reading gives primary importance to the novel's opposition between national enemies and the National Guard and the textual inscription of what looks like national security but, in Faulkner's novel, ends up as a form of local, racialized terrorism.

While *Light in August* functions as an exemplary modern American Gothic text, an analysis of how Percy Grimm, as both white supremacist and National Guardsman, enhances the novel's Gothic structure has been ignored in favor of psychoanalytic readings of Joe Christmas (as a "depressed narcissist") or the novel's representations of the "haunted house" (Jarraway 63; Polk 24, 29–30). Teresa Goddu has argued that "the gothic, like all discourses, needs to be historicized" and that "the gothic tells of the historical horrors that make national identity possible yet must be repressed in order to sustain it" (2, 10). Additionally, Eric Savoy has pointed out that, once the Gothic emerges, it does not provide a newer, more complete version of national history. Instead, the Gothic resists its telling in any complete and final form. It "irrupts by fits and starts in a semiotic that is fragmentary, one that is more suggestive than conclusive" of national history's frightening and forgotten past (Savoy 8). An analysis of Gothic whiteness in *Light in August*, therefore, requires understanding the novel's relationship to the historical development of new forms of military defense in the early twentieth century, and how this part of U.S. history converges with and is, in part, made possible by the more repressed story of white supremacy in the modern South. Digging up the history of the National Guard (however fragmented or suggestive such research might be), then, is like uncovering the buried parts of a Gothic secret.

THE NATIONAL GUARD

During the first two decades of the twentieth century, officially sanctioned, militarized actions inside the U.S. changed the look of the nation during times of civil unrest. With the passing of the Dick Act of 1903, the National Defense Act of 1916, and the National Defense Act Amendments of 1920, the federal government authorized the training and inspection of state and local militias so that members of each could officially become citizen-soldiers, or members of the National Guard—a presence that signals the militarized containment of national emergencies.[6] Members of the National Guard were, and still are, simultaneously enlisted in both the federal and state National Guard (each state having its own National Guard), thus creating double identities for their recruits: he who is both civilian and soldier, with an understanding of defense at both the local and national level.

Membership in the National Guard offered the promise of militarized modernization for white men.[7] The institutionalization of uniforms, camps, and drills, as well as the formation of ranks and the regulation of weapons, assisted in disciplining and federalizing a whiteness that belonged to the masses—the anonymous crowd, the unorganized militia, the mass of roiling strikers, or even the lynch mob—and thus resignified local or regional whiteness as the official domain of the U.S. military. According to a 1993 report by the U.S. Advisory Commission on Intergovernmental Relations, the primary duties of the modern National Guard are to "suppress insurrections" (guarding against internal rebellions and uprisings) and "repel invasions" (guarding against external threats) (8). The citizen-soldier's purpose is to militaristically patrol the nation during the time of national emergency, strategically configuring and reconfiguring the insides and outsides of the nation depending on where, exactly, the perceived national threat emerges. The force of the National Guard as a metaphor, therefore, depends on the second term of its phrase, "guard," which connotes a border position designed to seal national meaning into a protected geopolitical totality.

During the height of literary modernism, four kinds of national emergency narratives produced the National Guard: natural disasters; those involving labor disputes and striking workers; those involving race, gender, and sexuality; and those in which the National Guard is mobilized on or over the border as a reserve force supplementing the regular army (Cooper 146–52). The narration of the Nationally Guarded event takes place within a peculiar temporal structure, one that builds with an alarmingly steady momentum and which speeds forward by moments of panic and violence. The violent movement from local crisis to national emergency suggests that, when the National Guard shows up in the political landscape, the nation itself threatens to burst, turning itself inside out. The borders of the nation are redefined in the emergency moment, a moment that contains a peopled excess whose violent destruction satiates America's desire for imaginary political and narrative safety.

As the National Guard entered into its third official decade of existence, the 1930s, Faulkner published *Light in August*, a novel that calls in the National Guard to oversee what can be understood, in the light of the above information, as a national emergency narrative.[8] Central to the plot is the mysteriously dead body of a white woman, Joanna Burden, who is assumed to have been murdered in cold blood at the hands of Joe Christmas, a character whose racial ambiguity puzzles other characters in the text as well as Joe himself.[9] Christmas is assumed to have raped Burden. At the end of the novel, Christmas ends up incarcerated and draws an angry white mob that clamors for his lynching. He also ends up under the "protection" of the National Guard. A narrative that involves the accusation of interracial murder and rape constitutes a national emergency, a narrative familiar enough to 1930s readers who knew that the National Guard was regularly called out during the early twentieth century to prevent the lynching of black men accused of interracial rape or murder (Cooper 46–49). While the presence of the National Guard in *Light in August* guarantees that the story of Joe

Christmas and Joanna Burden is, indeed, a national emergency narrative, the presence of the National Guard does not guarantee that the meaning of the modern nation in the time of emergency is ever anything more than a horrifying reminder of how the state has absolute power over who counts as worth guarding in the name of the nation and who does not.

Because, as far as I can tell, there has been very little work done on the National Guard as an object of literary and cultural studies, I preface my analysis of Faulkner's novel with a re-presentation of early-twentieth-century texts written by or for U.S. National Guardsmen to show how the state tries to breathe life into the otherwise stagnant bodies of rural white men who made up its early configurations.[10] Such an approach explains two things: 1) how the National Guard makes citizen-soldiers out of armed residents, and 2) how National Guard narratives characterize those marked as Other to the nation in times of emergency. National Guard narratives, I argue, call attention to how the borders of the body and the borders of the nation are, in military discourse, as in Faulkner's Gothic novel, always the same thing.

A CLEAN AND ORDERLY WHITE MOB

As local militias turned into National Guard units, a number of publications were printed to assist the citizen-soldier with his duties as a combatant, as well as to remind him of what it means to take on an identity that is attached to national importance. Such publications stress the important overlap between the proper, hygienic male body and the disciplined, obedient body of the soldier.[11] The Gothic materializes in the National Guardsmen's training, however, in three different ways: as corporeal abjection, as a paranoid threat that the guardsman will turn into a member of an anarchic mob, and as a polluting, national Other that lurks at the borders of the nation.

Captain Cromwell Stacey, for example, published a handbook for new National Guardsmen in 1916 called *Company Training (Infantry)*. *Company Training* begins with "The Rules of the Game for Enlisted Men of the National Guard," a list that tells recruits how to behave like citizen-soldiers (Stacey 5).[12] Rule One declares that "[t]he first duty of a soldier is loyalty, unhesitating obedience. Without this quality an army is no better than a mob.... One hundred disciplined men are always superior to a thousand undisciplined men" (5). Rule Four repeats this admonition; the citizen-soldier should "[g]et the reputation of being a fine military organization, and not that of a uniformed mob" (5). Throughout Stacey's training manual, there exists a primary anxiety over the collapse of the National Guard into an inefficient mob of untrained men: "I have heard many National Guard officers say: 'This is not the Regular Army and we can't have the same discipline.' True, *but you can try.* The nearer you approach to the Regular Army standard the better organization you will have and the more efficient your company will be" (9). The difference between mob, National Guard, and army is only a matter of degrees. According to Stacey, the National Guard aspires to army status, but worries it might actually be nothing more than a mob in uniform. The training manual, therefore, is crucial for determining the difference between a mob and the National Guard; it is a literary reminder of how to discipline the body, how to make the body look like and act like a nation. As a result, the manual reviews the kinds of training citizen-soldiers need for attack and defense—how to march, patrol, lunge, strike, parry, thrust, point, and guard, as well as how to take care of parts of the body most susceptible to invasion: its orifices.

The cleanliness of the military body begins, as it were, in the kitchen and ends, surely, in the outhouse or latrine. Stacey's training manual orders the care of the mouth and the anus, of knowing the difference between food and feces, as a part of training the National Guard: "Watch your kitchens like a hawk. They must be clean as a pin. Watch your cooks and see that they bathe daily and always have on clean clothes" (114).[13] To guard the kitchen is to protect the body from a filthy oral invasion. The threat to the body lies outside its borders and is brought into the body only if one is caught off guard. In addition to the mouth, the National Guard needs to be reminded of how to be on guard against anything that might cling to its uncanny double, the anus: "You must secure toilet paper; no matter how you get it, but you must have it.... If you don't do this, men will use newspaper, or more frequently not use any paper at all, none being available. This method will soon produce piles, and you will have men on sick report as a result. Rears must be made comfortable; otherwise men will not use them and will get in the habit of going off in the bushes and defiling the campsite" (115). Here the threat comes from inside the body. The threat, in this case, involves not being able to fully eliminate the body's excess, a threat of producing so much shit around the campsite that the whole place reeks of it, drawing disease and contaminating the otherwise pure site of modern national-military body building. The National Guard grooms the animalistic, rural bodies of white men, refining their rituals and habits so that each will fit into a more respectable, civilized national culture.

WHITE BORDERS AND HEMISPHERIC FILTH

As the sanitary body of the soldier emerges from the provincial body of the citizen, so too does "America," as a narrative about the good, clean home, emerge as the National Guard polices the internal and external borders of the United States.[14] The first national emergency during which the National Guard was mobilized was the result of an attack from below, just south of the U.S. border. In March 1916, President Woodrow Wilson called out National Guardsmen to—literally—line the U.S.-Mexico border and guard against Mexican revolutionary Pancho Villa, whose army crossed the border into Columbus, New Mexico, and killed nineteen U.S. citizens (Cooper 156–63).[15]

During that time, Irving Goff McCann, a captain in the Illinois State National Guard, wrote a short book that chronicles his travels to and experiences at Camp Wilson (now Camp Travis), just outside of San Antonio, Texas. McCann's book, *With the National Guard on the Border: Our National Military Problem* (1917), is a record of his life with the National Guard as it was stationed in close proximity to the U.S.-Mexico border. Much like the training manual's investment in the hygienic body of the citizen-soldier, McCann's narrative describes the border between the United States and Mexico as a division between clean and dirty. According to McCann, the U.S.-Mexico border is "[t]he boundary line between the heaven of American liberty and internal peace and the purgatory of Mexican filth, disease, illiteracy, despotism, and revolution. . . . Mexico is . . . a fresh wound and a clot of blood on the Western Hemisphere. . . . Under the direction of the sanitary experts of the United States Army, Mexico would receive its first national bath, and its health conditions be vastly improved" (22, 23, 43). McCann's nationalist idiom finds expression in bodily abjection. He imagines the Western Hemisphere as a body of which Mexico is a part—filthy, bloodstained, and disease-ridden—and then conjures an image of American military devastation as that which would not only do some cleaning, but that which would give dirty parts of the hemispheric body a bath.

I call attention to Captain Stacey's and Captain McCann's National Guard narratives in order to show how the project of making the citizen-soldier overlaps with the project of constructing national borders during times of "emergency." What emerges, in both of the above narratives, is matter that must be eliminated, and the projection of that filth onto a national Other across the border—a process of U.S. abjection that keeps nation and body whole and pure or, as McCann would have it, a "heaven of liberty and internal peace." It is with these representations of the National Guard in mind that I turn to Faulkner's *Light in August*, a novel that waits to introduce its one National Guardsman until the end of the book, in the second-to-last chapter.

Percy Grimm appears quite suddenly, materializing out of nowhere, so it seems, and commits an act of violence so brutal that it might easily distract the reader from the fact that he, like Captain McCann and Captain Stacey, is a military captain—a captain in the Mississippi National Guard.[16] His membership in the National Guard matters, I suggest, not only because he is one of several characters for whom, as one Faulkner scholar puts it, "filth and abomination provide the categories in terms of which they understand most of life," but also because his presence marks the story of Joanna Burden and Joe Christmas as a national emergency narrative (Minter, *William Faulkner* 132). And like many authors who are writing modern Gothic novels in the U.S. South, Faulkner is less interested in representing "America" as the "heaven of liberty and internal peace," as McCann sees it, and more interested in writing a novel about how the nation generates its own terrifying and uncanny specters of difference, detailing, as he does, the body and its fluids to serve as a metaphor for what Laura Doyle has recently called "a living entity under siege from itself yet constituting itself in the process" (339). Because I am interested in both the representation of the National Guard and the Gothic narrative that produces its presence, I will first sketch the emergencies of race and gender that surround the coming together of Joanna Burden and Joe Christmas, so that we can see why it is that the National Guard is that which joins them, finally, in death. The critical transformation of both characters in the minds of Jefferson's white public signals the emergence of a new fantasy about whiteness that, in turn, drives the novel's emergency forward to its bloody end. I begin with an analysis of Joanna Burden's transformation from white foreigner and enemy to southern white lady, go on to explain the inversion of Joe Christmas's identity from foreigner to "nigger," and then interpret Percy Grimm as the emergency narrative's nearly dead white citizen turned live National Guardsman.

THREATENING WHITE SUPREMACY

Light in August revolves around a gruesome event that takes place in the small town of Jefferson, Mississippi, one that escalates into an emergency of national proportions: the butchering of Joanna Burden (nearly severing her head from her body, but leaving intact a bit of gristle that connects the two) and the torching of her family's property. Joanna Burden's slaughter produces a local crisis and, ultimately, a national emergency not only because she is a white woman who lives alone in a small southern town, but also because she is a white woman who, in keeping with a long family tradition, turns Mississippi racial relations inside out because she associates with and advocates for blacks living in the U.S. South. No matter how much time the Burden family has lived, worked, and reproduced in Mississippi, the town of Jefferson does not consider them southerners, but a regionally defined enemy who has erupted from within.

And here's why: from at least the early nineteenth century, Joanna's grandfather, Calvin Burden, raucously speaks out against slavery, and eventually kills another white man in the name of abolitionism (242). During the Reconstruction, Joanna's grandfather and father travel "east, to Washington, and [get] a commission from the government to come down [to Jefferson, Mississippi] to help with the freed negroes" (251). The Burdens, therefore, act as agents of the Freedmen's Bureau. Finally, years later, in Jefferson, the second Calvin Burden (Joanna's half-brother, grandson of the first) is killed (by a white man) over "a question of negro voting" (248). Joanna Burden explains what this means very clearly. She tells Christmas,

"They hated us here. We were Yankees. Foreigners. Worse than foreigners: enemies. Carpet baggers. And it—the [Civil] War—still too close for even the ones that got whipped to be very sensible. Stirring up the negroes to murder and rape, they called it. Threatening white supremacy" (249). In the early part of the twentieth century, Joanna Burden continues her family's legacy as a sign of that which "threatens white supremacy" by working as a liaison between the administrators of southern black schools and universities and African American female citizens. Even though Joanna was born and raised in Jefferson, her labor and history sully her whiteness, differentiating it from the purity of whiteness that belongs to other white southerners. Publicly, her nonsouthern whiteness makes her a foreigner, a Yankee, and an enemy who is "mixed up with niggers" (53). As a result, she lives in isolation from other whites while she continues to provide advice to "the presidents and faculties and trustees [of black schools], [as well as] advice personal and practical to young girl students and even alumnae, of a dozen negro schools and colleges throughout the [S]outh" (233). Joanna Burden's death, therefore, signals the end of generation upon generation of white patronage of blacks in the midst of a region saturated by white supremacy.[17]

Burden's position outside of white normativity ("a foreigner, an outlander" [289]) instantly changes the day that her nearly beheaded white body is dragged out of its burning home and into the light of the morning sun (91–92). In addition to white law and order (the sheriff, deputy, and marshal, along with firefighters), Burden's body brings with it the attention of a white mob that arrives "within thirty minutes ... as though out of thin air ... parties and groups ranging from single individuals to entire families. Still others came out from town in racing and blatting cars" (287). In the novel's economy of race and gender, Burden's public identity, at the moment of her death, transforms from Yankee-foreigner-enemy to violated southern white woman whom the mob instantly identifies as one of their own. The narrator tells us that "[w]hile she was alive they [white men] would not have allowed their wives to call on her. When they were younger, children ... they had called after her on the street, 'Nigger lover! Nigger lover!'" (291-92). Now, however, the spectacle of a dead white woman, with her throat cut, sends the white mob into a frenzy, collectively believing that "the body ... cried out for vengeance," collectively asking, "*Who did* it? Who did it? . . . Is he still free? Ah. Is he? Is he? . . . Is that him? Is that the one that did it? . . . By God, if that's him, what are we doing, standing around here? Murdering a white woman the black son of a . . ."* (290–91). In the instant that the mob discovers that she has been nearly decapitated, the historical specificity of Joanna Burden disappears; instead, mob logic rules, replacing the foreigner-enemy stigma with the mythic cover story of the unguarded southern white lady. Her death puts into motion the beginnings of a lynching narrative, and the lynching narrative turns, finally, into a national emergency once it is discovered that the man whom everyone thought was a "foreigner" is actually a "negro" who has been sleeping and living with Joanna.[18]

Christmas's white cabinmate, Joe Brown, alerts the unsuspecting public to Christmas's racial blackness, transforming Christmas's identity from a mysterious "foreigner" into the "nigger" of the lynching narrative. When Brown reveals "the truth" of Christmas's race to a surprised white police force—that Christmas is not a foreigner, as previously assumed,[19] but that he is black—it not only secures Christmas's public role in the unfolding Gothic drama about interracial sex and murder, but also, importantly, exemplifies how racial blackness emerges out of national foreignness. Brown ridicules the white vigilantes and police force:

> "That's right," [Brown] says. "Go on. Accuse me. Accuse the white man that's trying to help you with what he knows. Accuse the white man and let the nigger go free. Accuse the white and let the nigger run."
>
> "Nigger?" the sheriff said. "Nigger?"
>
> . . . "You're so smart," he says. "The folks in this town is so smart. Fooled for three years. Calling him a foreigner for three years, when soon as I watched him three days I knew he wasn't no more a foreigner than I am. I knew before he even told me himself." . . .
>
> "You better be careful what you are saying, if it is a white man you are talking about," the marshal says. "I don't care if he is a murderer or not."
>
> "I'm talking about Christmas," Brown says. "The man that killed that white woman after he had done lived with her in plain sight of this whole town, and you all letting him get further and further away

while you are accusing the one fellow that can find him for you, that knows what he done. He's got nigger blood in him." (97–98)

Christmas's racial identity supplies the already-in-crisis town of Jefferson with the information it is looking for, a racial truth that fits in with the myth of the black rapist: "'A nigger,' the marshal said. 'I always thought there was something funny about that fellow . . . I'll attend to Christmas'" (99). The emerging truth of Christmas, that he has claimed to be part black, and that he has been having sex with Joanna Burden, assures the white police force that they have found their criminal, and that he will be "attended to" as the law sees fit. In the end, however, it is not the sheriff who attends to Christmas, but the sheriff does foreshadow who will: "[Christmas] better be careful, or Percy Grimm'll get him with that army of his" (423).

PERCY GRIMM AND "AMERICA"

The sheriff's ironic reference to an army foreshadows the eventual materialization of what can only be described as Percy Grimm's veteran-militia, composed of members of the American Legion who, as one of them points out, "are not soldiers now," but whose "Post" Grimm will transform into a platoon, with himself in command (452). Those who form the squads that patrol the town square are veterans of past wars, not National Guardsmen and not currently enlisted men, but they do move and act under the direction of Grimm and in the name of the nation. Grimm transforms Jefferson's veterans back into soldiers in order to make sure that no member of the Jefferson population decides to take the law into his own hands by lynching Christmas, who is, at this point, already in jail. Veterans reemerge as the soldiers they once were to make sure Jefferson's citizens do not emerge as a mob. This is a description of Percy Grimm talking to the American Legion:

> "We got to preserve order," he said. "We must let the law take its course. The law. The nation. It is the right of no civilian to sentence a man to death. And we, the soldiers in Jefferson, are the ones to see to that."

"How do you know that anybody is planning anything different?" the legion commander said. "Have you heard any talk?"

"I dont know. I haven't listened.... That's not the question. It's whether or not we, as soldiers, that have worn the uniform are going to be the first to state where we stand. To show these people right off just where the government of the country stands on such things.... I thought it might be a good thing if I wear my uniform until this business is settled. So [the town] can see that Uncle Sam is present in more than spirit." (451–53)

Grimm's first priority, therefore, is ignorantly preemptive. He establishes the difference between citizen and soldier, to make sure the military's presence installs a fear in Jefferson's citizens who might be thinking of acting outside of the law.

The narrator alerts the reader to how Grimm's insistence on the difference between citizen and soldier is symptomatic of his own journey from being a natural-born Mississippi citizen to fully saved National Guardsman:

> He was about twentyfive and a captain in the State national guard. He had been born in the town and had lived there all his life save for the periods of summer encampments. He was too young to have been in the European War, though it was not until 1921 or '22 that he realised that he would never forgive his parents for that fact.... It was the new civilian-military act which saved him. (449–50)[20]

The civilian-military act, explained above as the National Defense Act of 1916, "saves" Grimm, providing him with the national body he has been so desperately seeking. The narrator tells the reader that, prior to his enlistment in the National Guard, Grimm

> was like a man who had been for a long time in a swamp, in the dark. It was as though he not only could see no path ahead of him, he knew that there was none. Then suddenly his life opened definite and clear. The wasted years in which he had shown no ability in school,

in which he had been known as lazy, recalcitrant, without ambition, were behind him, forgotten. (450–51)

For Percy Grimm, any identity other than an American identity—a nationally militarized identity—is a wasted identity, one divorced from power. Before his identity as a citizen-soldier, Grimm absorbs those qualities attributed to the novel's "hot wet primogenitive Female" and "womanshenegro": the dark swamp, the unclear and sluggish, the unmanageable (115, 156). Membership in the National Guard gives Grimm power by loosening him from the constraints of this body:

> He could now see his life opening before him, uncomplex and inescapable as a barren corridor, completely freed now of ever again having to think or decide, the burden which he now assumed and carried as bright and weightless and martial as his insignatory brass: a sublime and implicit faith in physical courage and blind obedience. (451)

For Percy Grimm (as it is in McCann's memoir), identification with the state produces a pure and shining American identity, one tied to "a belief that the *white race* is superior to any and all other races and that the *American* is superior to all other white races and the *American uniform* is superior to all men" (451; emphasis added). Grimm's Gothic status as a "suffering," young, impoverished, southern white male who wants "to tell [his story], to open his heart to" someone transforms into a new, more powerful, nationally identified white male (450).

As a result, Grimm's patriotic purpose spreads like wildfire. Grimm brings Uncle Sam into the small town of Jefferson and nationalizes the town by militarizing it. Soon enough, "without knowing that they were thinking about it, the town had suddenly accepted Grimm with respect and perhaps a little awe and a deal of actual faith and confidence, as though somehow his vision and patriotism and pride in that town . . . had been quicker and truer than theirs" (456–57). Thus Percy Grimm, a National Guard of one (for he is the only member of the National Guard in the book), not only transforms this local southern region into a site of national pride (a site in which he will protect "America and Americans" [454]), but also enacts a Gothic collapse of the difference between the supposedly peacekeeping National Guard and the terroristic violence of the southern white lynch mob.[21] After Grimm organizes the American Legion into squads to prevent the townspeople from lynching Christmas, Christmas escapes into the crowd as a fire siren blares its "slow and sustained scream" (460). Grimm, in the name of the National Guard, hunts Christmas down, corners him, fires five shots into his body, slices off his genitals, and "fling[s] behind him the bloody butcher knife," exclaiming, "Now you'll leave white women alone, even in hell" (464).[22]

EMERGENCY'S ENDS

Faulkner's National Guardsman falls straight out of Captain Stacey's training manual. Grimm moves exactly from the Gothic, history-laden, rural, impoverished white southerner to the fetishistic fascist, hot for the American uniform and the flag and burning for the chance to waste whatever body troubles the order or crosses the borders of race and gender in Jefferson. Faulkner's National Guard is singular and intimate, a one-on-one, body-to-body experience.[23] Percy Grimm chases and shoots Christmas, then uses his hand to search inside of Christmas's clothing for genitals that are held, sliced off with a butcher's knife. For Faulkner, the National Guard's work is direct, a terrible touching of National Guard and National Other, of citizen-soldier and criminal-enemy, lawman and outlaw. Grimm's violation of bodily borders in the name of America mirrors the description of the national border provided by the National Guardsman McCann, a policing of the limits of the nation to expel what pollutes the sign of its most cherished interior (white women). Grimm generates a fiction that the National Guard will prevent citizens from turning into a mob, thwart the lynching of a black man, and protect women from rape and murder—none of which it does. Grimm's last words about white women ends the novel's three-part articulation of white supremacy, which includes the Bible-inspired holiness of the white race espoused by Doc Hines, the eugenic theory of the white race espoused by Gavin Stevens, and the white nationalism of Grimm himself. The novel's awful conflation of National Guard and southern lynch mob under the sign of whiteness acts as a powerful critique of modern

America, signifying, as it does, the monstrosity of, not the racially ambiguous Joe Christmas, nor the novel's construction of all sorts of Others in the text (including woman, Yankee, enemy, carpetbagger, foreigner, and "nigger"), but the monstrosity of the state itself as an unstoppable agent of death.

NOTES

Introduction: Situating Whiteness in Faulkner Studies, Situating Faulkner in Whiteness Studies
—Jay Watson

1. See Wiegman, "Whiteness Studies."

2. That this transparency is a historical phenomenon as well as a theoretical formulation should be clear from the opening sentences of Grace Elizabeth Hale's cultural history of segregation: "Central to the meaning of whiteness is a broad, collective American silence. The denial of white as a racial identity, the denial that whiteness has a history, allows the quiet, the blankness, to stand as the norm. This erasure enables many to fuse their absence of racial being with the nation, making whiteness their unspoken but deepest sense of what it means to be an American" (xi).

3. A generation ago, Myra Jehlen was pursuing a roughly similar point in arguing that black/white racial conflict was not the central tension at work in Faulkner's world but that the fundamental "organizing principle" in the social structure of Yoknapatawpha was instead "the division between two classes of white society, the planters and the 'rednecks'" (9). "His people," she elaborates, "are made of the stuff of class distinctions: they are planter or poor-white (some few in between and defined by that too) and become individual by being a variant of their type. Moreover their motivations and the plots of their stories most often have to do with maintaining, resisting, or refurbishing a social situation which is first of all class defined and only then regional or racial" (10), a claim Jehlen extends even to *Absalom, Absalom!* (67–68). "The secondary importance" of black/white race consciousness in Faulkner's writings "may be surprising," observes Jehlen (10). "But it should be recalled that the Yoknapatawpha saga is a white man's tale. White priorities prevail." The trouble, though, is that Jehlen approaches her planter and yeomen figures strictly in class terms rather than as thoroughly racialized white identities.

4. This typology is indebted to, but does not simply reproduce, Ruth Frankenberg's overview of the field in her introduction to the edited collection *Displacing Whiteness*. See especially 1–3.

5. See *White* 89–103, 110–121 for elaborations of this argument.

6. A very brief list of Morrison's and hooks's predecessors in this tradition would include Ida B. Wells, W. E. B. Du Bois, James Weldon Johnson, C. L. R. James, Frantz

Fanon, and James Baldwin. For an interesting discussion of how Du Bois's revisionist historiography of Reconstruction-era race relations in *Black Reconstruction in America* (1935) may have indirectly or osmotically influenced Faulkner's understanding of southern white male subject formation in such works as *The Unvanquished* (1938), see Hannon 34–49.

7. See 87–93. Important groundwork for this argument was laid in Weinstein's earlier monograph, *Faulkner's Subject: A Cosmos No One Owns*. See especially 82–109.

8. See especially 248–51.

9. For other valuable examples of contemporary Faulkner criticism that take up the issue of whiteness in a manner informed by critical race studies, see Atkinson, "Impenetrable," Brister, Donaldson, Palmer, Paradiso, Sugimori, "Racial Mixture," and Sugimori, "Signifying."

10. See, for instance, Cohn 45–93; the essays gathered in Smith and Cohn 303–445; and the essays in Trefzer and Abadie.

11. See especially 1–38, 55–76, 103–13, 197–208.

Negotiating the Marble Bonds of Whiteness: Hybridity and Imperial Impulse in Faulkner
—Taylor Hagood

1. I am indebted to Christopher Bundrick, Benjamin Fisher, Travis Montgomery, Suzanne Penuel, Annette Trefzer, Joseph R. Urgo, and Jay Watson for fruitful comments and insights regarding the ideas set forth in this essay. Also, the bulk of the research for this article was completed with the aid of funding provided by the Frances Bell McCool Dissertation Fellowship in Faulkner Studies.

2. See Jones and Monteith, and Smith and Cohn.

3. On Elgin, see St. Clair and Vrettos.

4. The urn as a usable object first in a Greek and then in a British context conforms to Lévi-Strauss's definition of "the significant images of myth, the materials of the bricoleur, [which] are elements which can be defined by two criteria: they have *had a use*, as words in a piece of discourse which mythical thought 'detaches' in the same way as a bricoleur, in the course of repairing them, detaches the cogwheels of an old alarm clock; and *they can be used again* either for the same purpose or for a different one if they are at all diverted from their previous function" (35).

5. Crook details the origins and development of the Greek revival in Britain, noting that the Greek revival was actually a Romantic-Classic hybrid that negotiated between rationalistic balance and emotional asymmetry in style.

6. In addition to Hamlin, see Maynard; and also McDowell and Meyer.

7. Regarding Greek Revival architecture in the South, see also Mills Lane.

8. Arthur Machen's "The Great God Pan" dramatizes this very dynamic in a text contemporary with Faulkner's *The Marble Faun*.

9. I am borrowing the concept of the "counterfeit" Other from Jonathan Dollimore via Diane Roberts. See Roberts 78.

10. Regarding the double performativity in these writers' works, see Schmidt, Romine, and my essay, "'Prodjickin', or mekin' a present to yo' fam'ly': Rereading Empowerment in Thomas Nelson Page's Frame Narratives."

11. Blotner connects the story to Anderson, noting that just as Wilfred Midgleston has his vision in the mountains of Virginia, "[w]hen Faulkner had seen Sherwood Anderson in early 1926, Anderson had just bought a farm in the ruggedly beautiful, isolated region of southwest Virginia close to Marion" (254).

12. See Roger M. and Diana Davids Olien for discussion of journalistic attacks on the Standard Oil Company and their enduring impact on public perception of it.

13. See Faulkner, Father Abraham: *Holograph*.

Genealogies of White Deviance: The Eugenic Family Studies, *Buck v. Bell*, and William Faulkner, 1926–1931
—Jay Watson

1. In addition to Woodward, King, and Handley, see, for instance, Glissant and Kinney.

2. I do not employ Leigh Anne Duck's enormously useful concept here lightly. For in many ways the U.S. eugenics movement "found" in the degenerate white clans of the family studies precisely what, as Duck painstakingly demonstrates, U.S. politicians and intellectuals of the period "found" in the South: a temporal Other to the modernizing nation. See especially 1–49 (on the construction of the South in terms of temporal alterity), and 96–101 (on eugenically oriented commentary on the region).

3. For more on the gender politics behind the classification *feebleminded*, see Black 110; Deutsch 5, 64; English 160–61, 169–73; Kevles 107; Kline 53–56, 71; Lancaster 17, 26; Noll, *Feeble-Minded* 21, 69, 112–13, 132; and Rafter, *Creating* 44.

4. Goddard coined the term *moron* in 1910 to designate feebleminded persons with a "mental age" of eight to twelve years. The term derived from the Greek word for "foolish" (Deutsch 112).

5. The bill was introduced in February, shortly after the inauguration of Governor Bilbo (Larson 117). Over the next two months, the proposed statute was debated in Jackson and in a number of the state's leading newspapers, including the *Jackson Daily News* and the *Daily Clarion-Ledger* (see 215–16 n168–76). The state senate approved the sterilization bill two weeks after the house, as the legislative session was coming to a close (118). Though the enactment of the new statute went unreported throughout the month of April in the weekly "Doings of the Legislature" column of the Oxford *Eagle* and unmentioned in an April 26 *Eagle* roundup of the 1928 legislative session, "Accomplishments of Solons Noted as They Adjourn," it is difficult to believe that Faulkner would have been unaware of the bill and its public discussion around the state, especially given his frequent contact with his politically connected lawyer friend Phil Stone during the spring of 1928.

6. The two lineages, stemming from the same sire but different consorts, were represented in the pseudonym "Kallikak," which Goddard fashioned by fusing together Greek terms for "good" (*kalos*) and "bad" (*kakos*).

7. "Tribe of Ishmael" was of course McCulloch's name for the Indiana subjects of his "study in social degradation." The name would be another excellent example of the pejorative pseudonyms so prevalent in eugenics literature but for the inconvenient fact that it wasn't a pseudonym at all. The family in question was actually named Ishmael. For more on this study and its legacy, see Deutsch.

8. Indeed, we will learn later in Faulkner's career that even sexually deviant Byron Snopes manages to out-reproduce the Sartoris twins by fathering four half-breed "waifs" upon "a Jicarilla Apache squaw in Old Mexico." See Faulkner, *The Town* 317.

9. See, for instance, "The Tall Men" (Faulkner, *Collected Stories* 45–62).

10. For more on this fear of "passing," especially by the feebleminded, see Deutsch 112, English 167–69, Kline 22–23, and Rafter, *Creating* 56.

11. On Indiana's role in U.S. eugenics history, see Black 64; Deutsch 102–103, 106, 113; Kevles 100; Larson 27; Noll, *Feeble-Minded* 65; and Wray 90. Home at one time or another to surgical sterilization pioneer Harry Clay Sharp, scholar David Starr Jordan, intelligence testing authority Lewis Terman, family study authors Oscar McCulloch and Arthur Estabrook, and other influential state and university officials, the state was also the site of the first compulsory vasectomy performed upon a person in custody, and passed the nation's first eugenic sterilization law in 1907. Deutsch calls Indiana "a laboratory for the eugenics movement" (106).

12. In another context, Elizabeth Yukins has addressed the way sterilization and lynching worked side by side (if not hand in hand) during the Jim Crow years as technologies of reproductive control over the South's undesirable populations, noting that while "racist neglect somewhat shielded African Americans from the *legal* sterilization procedures performed on 'feeble-minded' persons in state institutions," "illegal procedures, such as lynching, provided another, related type of social control" (183n5).

13. Certainly the predicament of Jason's wayward niece, Miss Quentin, in the Compson household also evokes that of the institutional inmate. Locked into her room at night, subjected to the most invasive and humiliating forms of interrogation and surveillance, and nominated herself as a candidate for sterilization (as we will see shortly) by her "warden" and uncle, she could be forgiven for seeing little difference between Compson space and the disciplinary spaces of the state mental health system. And when she graduates from inmate to escapee, the novel's thumbnail picture of the room she leaves behind evokes not only the assignation house (282) but the institutional ward.

14. See, for instance, Kevles 53, 108; and Rafter, *Creating* 153.

15. In his initial examination of Carrie Buck, superintendent A. S. Priddy of the Virginia Colony for Epileptics and Feeble-minded classified her as "the lowest grade Moron class" and, not incidentally, as "a moral delinquent" (quoted in Lombardo 107).

16. He is quick, however, to question whether "even that would do any good. Like I say once a bitch always a bitch" (263). Like some contemporary eugenicists, that is, Jason

recognizes that "cutting" his wayward kinswomen will address only half the problem—it will stop the "bitches" from propagating but not from "bitching" (fornicating) and thus continuing to dishonor the family name.

At other times, Jason seems to envision institutional segregation for his niece: "I think I know a place where they'll take her too and the name of it's not Milk street and Honey avenue either" (222). He could simply be thinking about a brothel, of course, but he could as easily have in mind a colony for the feebleminded. In the same passage Jason offers an economic rationale for institutionalizing Benjy—"why not send him there and get that much benefit out of the taxes we pay"—that was not unfamiliar to contemporary eugenics advocates.

17. Significantly, the one passage from the novel in which the vision of the male line achieves this sort of three-generational thickness directly invokes the Sartoris family *and* its genealogy of death: "It used to be I thought of death as a man something like Grandfather a friend of his a kind of private and particular friend like we used to think of Grandfather's desk not to touch it or even to talk loud in the room where it was I always thought of them being together somewhere all the time waiting for old Colonel Sartoris to come down and sit with them waiting on a high place beyond cedar trees Colonel Sartoris was on a still higher place looking out across at something and they were waiting for him to get done looking at it and come down" (176). By contrast, degeneracy, not death, is the specter associated with the female Compson line.

18. See, for instance, Kline 3, 16; Lancaster 17–18, 24, 49; Larson 35–36, 68, 92, 93, 130; Noll, *Feeble-Minded* 15–16, 40, 76, 132; Rafter, *Creating* 48, 160; and Yukins 178, 180–81.

19. Or perhaps I shouldn't be so quick to assign Jason a monopoly over sterilization fantasy, since Quentin in fact has one of his own: "Versh told me about a man who mutilated himself. He went into the woods and did it with a razor, sitting in a ditch. A broken razor flinging them backward over his shoulder the same motion complete the jerked skein of blood backward not looping. But that's not it. It's not not having them. It's never to have had them then I could say O That That's Chinese I dont know Chinese" (115–16). Though he seems to envision self-castration as a (not quite adequate) safeguard against the wounding action of desire, its eugenic overtones should not be lost on the reader.

20. The close connections in Quentin's imagination between his sister and the "dirty" immigrant girl he briefly squires around Cambridge (125–45) underscore the racial doubt that Caddy inspires.

21. Jason also echoes his brother in his emphasis on "the woods" as the site of this illicit, racialized female sexuality. "Who do you play out with?" he asks his niece. "Are you hiding out in the woods with one of those dam slick-headed jellybeans? Is that where you go?" (184). Later he vows to himself to catch Quentin's tent-show beau: "I'll make him think that dam red tie is the latch string to hell if he thinks he can run the woods with my niece" (241). Interestingly, the family studies, with their rural hill settings, often present the woods in similar terms, as a site of white sexual deviance and "unrestrained sensuality" (Rafter, *White Trash* 164).

22. Interestingly, this reconstitution of the Bundren family at novel's end leaves us with a patriarch affiliated over the course of the narrative with two different consorts *and*

with a reconfigured sibling cohort that follows the one-in-four Compson structure of a sister and three brothers. This reshuffling of the genealogical deck sets up the possibility of a Kallikak-style dual-lineage analysis (if we can assume that Anse and his new wife aren't done chapping yet), a Compson-style study of the distribution pattern of recessive traits, or both!

23. In the novel, this negotiation process also reflects powerful tensions between country and city and pervasive self-consciousness about rural and "town" identities and the ideologically charged differences between them. See, for instance, 7, 60, 66, 110, 171, 230, 241–42, 250.

On the links between Progressivism and eugenics ideology, see English 2–3; Larson 10–11; Lombardo 17, 34; Noll, *Feeble-Minded* 65, 77, 80; and Rafter, *White Trash* 7 and *Creating* 210.

24. We need not turn to Calvin Brown's *Glossary of Faulkner's South* to identify "feeb" as a term for a feebleminded person (80), but his entries for "crimp," which he defines as "a cheat" (63), and "spung," which he identifies as "a crook who preys or lives on other crooks" (187), are considerably more helpful than the *Dictionary of American Slang*.

25. On the social, political, and ideological uses of delinquency, see Foucault 257–92.

26. Likewise, Horace Benbow's Saturday stroll around the Jefferson square (111–12) presents a stock country-comes-to-town scenario, with rural folk milling in the streets and alleys to sample the new goods, services, and sensations available in the modern urban setting.

27. The portrait of the madwoman borders on white-trash stereotype, suggesting that Ruby and her baby are finding their level in the urban space that most closely resembles the rural one they left behind at the Frenchman place.

28. As noted many years ago by Thadious Davis (*Faulkner's "Negro"* 70–75).

29. Though for a different view, see Kline, who posits a turn among Depression-era eugenicists from strictly genetic toward more environmentalist explanations for unfitness within the crucible of the white family. See especially 94–100, 124–30.

Queering Whiteness, Queering Faulkner: Hightower's "Wild Bulges"
—*Alfred J. López*

1. For a more thorough explication of the assumptions of whiteness studies, see Dyer 1–40.

2. See Newitz and Wray, Introduction.

3. See Zettsu.

4. This is of course not an uncommon gesture in Spivak's work. For a recent example, see Spivak 93.

5. See, for example, the entry for "queer" in *The Faulkner Glossary*: "odd, unusual (not as in 'homosexual')."

6. For further explanation of the *tuché*-automaton, see Lacan 50–54. For a discussion of this concept within the context of whiteness, see Seshadri-Crooks 82.

7. See Faulkner 61–65.

8. For the Wolfman's famous dream of the white wolves, see Freud, "History" 29. For my own brief discussion of the significance of the window in that dream as a "staging" element, see López 163–64.

9. As in the Wolfman case, here the adult dreamer realizes the memory of the childhood scene, which as Freud explains "was able to show him what sexual satisfaction from his father was like; and the result was terror, *horror of the fulfillment of the wish*, and consequently a flight from his father." Although the dream distorts much of the material that informs it, it nevertheless "preserve[s] the essential connection" between his unsatisfied love and horror at the realization of his own forbidden longing. Thus, in short, the child's paradoxical response of excitement and nausea. Additionally, no small part of this horror is the dreamer's realization of the single most necessary condition of this satisfaction: he must be castrated like his mother, in order to receive the sexual satisfaction from his father that she obviously does or did. For the analyst's explanation in the context of the Wolfman case, see Freud, "History" 36.

10. See Freud, "History" 75–82.

11. See Freud, *Interpretation* 438–39.

12. There remains for me a perhaps unsolvable ambiguity in the developing dream-work of the vision, specifically whether the "neat folds" of the garment and parting of the "lid" belong imaginatively to the disrobing and submission of the mother—and thus his own—or the child's daydream of disrobing and discovering the nakedness of the father. Nevertheless, I do not believe it necessary to solve this particular point to allow the encoded sexual nature of the scene generally.

13. See Freud, *Interpretation* 340–44 and *Introductory* 173–75.

14. "Chicken hawk" actually has a long history of use in this context, going back to the Latin words *pullus* (chicken) and *pullarius* (chicken hawk, chaser of chickens). In English the latter translates roughly into "poulterer," or the more recent twentieth-century version, "chicken hawk." For more on the etymology of these and other gay slang terms, see Norton.

Passing as Miscegenation:
Whiteness and Homoeroticism in Faulkner's *Absalom, Absalom!*
—Betina Entzminger

1. Thanks to my colleague Dr. Cristina Mathews for helping me to articulate more clearly the ideas in this paragraph.

2. Similarly, examining *Light in August*, Ickstadt links the modernist form of the novel, "the deconstruction and reconstitution of narrative order," with Faulkner's attempts to blur artificial binaries: "the topos of 'passing' . . . is at once a reference to a social fact, a cultural fantasy, and a metaphor of the blurring and crossing of boundaries characteristic of the modernizing process as much as of the modernist text. . . . *Passing*, with its subversive implications that question (yet also reaffirm) existing hierarchies, could be regarded as a significant metaphor of modernism itself" (531).

3. As Lee Edelman notes, "The black body, as material supplement or signifier, as that which must be possessed in order to validate the dominant subject's putative possession of the phallus, must endure a symbolic inscription corresponding to that of the female body" (qtd. in Michele Wallace 88).

4. During the late nineteenth and early twentieth centuries, the minstrel show was a popular venue for blurring the boundaries of and exploring the connections between race and gender. In these often homoerotic performances, in which black face allowed the performers greater sexual freedom, "white men played not just black men but black women as well" (Hale 157). Offering further evidence of the historical association of gender with race, Robyn Wiegman cites the practice of castrating the male lynching victim: "in the disciplinary fusion of castration with lynching, the mob severs the black male from the masculine" (124). This practice not only removes the supposed threat of black male sexuality, but it also symbolically removes the power of the phallus, thereby feminizing the black male victim. In fact, male African Americans and Native Americans were not even called "men" in the late nineteenth and early twentieth centuries because manliness connoted civilization and whiteness (Bederman 50).

5. Michael Davidson points out that more recently, "The National Hemophilia Foundation's attempt to screen out homosexuals as blood donors in the early days of AIDS . . . was linked by many gays and lesbians to racist practices in the nineteenth century . . . that divided black blood from white blood" (44). Davidson also recalls that in the media's treatment of AIDS, believed then to be a gay disease, the predominantly black country Haiti "often function[ed] as an 'entry' point for the disease. . . . AIDS comes from the outside, entering the national body through unprotected borders" (50).

6. Though small differences in the timeline, characterizations of Quentin, and characterizations of Shreve (including the fact that Shreve's last name is McCannon in *The Sound and the Fury*, but in the appendix to *Absalom, Absalom!* his last name is MacKenzie) argue against reading these as the same two characters in each novel, Faulkner's retelling of stories throughout his career argues that we should read these two works together. In a *Paris Review* interview, Faulkner said, "He [the artist] must never be satisfied with what he does. It never is as good as it can be done. Always dream and shoot higher than you know you can do" (Holmes 11). Faulkner describes his approach to the story he tells in *The Sound and the Fury* in this way. He felt he had not gotten it right the first time, so he told the story again, and again, and again, each time from a different perspective. We see the same pattern in *Absalom, Absalom!* as each character adds to and revises the tale that is told to him. Given Faulkner's philosophy about rewriting and retelling tales and the fact that he practices it in each of these novels independently, it is no stretch to read *Absalom, Absalom!* as a type of prequel to *The Sound and the Fury* in which the author goes back in time to supply the background that may shed more light on the tale of Quentin Compson. The fact that Faulkner described Yoknapatawpha County, where these two and other major novels are set, as his own postage stamp of soil, further suggests that we should view this community and its inhabitants, across time and across the covers of books, as a whole.

7. According to De La Torre, in the eighteenth and nineteenth centuries, "Cuba's African population also was categorized as feminine.... Until emancipation, the plantation ratio of males to females" ranged from 2:1 to 4:1. "Usually, black women lived in the cities and towns. Hence, slave quarters, known as *barracónes*, consisted solely of men, creating the reputation of their non-*macho* roles. Skewed sex ratios made black males the targets of the white master who as *bugarrones* could rape them" (220–21). Often these acts were committed by men who considered themselves to be heterosexual.

8. As Jay Watson points out, "[T]he 'thrust' of spoken language itself ... further eroticizes this marriage." Watson explains that speaking is "an act of penetrating-with-the-word" and hearing is a matter of "being-penetrated-by-the-word."

9. Two females, Judith and Miss Rosa, also tell the story. Their narration is one-directional, instead of collaborative, as it is with the men, and the women's telling does not lessen, in fact may increase, their social isolation.

10. Dyer points out the many associations of whiteness with absence or death in Western art and letters. Around 1910, incidentally about the same time *Absalom, Absalom!* is set, the term "white death" referred to tuberculosis, accounts of which often referred to the "sublime pallor" of the victim with an implication of longing (*White* 209). Dyer's assertion that "the purity of whiteness may simply be the absence of being" (80) resonates with Quentin's eventual suicide at the end of his first year at Harvard.

11. I am indebted to Jay Watson for pointing out this connection.

12. Duvall notes a similar form of homosexual panic in *Light in August*. Percy Grimm conflates passing for white and passing for straight when he accuses Reverend Hightower of taking down his pants for Joe Christmas, and he removes Joe as a sexual threat by castrating him: "The 'black blood' that flows from Christmas's hips and loins is metaphorically and metonymically menstrual blood; Joe bleeds where women (and only women) bleed" (64). Also significant is the fact that the fire that destroys Henry, Clytie, and the remains of the Sutpen mansion begins in the mansion's closet.

13. In chapter 8, Faulkner has Shreve retell Quentin's account of visiting Sutpen's Hundred with Miss Rosa. Just as Quentin is about to climb the stairs, the narrative shifts without transition (280) into an imagined re-creation of the scene in which Thomas Sutpen tells Henry of Bon's Negro blood. The novel's structure suggests that Quentin learns of this conversation when he talks with Henry that night at the top of the stairs in Sutpen's Hundred.

14. According to the *Oxford English Dictionary*, in the mid-nineteenth century and beyond, the word "butt" was used to mean both "the thicker end" of a tool or weapon and a buttock. Faulkner may have included these double entendres consciously or unconsciously.

15. Hedges's homoerotic interpretation of the ending of Melville's *Billy Budd* seems relevant to explain Quentin's panic. According to Hedges, Budd's fate "highlights the links between homophobia and Jim Crow: a white man who is too visible, undisciplined, or colorful can almost at any time and regardless of his intentions become a white man lynched" (240). Such was the fate of Faulkner characters Bon and Christmas, and Quentin may fear the same fate for himself.

"A Strange Nigger": Faulkner and the Minstrel Performance of Whiteness
—John N. Duvall

1. Despite Gubar's attempts to work dialectically (at least to the extent that she often articulates what is progressive and what problematic in the excursions of cultural producers into racial impersonation), in the last instance her recurring conclusion is that black impersonations of whiteness are, if not always politically useful, at least justifiable, while white impersonations of blackness are inevitably gestures of bad faith. Her conclusion regarding John Howard Griffith's courageous *Black Like Me* is typical: "even the most highminded, idealistic motivations will not save white impersonators of blackness from violating, appropriating, or compromising black subjectivity in a way that will inevitably rebound against the ethical integrity of whites" (36).

2. Johnson, writing from the recognition that his own declared homosexuality may problematize his authority to write about blackness, much as certain African American critics from the 1960s marginalized James Baldwin, nevertheless takes on a number of striking instances of black performance, including a white, largely atheistic Australian choir that sings only gospel music.

3. Judith Sensibar places Faulkner's use of Pierrot in the context of other modernist uses of this figure and sees Pierrot speaking to Faulkner's own fragmented sense of self (xvi–xix).

4. My thinking here grows out of Weinstein's discussion of property, propriety, and the proper in relation to southern honorifics (*What Else* 87–97). For a fuller consideration of the way Ike becomes culturally black, see my essay "Was Ike Black?"

5. In "Why are you so black?" I consider more fully how Faulkner may have been responding to specific passages from Ellis's *Sexual Inversion*.

6. The most notable exception was the limited success of Arkansas's Southern Tenant Farmers Union in the 1930s. For a brief history of this union, see Egerton 154–58. For a reading that historicizes "Barn Burning" through the work of the STFU, see Lessig 82–96.

7. In his desire to own a gun, Dave's sense of the politics of racial identity is better than he knows. As Theodore W. Allen argues, gun ownership has been one of the constitutive structures of whiteness. Instantiated by a series of skin-privileging laws during the colonial period, gun ownership became one of the key guarantors of white identity. Every bit as much as voting rights, gun ownership was denied African Americans (2: 177–200). Dave's urge to own a gun (very like gun ownership among poor whites) is an urge to put on whiteface inasmuch as it challenges one of the defining material privileges of whiteness, a privilege that poor whites still call on to shore up their marginal whiteness. My thanks to Jay Watson for pointing out Allen's legal research and suggesting its implications to Wright's story.

8. Lessig concurs largely with Godden regarding Abner Snopes's relation to blackness, though he challenges Godden's claim that Abner's racism means that he fails to achieve full class consciousness (92).

9. For Lessig, the story "undermines the racial identity of the Snopes while asserting de Spain's claim to true 'whiteness'" (93). My reading of figurative blackness surrounding Abner and Sarty complements this claim, which Lessig develops more from historical context.

10. For a full account of the circumstances surrounding Faulkner's letter, as well as the full text of the letter, see McMillen and Polk.

Moonshine and Magnolias: *The Story of Temple Drake* and *The Birth of a Nation*
—Deborah E. Barker

1. In 1933, the furor over the release of *The Story of Temple Drake* helped to strengthen the Production Code—Hollywood's self-imposed code of censorship—and its enforcement under Joe Breen, who, in turn, prevented the movie's rerelease. The film was not shown again until 1958. It is still associated with the pre-Code period and was shown in 1999 as part of a pre-Code film festival. As recently as July 2005 it was shown in New York at the Film Forum.

2. Ramsey discusses the advertisements of *The Story of Temple Drake* that prominently link Faulkner's name to the film and even directly connect the film to *Sanctuary* despite Breen's order not to use the name of the novel (20).

3. As Bernardi explains, "Griffith's articulations of style and of race are involved in the same cinematic and discursive processes; pragmatically, they co-constitute the filmmaker's narrative system" ("Voice" 104).

4. As is true of his innovations in cinematic structure—Griffith did not invent the new techniques but he combined them in innovative ways—his *The Birth of a Nation* was not the first film to associate itself with "Art" in order to appeal to a white middle-class audience, but it was able to capitalize on the cinematic move to respectability in a way that captured the attention of the American public, both black and white. Many white Americans chose to see *The Birth of a Nation* as an unproblematic representation of the historical truth of white superiority; the National Association for the Advancement of Colored People (NAACP) and the black press, however, condemned the film for its racism and sought to prevent it from being shown. For an extensive discussion of the black press's response to the novel, play, and film, see Everett 59–106.

5. As Hall argues, the implied punishment for those who violate the taboos include white southern women (333–40). "A woman who had just been raped, or who had been apprehended in a clandestine interracial affair, or whose male relatives were pretending that she had been raped, stood on display before the whole community. Here was the quintessential Woman as victim: polluted, 'ruined for life,' the object of fantasy and secret contempt" (335).

6. Thomas Reid, an important Scottish realist philosopher, maintained that outward beauty is a sign of the goodness of the mind (Martin 42).

7. Before *The Birth of a Nation*, *The Leopard's Spots* and *The Clansman* were converted by Dixon into a successful play, which included the conflation of Flora and Marion. The scene in the cellar and the chase sequence with Gus, Flora, and Ben are Griffith's additions. This type of scene is very characteristic of Griffith's style; he often created a sense of the home, typically a place of security, as a claustrophobic scene of entrapment with crosscuts to the danger that confronts the home, in this case the black troops.

8. At the war's end many southern states established Black Codes, which required African Americans to have written proof of employment and prevented anyone from offering work to an African American already under contract (Foner 198–99). The Black Codes were abolished under Radical Reconstruction, but the end of Reconstruction brought back laws, especially vagrancy laws and "antienticement" laws, which were enforced primarily to control black labor (Foner 587–98).

9. Historian Arthur S. Link asserts that the cotton crisis of 1914–1915 "left deep scars upon the South and a residue of intense anti-British sentiment," making "the South one of the chief centers of resistance to military and naval expansion and to strong diplomacy vis-à-vis Germany between 1915 and 1917" (qtd. in Grantham 75). As late as 1917 one Texas congressman declared that Great Britain has "killed the cotton market of the South, robbed the Southland of nearly $400,000,000 [and] bought our cotton on a dead market at 5 and 6 cents a pound" (qtd. in Grantham 75–76).

10. A pound of cotton, which sold for eighteen cents in 1929, cost less than six cents by 1933 (Wolters 9).

11. Joel Williamson in *The Crucible of Race* maintains that by "the 1930s the depoliticalization and segregation of blacks in the South was virtually complete. [T]he white electorate, itself greatly reduced, was super-satisfied with its world. The exclusion of blacks from politics was not even thought about; it was accepted simply as the natural order of things" (248).

12. See Ayers 55–80.

13. Later, when Temple does express sexual desire for Red, she is portrayed as desperate and driven, not as a woman in control of her own sexuality (238–39).

14. F. Scott Fitzgerald's *The Great Gatsby* (1925) highlights the role of cars as showy symbols of money and bootlegged gin as the source of Gatsby's wealth.

15. Many critics have also been rather hard on Temple and seem to accept Ruby's characterization. Seidel suggests that Temple's hysterical reactions at the plantation reflect a narcissistic attempt to attract attention to herself at all costs (106).

16. In the press book ad, Ruby's lines are accompanied by the image of Trigger leaning over a worried-looking Temple, giving the impression that these are Trigger's words and further insinuating that the rape is a form of punishment for Temple's behavior as an upper-class tease.

17. For a discussion of the technological and aesthetic emphasis on whiteness in the development of photography and film, see Dyer, *White*. Dyer analyzes the way light has been used to reinforce the connection between whiteness and purity, especially regarding white female actresses, who are typically made to "glow from within," and who, in

heterosexual pairings, seem to "illuminate" the darker (yet still white) male (*White* 122–42). In applying these uses of light to *The Birth of a Nation,* Dyer shows how this contrast is heightened in the filming of white women and nonwhite men, who bleed into the shadows. This effect is created (unlike much of the film which is shot in natural light) through the use of a bright overhead light, "the epitome of the northern light so prized by Hollywood," causing Dyer to conclude that the film "betrays a feeling that the South is, after all, not quite white enough to give birth to the new nation" ("Into" 175).

18. The image of a cat would later be employed in *The Women* (1939) to condemn gossipers who threaten the marriage of the "good woman," but in the case of *The Women* there is a clear distinction between the meddling women (who also get their comeuppance) and the good woman, who gets her husband back.

19. Earlier in *The Sound and the Fury* (1929), Faulkner explicitly racializes the "wanton" belle, Caddy. Even though Caddy is still living at home, her promiscuous behavior threatens the reputation of the Compson family. Quentin thinks of this in racial terms as he asks, "*Why wont you bring him to the house, Caddy? Why must you do like nigger women do in the pasture the ditch the dark woods hot hidden furious in the dark woods*" (92). Caddy's desires can never be totally controlled by her brothers, despite their attempts to limit and contain her. Temple's father and brothers seem to do just that in the final courtroom scene in which they encircle the cringing Temple and she disappears as they walk as a unit out of the courtroom. Thanks to Jay Watson for pointing out the connection between Caddy and Temple.

20. Ramsey persuasively argues that Temple's bad side is an allusion to bisexuality that was also linked to rumors about Miriam Hopkins, but this does not seem to explain the "bad streak" in the Drakes, as homosexuality was not necessarily thought to be inherited (26).

21. For a recent discussion of Popeye's ambiguous racial representation, see Guttman 15–34.

22. J. W. Williamson traces the hillbilly back to George Washington Harris's character Sut Lovingood: "a tall lanky east Tennessee ridgerunner ... short on manners, intimate with dirt and ignorant of 'progress'" (33). The hillbilly according to Williamson "gives the horse-laugh to middle-class respectability. He's absurdly and delightfully free" (4). "He drinks hard liquor.... He's theatrically lazy but remains virile. He nearly always possesses the wherewithal for physical violence—especially involving dogs and guns.... He reminds us symbolically of filth, of disgusting bodily functions. Why else is he so frequently pictured with outhouses?" (*Hillbillyland* 2–3).

23. See Blotner 234–35; and Arnold and Trouard 5–6.

24. Mark Twain, in *Adventures of Huckleberry Finn*, divorces the issue of lynching from the issue of race and rape by depicting a white mob that goes after a white man, Colonel Sherburn, for killing another white man, Old Boggs. Furthermore, he has Colonel Sherburn belittle the mob as a bunch of cowards with only "half a man" as a leader. Almost fifty years later Faulkner, too, ostensibly takes race out of the equation, by setting the crime in an all-white context, but leaves in the rape of the belle.

25. For a discussion of the role of the "cracker" as both a source of contaminated whiteness and racial intolerance, see A. Graham 12–17.

26. The mass media, including the tabloids and the movies, helped to promote the image of the glamorized gangster (Rosow 113–18).

27. By 1933 the Depression had hit the movie industry as well, and Paramount, which helped to establish the gangster genre and produce *The Story of Temple Drake*, was bankrupt (Rosow 146).

28. Skal maintains that the European setting was a thinly veiled America, but *The Story of Temple Drake* brings the horror film directly to America (37–61).

29. The image of Trigger as a dark, menacing monster is captured in the press book ad which features a shot of Temple, with hands over her mouth in horror, and an oversized shot of Trigger's eyes (lit from below to cast ominous shadows) looming over Temple's shoulder.

30. For a discussion of the importance of staircases in German Expressionist films, see Eisner 131.

31. Though Universal Studios pioneered the horror film in the 1930s with its release of *Frankenstein* and *Dracula*, Paramount, which produced *The Story of Temple Drake*, responded with its own horror hit, *Dr. Jekyll and Mr. Hyde*, on which Struss was the cinematographer.

32. In shooting *The Story of Temple Drake*, Struss explained, "For night scenes I wanted enough underlying lights to get something on the film, because I didn't believe in pale gray for night. I wanted blacks with detail, highlights. If I got highlights, I could get blacks.... [T]here have been different schools of thought, different cinematographers have used little light, but then they got grays and mushy black—they were not black, they were not night, and they had no detail in them. I just didn't like to work that way" (qtd. in Harvith 17).

33. I would like to thank Judith L. Sensibar for alerting me to the reference to Mex in the storyboard. For an image of the storyboards, see James Watson, "Carve" 31.

34. Stephen Benbow in many ways lives up to Horace Benbow's potential as he is introduced in *Flags in the Dust*. As Jay Watson explains, "As a veteran, an aesthete, a southerner aristocrat, and an attorney, however, Horace represents the potential for a rare point of contact between old ways and new, antique certainties and contemporary indeterminacies. Horace's thorough grounding in the tenets and postures of modernity insures his skepticism and self-consciousness, yet his vocation demands commitment and selflessness. Horace should be the happiest of hybrids in *Flags in the Dust*: a modern man who, thanks to the rhetorical and ethical imperatives of his calling, manages to avoid the threat of solipsism" (*Forensic Fictions* 44).

35. In the novel, Gowan not only cannot protect Temple; his shame leads him to leave without her the next morning because he is afraid to face her: "[w]rithing inside his disreputable and bloody clothes in an agony of rage and shame," because he "passed out twice," Gowan imagines "the whispering eyes" in town until "the prospect of facing Temple again was more than he could bear" (85). Had he come to her aid, even at this late date, he would still have saved Temple from being raped.

36. Temple, in her innocence, assumes that being a man will protect her from rape, a belief that Faulkner undercuts in the lynching scene. In reference to the lynching, one of the men in the mob says, "we never used a cob. We made him wish we had used a cob" (296), implying that Goodwin, like Temple, was violated before his death, the manner in which is left to the reader's imagination.

37. The moment in the novel when Benbow most identifies with Temple as rape victim is directly linked to his own incestuous desire for his stepdaughter, Little Belle. As Sabine Sielke maintains, "[W]e repeatedly find Benbow in one particular position: bent over a watery surface or looking directly into a mirror from which the object of his incestuous desire stares back at him" (99).

38. Even though Narcissa is a respectable widow in *Sanctuary*, she still holds onto her status as a flirtatious and innocent belle, dating young men, but refusing to marry, even wearing "her customary white dress," a symbol of the belle (25).

39. Elsie's role as northern belle is suggested in Ben's first "encounter" with her and positively associates her with cotton, the flower of the South. Before the war, Phil has come from the North to visit his old friend. As they stand in the middle of the cotton field, Ben plucks a white flower and, as he gives it to Phil, he notices the picture of Elsie in a miniature frame. Ben completes the "exchange of women" by giving Phil the flower (which Phil gives to Margaret as a token of love) for the photo. As Phil attempts to take the photograph back, Ben shakes his head and puts the frame in his breast pocket and walks out of the shot to look at Elsie in "private." The intertitle reads, "He finds the ideal of his dream in the picture of Elsie Stoneman, his friend's sister, whom he has never seen." As Ben starts to open the picture, Flora, in the background, walks out of the shot. Flora is not the flower being exchanged in this scene; she is replaced with the image of Elsie. An insert shot of the photo shows Elsie in a series of frames: the close-up of Elsie is framed by an iris shot, then the white border on the frame, the frame itself, and within the photo, Elsie's white tulle veil frames her face and she looks off camera in a dreamy and sentimental pose. Ben, the southern soldier, takes the photo into battle with him.

Inside and Outside Southern Whiteness: Film Viewing, the Frame, and the Racing of Space in Yoknapatawpha
—Peter Lurie

1. See Matthews, "*As I Lay Dying*," for a similar focus on the novel's emphasis on elements of modernity such as consumerism and commercial exchange.

2. O'Donnell sees this ending in rather stark terms. He uses Deleuze and Guattari's notions of the state to suggest that "in this novel Faulkner sacrifices psychological depth (embodied by Darl) to a comprehension of the family as a commodified entity that works [...] according to the law, within the confines of the State and its striations, its systems of communication and exchange" (93).

3. Bruce Kawin was the first Faulkner critic to note this particular strategy and its affinities with what he termed the modernist "crisis" and, specifically, with *As I Lay Dying* ("Montage" 106, 124–25). More recently, Susan McCabe makes a similar point in *Cinematic Modernism*. She connects post–World War I sufferers of psychic and physical trauma to the "dismemberment" of montage, one that is equally apposite to *As I Lay Dying*'s formal and familial disjunctions.

4. See Dyer, *White*, as well as "Into the Light."

5. See Gunning and also Ray, who describes early film's capitulation to a bourgeois "taste for the *representational*" constraints of narrative realism (125).

6. As May describes, in 1912 "[l]aborers still comprised 70 percent of the ... [movie] audience; but 20 percent were now clerical workers and 5 percent were respectable bourgeois men and women. Without losing the original audience of immigrants ... the Protestant filmmakers and censors ... had created a medium that cut across class, sex, and (political) party lines" (30–31).

7. As Rogin puts it, "The rapid transformation of the North after the Civil War ... generated compensatory celebrations of the antebellum South. At the same time, the massive influx of immigrants from southern and eastern Europe ... created Northern sympathy for Southern efforts to control an indispensible but [supposedly] inferior work force" ("Sword" 253). Cf. Michaels, particularly his discussion of 1920s patterns of thought about ethnicity, "the family," and nationhood.

8. In his memoir *The Falkners of Mississippi*, Faulkner's brother Murry indicated that as young men he and William went to the movies in Oxford as often as they could, generally once or twice a week (Falkner 49–51).

9. See Kasson, *Amusing the Million*, for an account of how Coney Island and other amusement parks offered opportunities for class (but not racial) mixing and "refabrication."

10. Rogin quotes Ralph Ellison from *Invisible Man* on the notion of a kind of national, racial "masquerade" in a country made of up of "former colonials and immigrants: The Declaration of an American identity meant the taking on of a mask" (*Blackface* 49). See also Doane and her discussion of *Birth of a Nation*. "Blackness is a costume which is worn or removed at will by whites [through blackface], while whiteness in its symbolic dimension (the white robes of the Ku Klux Klan) is also a form of masquerade which conceals an identity" (229).

11. See Matthews, "Shortened Stories," for an account of Faulkner's "retailing" of various narrative elements in connection with his modernism and so-called "art fiction."

12. See also Hale and her deeply considered analysis of the spectacular and public nature of lynching, which includes important attention to the sexual dynamics of power and display involved in the practice of lynching. As she succinctly puts it, "No one is ever more white than the members of a lynch mob" (367 n55).

13. As is often recognized, *Light in August* in particular shows Faulkner's awareness of Jefferson as a community and its felt presence in characters' lives. The town is named more often than in Faulkner's other major novels. And Faulkner's frequent references to what its inhabitants "knew," "believed," or felt, particularly in those sections dealing with Hightower

(e.g., "the town was sorry for being glad, as people sometimes are for those whom they have at last forced to do as they wanted them to" [70]), treat Jefferson as nearly a character in its own right.

14. As Shawn Michelle Smith and others have shown, the same "Fair Day" atmosphere attended southern lynchings. She notes that six thousand white Georgians "attended" the lynching of "Sam Hose" (Samuel Wilkes) in Newnan, Georgia, on April 23, 1899, with many travelling to the site on trains with specific reservations for "the event" (113). See also Hale 229.

15. Horkheimer and Adorno imply a similar homology in their famous essay "The Culture Industry," written with the specter of European fascism in mind—specifically, the Third Reich's use of film and mass spectacle (and films *of* mass spectacle) to mobilize its following with pictures like Leni Riefenstahl's *Triumph of the Will*.

16. That "civilizing" and modernizing process is like the one at work in the Bundrens' trip to Jefferson. Becoming part of a national culture through their moves northward and into metropolitan and civic life, the Bundrens lose parts of their more specifically regional otherness (as figured, O'Donnell suggests, in their "sacrifice" of Darl). In the context of mass cultural depictions of immigration, Lauren Berlant similarly discusses the kinds of transformations demanded of national identity. Referring to "what happens to the immigrant's sensuous body in the process of" naturalizing, she writes "that to be an American citizen is to be anesthetized, complacent, unimaginative" (*The Queen* 198–99).

17. Many critics have noted this nation-region conjunction and its reliance on whiteness. In addition to Jackson, see Doane 229, Michaels 7–9, Hale 281–96 (and especially 281–83), and Duck. Grimm's "national" whiteness prevails through this section of the novel, that is, despite the remark by Jefferson's commander of the local Post of the American Legion that Christmas "'is Jefferson's trouble, not Washington's'" (454).

18. See Dyer's comments about the film's reliance on what he calls "North lighting," a visual technique he claims Griffith borrowed from European portrait painters like Rembrandt and Vermeer ("Into the Light" 171–73). See also Taylor. Taylor sees *Birth*'s long critical history as marked by an eliding of the film's ideological (and racist) content by its aesthetic aspects, a process that Taylor claims is foundational in film studies as a discipline (15–16).

19. We might then consider the physical or material as well as "metaphysical" aspects of cinematic light here. Particularly in the context of the segregated southern cinemas, the moviehouse becomes a kind of "storehouse of light," a social institution that constitutes whiteness by its dual operations of "dispensing" light, with its connotations of a spiritual, "pure" whiteness, and of constructing white subjectivity in and through the theater space. I am thankful to Jay Watson for offering this suggestion.

20. While Faulkner's biographers do not refer to his having seen this film, it is hard to imagine that he missed it, either in its initial run in 1915, when Faulkner was eighteen and already an avid moviegoer, or when it was rereleased in 1930, in the midst of Faulkner's most important period of writing. Without offering sources for the assertion, Bruce Kawin maintains that Faulkner not only had seen *Birth* but admired it (*Faulkner and Film* 72, 125).

21. Dyer's work in particular, which stresses the deathliness of whiteness and points to the Klan's role and depiction in *Birth* as death-delivering in conjunction with the cinematic elements of lighting, composition, and editing rhythms, offers a striking critique of the cinema's racial workings, its fashioning of an "interior" space defined as white (*White* 209). As one example of such an editing technique and its effects on viewers, Griffith's crosscutting toward the end of the film between shots of a white frontier family under siege by "unruly" freed blacks and the "heroic" Klan riding to their rescue enacts a powerful affect, as viewers are drawn into the screen and narrative space and, as Griffith accelerates his cutting, "spirited" into an enthrallment with the rescue. A similar process of viewer recruitment occurs, as we have seen, in lynching photos and in "Dry September." Jackson refers to the emergency narrative in terms that seem borrowed from Griffith's highly dynamic formalism. "The narration of the Nationally Guarded event takes place within a peculiar temporal structure, one that builds with an alarmingly steady momentum and which speeds forward by moments of panic and violence" (193).

22. As Metz writes, "[T]he cinema, 'more perceptual' than certain arts according to the list of its sensory registers, is also 'less perceptual' than others once the status of these perceptions is envisaged . . . ; for its perceptions are all in a sense 'false.' Or rather, the activity of perception which [film] involves is real (the cinema is not a phantasy), but the perceived is not really the object, it is its shade, its phantom, its double, its replica in a new kind of mirror" (44–45).

23. Consider Metz's remarks about the "credulous" film spectator, which have particular relevance to southern "credulity" about whiteness: "behind any fiction there is a second fiction: the diegetic events are fictional, that is the first; but everyone pretends to believe that they are true, and that is the second; there is even a third: the general refusal to admit that somewhere in oneself one believes they genuinely are true" (72). It is this "truth" about whiteness (and blackness) that many film audiences and southerners "credulously" believed.

24. As Hale puts it, "These 'lynching carnivals' . . . were . . . about strengthening the culture of segregation, creating a new southern future in which an expanding consumer culture created and maintained rather than blurred or transformed racial difference" (229).

25. Patricia McKee has written insightfully about the optics and politics of whiteness in Faulkner and in U.S. social reality generally. "The power of whiteness is not visible," she points out. "Whiteness . . . maintains the properties of media productivity without maintaining properties of physical objects. . . . This removal from the realm of the visible . . . has been crucial to whites' domination of visuality in Western culture" (11). I will return to the specific ways Faulkner restores to whiteness the "properties of physical objects."

26. As Rogin points out, in ruling on whether to uphold protests against *Birth*'s screening, "The National Board of Review . . . applauded *Birth*, not on free-speech grounds but because of its [supposed] historical accuracy and educational value. . . . Censors found truthful and educational the suggestions of black sexual violence . . . but they wanted to bury the (more accurate) representations of white racist speech and action" ("Sword" 277).

White Disavowal, Black Enfranchisement, and the Homoerotic in William Faulkner's *Light in August*
—Aliyyah I. Abdur-Rahman

1. See Eng for a thoughtful account of Sigmund Freud's theories linking notions of cultural primitivism and ideas about the white psyche.

2. Some prominent twentieth-century African American authors have made this point. See, for example, James Baldwin's essays in *The Price of the Ticket*, especially "Many Thousands Gone" and "In Search of a Majority." See also Morrison for a discussion of prominent twentieth-century novelists who use tropes of racial blackness to substantiate the development of white characters.

3. For more on the ways in which the failure to extend patriarchal recognition to black men has hampered their masculine development, see Harper and Ferguson.

4. Much has been written about whiteness, its self-characterization as universal and "race-free"—specific only in terms of its cultural and racial dominance over all raced "others." A crucial component of the character of whiteness is its reliance on serviceable raced "others" whose particularity enables its "race-less" emergence and prominence. For more on this, especially its manifestation in American literature, see Morrison.

5. To explore this point further, see Ginsburg.

6. For a groundbreaking, in-depth discussion of this point, see Somerville.

7. I want to add two things: first, sexual criminality encompasses all outlaw sexual practices, including interracial sex, rape, incest, and homosexuality. Second, I do mean to posit a rigid distinction between black service to and sexual engagement with white people. As we know from black women's plight as domestic workers in much of the twentieth century, black labor in white homes and white establishments often included sexual service to white employers.

8. Before the sheriff knows about Christmas, Brown is the main suspect in the killing of Joanna Burden. Brown discloses Christmas's putative black racial origins to divert suspicion from himself—"'That's right,' he says. . . . 'Accuse the white man and let the nigger go free'" (97). To gain the social advantage over Christmas, Brown also announces his whiteness, thereby securing it and summoning the authority conferred by it.

9. John Duvall elucidates the homoeroticism and the homosexual panic that subtend Joe Christmas's murder and dismemberment. He writes, "A clear portrait of homosexual panic emerges . . . in Grimm's killing and castration of Joe Christmas. . . . But a homoerotic subtext is also at play in this moment" (62).

10. For more on the representation of the black eunuch as the comforting diminishment of black masculine prowess and authority, see Gubar 169–202.

11. I should add that this is attributable in part to the perceived failure of white southern manhood, evidenced, first and foremost, by southern white men's defeat in the Civil War and, finally, in the decline of the agricultural plantation system upon which both their identities and their wealth depended.

American Emergencies: Whiteness, the National Guard, and *Light in August*
—*Chuck Jackson*

1. By "classic Gothic," I mean a tale of terror designed to thrill its reader with its representations of evil, shadows, and fear. See Fiedler's description of the early-American Gothic as a literature replete with "images of alienation, flight, and abysmal fear" (143). Toni Morrison explains racial fetishization as a narrative technique by which the author "evok[es] erotic fears or desires and establish[es] fixed or major difference where difference does not exist or is minimal. Blood, for example, is a pervasive fetish: black blood, white blood, the purity of blood; the purity of white female sexuality, the pollution of African blood and sex. Fetishization is a strategy often used to assert the categorical absolutism of civilization and savagery" (68).

2. Harry Levin and Fiedler, as well as the more recent work of Teresa Goddu, name Charles Brockden Brown, Edgar Allan Poe, Nathaniel Hawthorne, Herman Melville, among others, as classic American Gothic writers. For a reevaluation of how Gothic blackness and whiteness must be understood in racial terms, in particularly in terms of the haunting of early-American literature by slavery, see Goddu and Morrison.

3. For more on the representation of whiteness as terrorizing, see hooks and McLaren.

4. See Wiegman and Stokes for an important critical articulation of the academic rise of whiteness studies in the U.S. academy.

5. My understanding of white, abstract personhood comes directly from Lauren Berlant's by now familiar argument about the national body and white male privilege: "[W]hite male privilege has been veiled by the rhetoric of the bodiless citizen, the generic 'person' whose political identity is *a priori* precisely because it is, in theory, non-corporeal" ("National Brands" 112).

6. For a full history of the transformation of local American militias into the National Guard, see Cooper. See also the U.S. Advisory 7–12.

7. On the working-class status of National Guardsmen, see Cooper 151. I racialize early formations of the National Guard as "white" to stress how Jim Crow laws prevented African Americans from fully achieving National Guardsman status. Lt. Col. (Ret.) Michael Lee Lanning explains how, just as black soldiers were segregated from whites in the formation of troops for battle during World War I: "Blacks also realized fewer opportunities to serve in the state militia—now known as the National Guard. Both the military and the state governments defined the Militia Act of 1903 as limiting federal control of the National Guard. All agreed that the racial composition of the National Guard remained a state prerogative and, as a result, many state units no longer accepted blacks. By the time the United States entered WWI in 1917, the National Guard contained only five thousand African American men, less than three percent of its total.... No black unit or black man served in the National Guard of any of the Deep South states" (102). Lanning describes the absence of African American National Guardsmen during the 1930s in a similar way: "All thirty of the National Guard regiments that formed its sixteen authorized divisions were all white.... By 1939 blacks totaled only about 2 percent of the strength of the Regular Army

and National Guard" (157). On the "purging" of black men from southern state National Guards during the first decade of the twentieth century, see Cooper 137.

8. Richard Wright's novel *Native Son* might also be thought of as a national emergency narrative, with its representation of the National Guard protecting the prison that houses Bigger Thomas from white mobs who scream for his lynching. Wright's posthumously published novel, *Lawd Today!* (written in the 1930s, but published in the 1960s), features a character, Al, who is an African American member of the National Guard. *Lawd Today!* follows its main character, Jake Jackson, and three of his buddies, Bob, Al, and Slim, all of whom are postal workers who drink, talk, play cards, chase women, and get into fights. Al, the National Guardsman, has the largest body of the four men, weighing in at "two hundred and fifty pounds" (76). See also *Native Son* 367, 377, 381, 383, and 405.

9. Joe Christmas's "black" body is actually "parchmentcolored" (120).

10. One notable exception is James Gibson's analysis of the culture of violence and contemporary U.S. masculinity. For more on how militarism finds its way into men's recreation and leisure activities, see Gibson.

11. See, in particular, Donovan and Dieges, as well as the U.S. Militia Bureau, *Questions* and *National*.

12. Stacey was *not* a National Guardsman, but rather a captain in the regular army, a U.S. infantry inspector and instructor. As he puts it in his introduction, "I know the trials and tribulations of the National Guard captains as well as if I had been one myself" (4). An uncanny identification with the National Guard identity is what makes this captain the authority on, and the author of, National Guardsmen training.

13. As hawkishly as National Guardsmen are asked to watch their kitchens, so, too, must the reader keep a close eye on kitchens and the kitchenesque in *Light in August*. The novel begins the story of Christmas with his vomiting of toothpaste in the dietician's closet (122); he trashes the food Mrs. McEachern brings him after his beating, then eats it in the corner of his room "with his hands ... like a savage, like a dog" (155); at eighteen, he begins a relationship with the waitress Bobbie Allen at the diner's kitchen lunch counter (179); in his thirties, he breaks into the Burden house through an open window leading to the kitchen (229); and, finally, he ends up shot and then mutilated with a butcher knife by Percy Grimm on the floor of Reverend Hightower's kitchen (464). Like the instructions that train the National Guard, this series of beginnings set in kitchens also act as scenes of discipline for Christmas; however, unlike the bodies of trained citizen-soldiers, Christmas's unruly body ends up, in all cases, unable to swallow the rules of others.

14. My reading of "America" stems from Wiegman's analysis of "the story of America" as "that infinitely rhetorical figure that secures itself through multiple historicizing narratives of geopolitical destiny and chosen peoples," a "mythological text that functions to weld disparities together" (115). This mythological text "offers the singularity of identity as its triumphant resolution, a resolution that incorporates the fragmented excesses of social scripting into a narrative of continuity and unification [where] fragmentation is transformed into fusion, and 'America' emerges as the integrating sign for a more encompassing definition" (174).

15. For a cultural analysis of the representation of the border and Pancho Villa, see Wilson 340–61.

16. With the important exception of Jay Watson's groundbreaking essay "Writing Blood," there are no critical accounts of Percy Grimm as National Guardsman (see note 22 below). Even Watson, in his earlier essay "Overdoing Masculinity in *Light in August*," posits that Joe Christmas "dies at the hands of Jefferson's gender guard," and that the hunting for and castration of Christmas "should be read as the single sustained performance of a communal gender guard seeking to police the vertiginous masculine difference of Joe Christmas" (158). In "Overdoing," Watson builds his thesis around what he calls the "gender guard" but, like all critics, does not mention the National Guard. Such a critical displacement raises two interrelated questions: Why does the National Guard resist interpretation? Why is the National Guard a trope that shuts down critical imagination about its own particularity? It is almost as if, even in its textual form, the National Guard imperceptibly enforces an interpretive order, and a fear of this order, that contains the reading of its own production as if it were a dangerous, emergent excess.

17. I hesitate to describe the Burden family's work as "antiracist" since the Burden family history is conflicted: even as they die in the name of antislavery and in the name of electoral reform, the family understands blacks to be the white man's "burden," in need of white economic and political assistance.

18. The dead body of a white woman in the South instantly conjures, in the minds of Jefferson's white inhabitants, the specter of the black rapist, so that, in addition to the slashing of her throat, the white mob "knew, believed, and hoped that she had been ravished, too: at least once before her throat was cut and at least once afterward" (288). The combination of certain murder and fantasized rape licenses the town's white inhabitants to find a racialized scapegoat, thus rendering all black men suspects (291).

19. The novel introduces Christmas as a "foreigner" at the planing mill, where the workers are distressed about Christmas's appearance: "something definitely rootless about him, as though no town nor city was his, no street, no walls, no square of earth his home" (31). When the workers find out his name is Christmas, they add another layer of foreignness to him, differentiating "foreign" from "white": "'Did you ever hear of a white man named Christmas?' the foreman said. 'I never heard nobody a–tall named it,' the other said" (33). Later, Byron remembers that "[t]hey just thought that he was a foreigner, and as they watched him for the rest of that Friday, working in that tie and the straw hat and the creased trousers, they said among themselves that that was the way men in his country worked" (33–34).

20. Notice that Faulkner capitalizes "State" instead of "national" and "guard," a reversal of how it is usually written: state National Guard. This unusual capitalization suggests that, in this scene, the nation is being rewritten not as a representation of the nation-state, but of something more like a state-nation, a nation top-heavy with the coercive power of the State as well as a nation in which the power of localized states—like the state of Mississippi—constructs the meaning of the nation on its own terms.

21. For more on the Gothic collapse of discrete binaries, see Halberstam 23.

22. Jay Watson nimbly argues that Grimm's modern nativist ideology, which combines national and racial supremacy and pride, motivates Grimm's slide from peacekeeper to butcher ("Writing" 83). According to Watson, Grimm agrees to guard Christmas "as long as he agrees to act white, to accept the constitutional protection afforded to all whites under nativist ideology." But as soon as Christmas races out of the white hands of the law, his mobility signals his refusal of national protection, making him both un-American and therefore, in the eyes of Grimm, black and also someone against whom more and more violence must be used to reprotect the (white) nation (83). See Watson, "Writing," especially 82–84.

23. Elaine Scarry proposes that, during times of both war and peace, the body is where political learning and national identification register. From involuntary gestures like raising one's eyebrows to the dismemberment of soldiers on the battlefield, Scarry argues that what is most visible during war is "the extremity or extreme literalness with which the nation inscribes itself in the body; or . . . literalness with which the human body opens itself and allows 'the nation' to be registered there in the wound" (112). This, I would argue, is what drives Percy Grimm's actions against Joe Christmas.

WORKS CITED

Abate, Michelle Ann. "Reading Red: The Man with the (Gay) Red Tie in Faulkner's *The Sound and the Fury*." *Mississippi Quarterly* 54.3 (2001): 293–312.
Adorno, Theodor W., and Max Horkheimer. *Dialectic of Enlightenment*. 1944. New York: Continuum, 1988.
Allen, James. *Without Sanctuary: Lynching Photography in America*. Sante Fe: Twin Palm Publishers, 2000.
Allen, Robert C. "Decentering Historical Audience Studies: A Modest Proposal." *Hollywood in the Neighborhood: Historical Case Studies of Local Moviegoing*. Ed. Kathryn H. Fuller-Seeley. Berkeley: U of California P, 2008. 20–33.
———. "Relocating American Film History: The 'Problem' of the Empirical." *Cultural Studies* 20.1 (January 2006): 48–88.
Allen, Theodore. *The Invention of the White Race, Vol. 1: Racial Formation and Social Control*. New York: Verso, 1994.
———. *The Invention of the White Race, Vol. 2: The Origin of Racial Oppression in Anglo-America*. New York: Verso, 1997.
Altman, Dennis. *Homosexual: Oppression and Liberation*. New York: New York UP, 1993.
Anderson, Sherwood. *Dark Laughter*. New York: Boni, 1925.
Arnold, Edwin T., and Dawn Trouard. *Reading Faulkner: Sanctuary*. Jackson: UP of Mississippi, 1996.
Atkinson, Ted. *Faulkner and the Great Depression: Aesthetics, Ideology, and Cultural Politics*. Athens: U of Georgia P, 2006.
———. "The Impenetrable Lightness of Being: Miscegenation Imagery and the Anxiety of Whiteness in Faulkner's *Go Down, Moses*." *Faulkner and the Returns of the Text: Faulkner and Yoknapatawpha, 2008*. Ed. Annette Trefzer and Ann J. Abadie. Jackson: UP of Mississippi, forthcoming.
Ayers, Edward. *The Promise of the New South: Life After Reconstruction*. New York: Oxford UP, 1993.
Babb, Valerie. *Whiteness Visible: The Meaning of Whiteness in American Literature and Culture*. New York: New York UP, 1998.
Baldwin, James. *The Price of the Ticket: Collected Nonfiction, 1948–1985*. New York: St. Martin's, 1985.

Barkan, Elazar, and Ronald Bush, eds. *Prehistories of the Future: The Primitivist Project and the Culture of Modernism.* Stanford: Stanford UP, 1995.

Bederman, Gail. *Manliness and Civilization: A Cultural History of Gender and Race in the United States, 1880–1917.* Chicago: U of Chicago P, 1995.

Bentley, Nancy. "Slaves and Fauns: Hawthorne and the Uses of Primitivism." *ELH* 57.4 (1990): 901–37.

Berlant, Lauren. "National Brands/National Body: *Imitation of Life.*" *Comparative American Identities: Race, Sex, and Nationality in the Modern Text.* Ed. Hortense Spillers. New York: Routledge, 1991. 110–40.

———. *The Queen of America Goes to Washington City.* Durham: Duke UP, 1997.

Bernardi, Daniel, ed. *The Birth of Whiteness: Race and the Emergence of U.S. Cinema.* New Brunswick: Rutgers UP, 1996.

———. "The Voice of Whiteness: D. W. Griffith's Biograph Films (1908–1913)." Bernardi 103–28.

Bhabha, Homi K. *The Location of Culture.* New York: Routledge, 1994.

Black, Edwin. *War Against the Weak: Eugenics and America's Campaign to Create a Master Race.* New York: Four Walls Eight Windows, 2003.

Blackmer, Corinne E. "The Veils of the Law: Race and Sexuality in Nella Larsen's *Passing.*" *Racing Representation: Voice, History, Sexuality.* Ed. Kostas Myrsiades and Linda Myrsiades. New York: Rowman, 1998. 98–118.

Blotner, Joseph. *Faulkner: A Biography.* 1 vol. New York: Random House, 1984.

Breeden, James O. "States-Rights Medicine in the Old South." *Bulletin of the New York Academy of Medicine* 52 (1976): 348–72.

Brickhouse, Anna C. "'I Do Abhor an Indian Story': Hawthorne and the Allegorization of Racial 'Commixture.'" *ESQ* 42.4 (1996): 233–53.

Brister, J. G. "*Absalom, Absalom!* and the Semiotic Other." *Faulkner Journal* 22.1–2 (Fall 2006/Spring 2007): 39–53.

Brown, Calvin S. *A Glossary of Faulkner's South.* New Haven: Yale UP, 1976.

Butler, Judith. *Bodies that Matter: On the Discursive Limits of "Sex."* New York: Routledge, 1993.

Carby, Hazel V. *Reconstructing Womanhood: The Emergence of the Afro-American Woman Novelist.* Oxford: Oxford UP, 1987.

Cash, W. J. *The Mind of the South.* 1941. New York: Vintage, 1991.

Chambers, Ross. "The Unexamined." Hill, *Whiteness* 187–203.

Cohn, Deborah N. *History and Memory in the Two Souths: Recent Southern and Spanish American Fiction.* Nashville: Vanderbilt UP, 1999.

Cooper, Jerry. *The Rise of the National Guard: The Evolution of the American Militia, 1865–1920.* Lincoln: U of Nebraska P, 1997.

Crook, J. Mordaunt. *The Greek Revival: Neo-Classical Attitudes in British Architecture, 1760–1870.* London: Murray, 1972.

Davidson, Michael. "Strange Blood: Hemophobia and the Unexplored Boundaries of Queer Nation." *Beyond the Binary: Reconstructing Cultural Identity in a Multicultural Context.* Ed. Timothy B. Powell. New Brunswick: Rutgers UP, 1999. 39–60.

Davis, Angela Y. *Women, Race & Class.* New York: Random House, 1983.
Davis, Thadious. *Faulkner's "Negro": Art and the Southern Context.* Baton Rouge: Louisiana State UP, 1983.
———. *Games of Property: Law, Race, Gender, and Faulkner's* Go Down, Moses. Durham: Duke UP, 2003.
Degenfelder, E. Pauline. "The Four Faces of Temple Drake: Faulker's *Sanctuary*, *Requiem for a Nun*, and the Two Film Adaptations." *American Quarterly* 28.5 (1977): 544–60.
De La Torre, Miguel A. "Beyond Machismo." *Annual of the Society of Christian Ethics* 19 (1999): 213–33.
Deutsch, Nathaniel. *Inventing America's "Worst" Family: Eugenics, Islam, and the Fall and Rise of the Tribe of Ishmael.* Berkeley: U of California P, 2009.
Dixon, Thomas, Jr. *The Clansman.* New York: Doubleday, 1905.
———. *The Sins of the Father: A Romance of the South.* 1912. Lexington: UP of Kentucky, 2004.
Doane, Mary Ann. *Femmes Fatales: Feminism, Film Theory, Psychoanalysis.* New York: Routledge, 1991.
Donaldson, Susan V. "*Light in August*, Faulkner's Angels of History, and the Culture of Jim Crow." *Faulkner's Inheritance: Faulkner and Yoknapatawpha, 2005.* Ed. Joseph R. Urgo and Ann J. Abadie. Jackson: UP of Mississippi, 2007. 101–25.
Donovan, Liet. Col. T. F., and Capt. Charles J. Dieges. *The Home Guard Manual: Embracing the essential parts of the School of Citizen-Soldiery, Manual of Arms, and that portion of the Field Regulation relating to Military Police.* New York: Sherwood, 1917.
Doyle, Don. *Faulkner's County: The Historical Roots of Yoknapatawpha.* Chapel Hill: U of North Carolina P, 2001.
Doyle, Laura. "The Body Against Itself in Faulkner's Phenomenology of Race." *American Literature* 73.2 (2001): 339–64.
Duck, Leigh Anne. *The Nation's Region: Southern Modernism, Segregation, and U.S. Nationalism.* Athens: U of Georgia P, 2006.
Dugdale, Richard L. "Hereditary Pauperism as Illustrated in the 'Juke' Family." 1877. *White Trash: The Eugenic Family Studies, 1877–1919.* Ed. Nicole Hahn Rafter. Boston: Northeastern UP, 1988. 35–47.
Duvall, John N. "Faulkner's Crying Game: Male Homosexual Panic." *Faulkner and Gender: Faulkner and Yoknapatawpha, 1994.* Ed. Donald M. Kartiganer and Ann J. Abadie. Jackson: UP of Mississippi, 1996. 48–72.
———. *Faulkner's Marginal Couple: Invisible, Outlaw, and Unspeakable Communities.* Austin: U of Texas P, 1990.
———. "Was Ike Black? Avuncular Racechange in *Go Down, Moses*." *Misrecognition, Race, and the Real in Faulkner's Fiction.* Ed. Michael Zeitlin, et al. Etudes Faulknériennes 4. Rennes, France: Presses Universitaires de Rennes, 2004. 39–51.
———. "'Why are you so black?' Faulkner's Whiteface Minstrels, Primitivism, and Perversion." *A Companion to William Faulkner.* Ed. Richard C. Moreland. Malden, MA: Blackwell Publishing, 2007. 148–64.
Dyer, Richard. *The Culture of Queers.* New York: Routledge, 2002.

———. "Into the Light: The Whiteness of the South in *The Birth of a Nation*." King and Taylor 165–76.

———. *White*. New York: Routledge, 1997.

East, Edward M. *Heredity in Human Affairs*. 1927. New York: Charles Scribner's Sons, 1935.

Egerton, John. *Speak Now Against the Day: The Generation Before the Civil Rights Movement in the South*. Chapel Hill: U of North Carolina P, 1994.

Eisner, Lotte H. *The Haunted Screen: Expressionism in the German Cinema and the Influence of Max Reinhardt*. Berkeley: U of California P, 1969.

Ellison, Ralph. *Shadow and Act*. New York: Random House, 1964.

Eng, David. *Racial Castration: Managing Masculinity in Asian America*. Durham: Duke UP, 2001.

English, Daylanne K. *Unnatural Selections: Eugenics in American Modernism and the Harlem Renaissance*. Chapel Hill: U of North Carolina P, 2004.

Estabrook, Arthur H., and Ivan E. McDougle. *Mongrel Virginians: The Win Tribe*. Baltimore: The Williams and Wilkins Co., 1926.

Everett, Anna. *Returning the Gaze: A Genealogy of Black Film Criticism, 1909–1949*. Durham: Duke UP, 2001.

Falkner, Murry C. *The Falkners of Mississippi: A Memoir*. Baton Rouge: Louisiana State UP, 1967.

Faulkner, William. *Absalom, Absalom!* 1936. *The Corrected Text*. New York: Vintage International, 1990.

———. *As I Lay Dying*. 1930. *The Corrected Text*. New York: Vintage International, 1990.

———. "Barn Burning." 1939. *Collected Stories of William Faulkner*. 1950. New York: Vintage, 1977. 3–25.

———. *Collected Stories of William Faulkner*. 1950. New York: Vintage, 1977.

———. "Dry September." 1931. *Collected Stories of William Faulkner*. 1950. New York: Vintage, 1977. 169–83.

———. *A Fable*. 1954. *William Faulkner: Novels 1942–1954*. New York: Library of America, 1994. 665–1072.

———. *Father Abraham*. Ed. James B. Meriwether. New York: Random House, 1984.

———. *Father Abraham: Holograph Manuscript, Typescripts, and Miscellaneous Pages; and The Wishing Tree: Ribbon and Carbon Typescripts*. Int. and Arr. Thomas L. McHaney. New York: Garland, 1987.

———. *Flags in the Dust*. *William Faulkner: Novels 1926–1929*. New York: Library of America, 2006. 541–875.

———. *Go Down, Moses*. 1942. New York: Vintage International, 1990.

———. *The Hamlet*. 1940. *The Corrected Text*. *William Faulkner: Novels 1936–1940*. New York: Library of America, 1990. 727–1075.

———. *Light in August*. 1932. *The Corrected Text*. New York: Vintage International, 1990.

———. *The Marble Faun and A Green Bough*. New York: Random House, 1965.

———. *The Marionettes* (Ms facsimile). 1920. Charlottesville: UP of Virginia for the Bibliographical Society of the U of Virginia, 1977.

———. *Mayday*. South Bend: U of Notre Dame P, 1977.
———. *Mosquitoes*. 1927. New York: Liveright, 1955.
———. *Sanctuary*. 1931. *The Corrected Text*. New York: Vintage International, 1993.
———. *Soldiers' Pay*. New York: Boni, 1926.
———. *The Sound and the Fury*. 1929. *The Corrected Text*. New York: Vintage International, 1990.
———. *The Town*. 1957. *William Faulkner: Novels 1957–1962*. New York: Library of America, 1999. 1–326.
The Faulkner Glossary. 2005. Harpo Productions. 31 Oct. 2005. http://www.oprah.com/obc_classic/featbook/asof/books/books_glossary_06.jhtml.
Felman, Shoshana. *The Literary Speech Act: Don Juan with J. L. Austin, or Seduction in Two Languages*. Trans. Catherine Porter. Ithaca: Cornell UP, 1983.
Ferguson, Roderick A. *Aberrations in Black: Toward a Queer Color of Critique*. Minneapolis: U of Minnesota P, 2004.
Fiedler, Leslie A. *Love and Death in the American Novel*. 1960. Normal, IL: Dalkey Archive, 2003.
Fitzgerald, F. Scott. *The Great Gatsby*. 1925. New York: Macmillan, 1988.
Foner, Eric. *Reconstruction: American's Unfinished Revolution, 1863–1877*. New York: Perennial, 1989.
Foucault, Michel. *Discipline and Punish: The Birth of the Prison*. 1975. Trans. Alan Sheridan. New York: Vintage, 1979.
Fowler, Doreen. *Faulkner: The Return of the Repressed*. Charlottesville: U of Virginia P, 1997.
Frankenberg, Ruth. "Introduction: Local Whitenesses, Localizing Whiteness." *Displacing Whiteness: Essays in Social and Cultural Criticism*. Ed. Frankenberg. Durham: Duke UP, 1997. 1–33.
Freud, Sigmund. "From the History of an Infantile Neurosis." 1918. Strachey Vol. 17. 7–122.
———. *The Interpretation of Dreams*. 1900. Strachey Vol. 4–5.
———. *Introductory Lectures on Psychoanalysis*. 1917. Strachey Vol. 15–16.
Friday, Krister. "Miscegenated Time: The Spectral Body, Race, and Temporality in *Light in August*." *The Faulkner Journal* 16.3 (2000/2001): 41–64.
Gibson, James. *Warrior Dreams: Violence and Manhood in Post-Vietnam America*. New York: Farrar, 1994.
Gilroy, Paul. *Against Race: Imagining Political Culture Beyond the Color Line*. Cambridge: Harvard UP, 2000.
Ginsburg, Elaine. *Passing and the Fictions of Identity*. Durham: Duke UP, 1996.
Glissant, Edouard. *Faulkner, Mississippi*. 1996. Trans. Barbara Lewis and Thomas C. Spear. New York: Farrar, 1999.
Godden, Richard. *Fictions of Labor: William Faulkner and the South's Long Revolution*. Cambridge: Cambridge UP, 1997.
———, and Noel Polk. "Reading the Ledgers." *Mississippi Quarterly* 55.3 (2002): 301–59.
Goddu, Teresa. *Gothic America: Narrative, History, and Nation*. New York: Columbia UP, 1997.

Goldfield, Michael. *The Color of Politics: Race and the Mainsprings of American Politics*. New York: New P, 1997.

Graham, Allison. *Framing the South: Hollywood, Television, and Race During the Civil Rights Struggle*. Baltimore: Johns Hopkins UP, 2001.

Graham, Cooper C., et al. *D. W. Griffith and the Biograph Company*. Metuchen, NJ: Scarecrow, 1985.

Grantham, Dewey W. *The South in Modern America: A Region at Odds*. 1994. Fayetteville: U of Arkansas P, 2001.

Gubar, Susan. *Racechanges: White Skin, Black Faces in American Culture*. New York: Oxford UP, 1997.

Gunning, Sandra. *Race, Rape, and Lynching: The Red Record of American Literature, 1890-1912*. New York: Oxford UP, 1996.

Gunning, Tom. "The Cinema of Attractions: Early Film, Its Spectator, and the Avant-Garde." *Wide Angle* 8.3-4 (1986): 63-70.

Guttman, Sondra. "Who's Afraid of the Corncob Man? Masculinity, Race, and Labor in the Preface to *Sanctuary*." *The Faulkner Journal* 15.1-2 (1999/2000): 15-34.

Gwin, Minrose. "Did Ernest Like Gordon?: Faulkner's *Mosquitoes* and the Bite of Gender Trouble." *Faulkner and Gender: Faulkner and Yoknapatawpha, 1994*. Ed. Donald M. Kartiganer and Ann J. Abadie. Jackson: UP of Mississippi, 1996. 120-44.

Hagood, Taylor. "'Prodjickin', or mekin' a present to yo' fam'ly': Rereading Empowerment in Thomas Nelson Page's Frame Narratives." *Mississippi Quarterly* 57.3 (2004): 423-40.

Halberstam, Judith. *Skin Shows: Gothic Horror and the Technology of Monsters*. Durham: Duke UP, 1995.

Hale, Grace Elizabeth. *Making Whiteness: The Culture of Segregation in the South, 1890-1940*. New York: Pantheon, 1998.

Hall, Jacqueline Dowd. "'The Mind That Burns in Each Body': Women, Rape, and Racial Violence." *Powers of Desire: The Politics of Sexuality*. Ed. Ann Snitow, Christine Stansell, and Sharon Thompson. New York: Monthly Review, 1983. 328-49.

Hamlin, Talbot. *Greek Revival Architecture in America: Being an Account of Important Trends in American Architecture and American Life Prior to the War Between the States*. London: Oxford UP, 1944.

Handley, George B. *Postslavery Literatures in the Americas: Family Portraits in Black and White*. Charlottesville: UP of Virginia, 2000.

Haney López, Ian F. *White By Law: The Legal Construction of Race*. New York: New York UP, 1996.

Hannon, Charles. *Faulkner and the Discourses of Culture*. Baton Rouge: Louisiana State UP, 2005.

Harper, Phillip Brian. *Are We Not Men?: Masculine Identity and the Problem of African-American Identity*. New York: Oxford UP, 1996.

Harris, Cheryl I. "Whiteness as Property." *Harvard Law Review* 106 (1993): 1709-91.

Harris, Joel Chandler. *Uncle Remus: His Songs and His Sayings*. New York: Appleton, 1895.

Harris, Trudier. *Exorcising Blackness: Historical and Literary Lynching and Burning Rituals*. Bloomington: Indiana UP, 1984.

Harvith, Susan, and John Harvith. *Karl Struss: Man with a Camera*. Lansing: Henry, 1976.
Hawthorne, Nathaniel. *The Marble Faun: Or The Romance of Monte Beni*. New York: Signet, 1961.
Hay, John. "Piecing Together What Remains of the Cinematic City." *The Cinematic City*. Ed. D. B. Clarke. London: Routledge, 1977. 209–29.
Hedges, Warren. "If Uncle Tom is White, Should We Call Him 'Auntie'? Race and Sexuality in Postbellum U. S. Fiction." *Whiteness: A Critical Reader*. Ed. Mike Hill. New York: New York UP, 1997. 226–47.
Hill, Mike. "Introduction: Vipers in Shangri-la, Whiteness, Writing, and Other Ordinary Terrors." Hill 1–18.
———, ed. *Whiteness: A Critical Reader*. New York: New York UP, 1997.
Hobson, Fred. *Tell About the South: The Southern Rage to Explain*. Baton Rouge: Louisiana State UP, 1983.
Hodes, Martha. *White Women, Black Men: Illicit Sex in the Nineteenth-Century South*. New Haven: Yale UP, 1997.
Holmes, Edward M. *Faulkner's Twice-Told Tales: His Re-Use of His Material*. Paris: Mouton, 1966.
hooks, bell. "Representations of Whiteness in the Black Imagination." *Black Looks: Race and Representation*. Boston: South End, 1992. 165–78.
Hurston, Zora Neale. *The First One. Black Female Playwrights: An Anthology of Plays before 1950*. Ed. Kathy A. Perkins. Bloomington: Indiana UP, 1990. 80–88.
Ickstadt, Heinz. "The Discourse of Race and the 'Passing' Text: Faulkner's *Light in August*." *Amerikastudien* 42.4 (1997): 529–36.
Ignatiev, Noel. *How the Irish Became White*. New York: Routledge, 1995.
———. Interview. "Treason to Whiteness is Loyalty to Humanity." *Utne Reader* 66 (Nov./Dec. 1994): 82–86.
Irwin, John T. *Doubling and Incest/Repetition and Revenge: A Speculative Reading of Faulkner*. Baltimore: Johns Hopkins UP, 1975.
Jacobson, Matthew Frye. *Whiteness of a Different Color: European Immigration and the Alchemy of Race*. Cambridge: Harvard UP, 1998.
Jarraway, David R. "The Gothic Import of Faulkner's 'Black Son' in *Light in August*." Martin and Savoy 57–74.
Jehlen, Myra. *Class and Character in Faulkner's South*. New York: Columbia UP, 1976.
Johnson, E. Patrick. *Appropriating Blackness: Performance and the Politics of Authenticity*. Durham: Duke UP, 2003.
Jones, Anne Goodwyn. "Male Fantasies?: Faulkner's War Stories and the Construction of Gender." *Faulkner and Psychology: Faulkner and Yoknapatawpha, 1991*. Ed. Donald M. Kartiganer and Ann J. Abadie. Jackson: UP of Mississippi, 1994. 21–55.
———. "The Work of Gender in the Southern Renaissance." *Southern Writers and Their Worlds*. Ed. Christopher Morris and Steven G. Reinhardt. College Station: Texas A&M UP, 1996. 41–56.
Jones, Suzanne W., and Sharon Monteith, eds. *South to a New Place: Region, Literature, Culture*. Baton Rouge: Louisiana State UP, 2002.

Jordan, Winthrop. *White Over Black: American Attitudes Toward the Negro, 1550–1812.* Chapel Hill: U of North Carolina P, 1968.

Keats, John. *Selected Poems.* Ed. Elizabeth Cook. Oxford: Oxford UP, 1996.

Kawin, Bruce. *Faulkner and Film.* New York: Frederick Ungar, 1977.

———. "The Montage Element in Faulkner's Fiction." *Faulkner, Modernism, and Film: Faulkner and Yoknapatawpha, 1978.* Ed. Evans Harrington and Ann J. Abadie. Jackson: UP of Mississippi, 1979. 103–126.

Kasson, John. *Amusing the Million: Coney Island at the Turn of the Century.* New York: Hill & Wang, 1978.

Kevles, Daniel J. *In the Name of Eugenics: Genetics and the Uses of Human Heredity.* New York: Knopf, 1985.

King, Richard H. *A Southern Renaissance: The Cultural Awakening of the American South, 1930–1955.* New York: Oxford UP, 1980.

———, and Helen Taylor, eds. *Dixie Debates: Perspectives on Southern Culture.* New York: New York UP, 1996.

Kinney, Arthur F. "Faulkner's Families." *A Companion to William Faulkner.* Ed. Richard C. Moreland. Malden, MA: Blackwell Publishing, 2007. 180–201.

Kline, Wendy. *Building a Better Race: Gender, Sexuality, and Eugenics from the Turn of the Century to the Baby Boom.* Berkeley: U of California P, 2001.

Kristeva, Julia. *Powers of Horror: An Essay on Abjection.* Trans. Leon S. Roudiez. New York: Columbia UP, 1982.

Lacan, Jacques. *The Four Fundamental Concepts of Psychoanalysis: The Seminar of Jacques Lacan, Book XI.* Ed. Jacques Alain-Miller. Trans. Alan Sheridan. New York: Norton, 1998.

Lancaster, Ashley Craig. "Altruistic Mothers and Sexual Predators: Creating the Poor-White Woman in Twentieth-Century Southern Literature." Ph.D. diss., U of Mississippi, 2007.

Lane, Christopher. *The Ruling Passion: British Colonial Allegory and the Paradox of Homosexual Desire.* Durham: Duke UP, 1995.

Lane, Mills. *Architecture of the Old South.* Savannah: Beehive Foundation, 1996.

Lanning, Lt. Col. (Ret.) Michael Lee. *The African-American Soldier: From Crispus Attucks to Colin Powell.* Seacaucus, NJ: Citadel, 1999.

Larson, Edward J. *Sex, Race, and Science: Eugenics in the Deep South.* Baltimore: Johns Hopkins UP, 1995.

Lenning, Arthur. "Myth and Fact: The Reception of *The Birth of a Nation.*" *Film History* 16.2 (2004): 117–41.

Lessig, Matthew. "Class, Character, and 'Croppers: Faulkner's Snopeses and the Plight of the Sharecropper." *Arizona Quarterly* 55.4 (1999): 79–113.

Levin, Harry. *The Power of Blackness: Hawthorne, Poe, Melville.* 1958. Athens: Ohio UP, 1980.

Lévi-Strauss, Claude. *The Elementary Structures of Kinship.* Trans. James Harle Bell and John Richard von Sturmer. Boston: Beacon, 1969.

———. *The Savage Mind.* Trans. George Weidenfeld. Chicago: U of Chicago P, 1966.

Lipsitz, George. *The Possessive Investment in Whiteness: How White People Profit from Identity Politics.* Philadelphia: Temple UP, 1998.

Lombardo, Paul A. *Three Generations, No Imbeciles: Eugenics, the Supreme Court, and* Buck v. Bell. Baltimore: Johns Hopkins UP, 2008.

López, Alfred J. "The Gaze of the White Wolf: Psychoanalysis, Whiteness, and Colonial Trauma." *Postcolonial Whiteness: A Critical Reader on Race and Empire*. Ed. López. Albany: SUNY P, 2005. 155–82.

——. "Introduction: Whiteness After Empire." *Postcolonial Whiteness: A Critical Reader on Race and Empire*. Ed. López. Albany: SUNY P, 2005. 1–30.

Lott, Eric. *Love and Theft: Blackface Minstrelsy and the American Working Class*. New York: Oxford UP, 1993.

Lurie, Peter. *Vision's Immanence: Faulkner, Film, and the Popular Imagination*. Baltimore: Johns Hopkins UP, 2004.

Machen, Arthur. "The Great God Pan." *The Great God Pan*. Short Story Index Reprint Ser. Freeport, NY: Books for Libraries, 1926. 9–87.

MacKethan, Lucinda. *The Dream of Arcady: Place and Time in Southern Literature*. Baton Rouge: Louisiana State UP, 1980.

Martin, Robert K., and Eric Savoy. Introduction. *American Gothic: New Interventions in a National Narrative*. Ed. Martin and Savoy. Iowa City: U of Iowa P, 1995. vii–xii.

Martin, Terence. *The Instructed Vision: Scottish Common Sense Philosophy and the Origins of American Fiction*. Bloomington: Indiana UP, 1961.

Matthews, John T. "*As I Lay Dying* and the Machine Age." *boundary 2* 19.1 (1992): 69–94.

——. "Shortened Stories: Faulkner and the Market." *Faulkner and the Short Story: Faulkner and Yoknapatawpha, 1990*. Ed. Evans Harrington and Ann J. Abadie. Jackson: UP of Mississippi, 1992. 3–37.

May, Lary. "Apocalyptic Cinema: D. W. Griffith and the Aesthetics of Reform." *Movies and Mass Culture*. Ed. John Belton. New Brunswick: Rutgers UP, 1996. 25–58.

Maynard, W. Barksdale. *Architecture in the United States, 1800–1850*. New Haven: Yale UP, 2002.

McCabe, Susan. *Cinematic Modernism: Modernist Poetry and Film*. Cambridge: Cambridge UP, 2005.

McCann, Cpt. Irving Goff. *With the National Guard on the Border: Our National Military Problem*. St. Louis: CV Mosby, 1917.

McDowell, Deborah E. Introduction. Quicksand *and* Passing. By Nella Larsen. New Brunswick: Rutgers UP, 1986. ix–xxxv.

McDowell, Peggy, and Richard E. Meyer. *The Revival Styles in American Memorial Art*. Bowling Green: Bowling Green State U Popular P, 1994.

McKee, Patricia. *Producing American Races: Henry James, William Faulkner, Toni Morrison*. Durham: Duke UP, 1999.

McLaren, Peter. "White Terror and Oppositional Agency: Towards a Critical Multiculturalism." *Multiculturalism: A Critical Reader*. Ed. David Theo Goldberg. New York: Oxford UP, 1994. 45–74.

McMillen, Neil R., and Noel Polk. "Faulkner on Lynching." *The Faulkner Journal* 8.1 (1992): 3–14.

Melville, Herman. *Moby Dick, or, The Whale.* 1851. New York: Penguin, 1992.
Meriwether, James B. Introduction. *Father Abraham.* By William Faulkner. Ed. Meriwether. New York: Random, 1984. N.p.
Metz, Christian. *The Imaginary Signifier.* 1977. Trans. Celia Britton, Annwyl Williams, Ben Brewster, and Alfred Guzzetti. Bloomington: Indiana UP, 1982.
Michaels, Walter Benn. *Our America: Nativism, Modernism, and Pluralism.* Durham: Duke UP, 1995.
Miller, Dan B. *Erskine Caldwell: The Journey from Tobacco Road.* New York: Knopf, 1995.
Minter, David. *Faulkner's Questioning Narratives: Fictions of His Major Phase, 1929–1942.* Urbana: U of Illinois P, 2001.
———. *William Faulkner: His Life and Work.* Baltimore: John Hopkins UP, 1980.
Morrison, Toni. *Playing in the Dark: Whiteness and the Literary Imagination.* 1992. New York: Vintage, 1993.
Murray, Albert. *South to a Very Old Place.* 1971. New York: Vintage, 1991.
Newitz, Annalee, and Matt Wray. Introduction. *White Trash: Race and Class in America.* Ed. Wray and Newitz. New York: Routledge, 1997. 1–12.
———. "What is 'White Trash'? Stereotypes and Economic Conditions of Poor Whites in the United States." Hill, *Whiteness* 168–84.
Noll, Steven. "'A Far Greater Menace': Feebleminded Females in the South, 1900–1940." *Hidden Histories of Women in the New South.* Ed. Virginia Bernhard et al. Columbia: U of Missouri P, 1994. 31–51.
———. *Feeble-Minded in Our Midst: Institutions for the Mentally Retarded in the South, 1900–1940.* Chapel Hill: U of North Carolina P, 1995.
North, Michael. *The Dialect of Modernism: Race, Language & Twentieth-Century Literature.* New York: Oxford UP, 1994.
Norton, Rictor. "The Sodomite and the Lesbian." *A Critique of Social Constructionism and Postmodern Queer Theory.* 12 July 2002. Rictor Norton Homepage. 21 Oct. 2005. http://www.infopt.demon.co.uk/social22.htm.
O'Donnell, Patrick. "Between the Family and the State: Nomadism and Authority in *As I Lay Dying*." *Faulkner Journal* 7.1–2 (1991–1992): 83–94.
Olien, Roger M., and Diana Davids Olien. *Oil and Ideology: The Cultural Creation of the American Petroleum Industry.* Chapel Hill: U of North Carolina P, 2000.
Omi, Michael, and Howard Winant. *Racial Formation in the United States: From the 1960s to the 1990s.* 2nd ed. New York: Routledge, 1994.
Page, Thomas Nelson. *In Ole Virginia, Or, Marse Chan and Other Stories.* Chapel Hill: U of North Carolina P, 1969.
Palmer, Louis. "Bourgeois Blues: Class, Whiteness, and Southern Gothic in Early Faulkner and Caldwell." *Faulkner Journal* 22.1–2 (Fall 2006/Spring 2007): 120–139.
Paradiso, Sharon Desmond. "Terrorizing Whiteness in Yoknapatawpha County." *Faulkner Journal* 23.2 (Spring 2008): 23–42.
Payne, Arthur Frank. "Temple Drake Mirror for All Women Now, Psychologist Declares." *Publicity Features-Advances.* The Story of Temple Drake *Press Book.* Hollywood: Paramount Pictures, 1933.

Poe, Edgar Allan. *The Narrative of Arthur Gordon Pym, of Nantucket.* New York: Hill, 1960.
Polk, Noel. *Children of the Dark House: Text and Context in Faulkner.* Jackson: UP of Mississippi, 1996.
———. "'The Dungeon Was Mother Herself': William Faulkner: 1927–1931." *New Directions in Faulkner Studies: Faulkner and Yoknapatawpha, 1983.* Ed. Doreen Fowler and Ann J. Abadie. Jackson: UP of Mississippi, 1984. 61–93.
———. "Faulkner: The Artist as Cuckold." *Faulkner and Gender: Faulkner and Yoknapatawpha, 1994.* Ed. Donald M. Kartiganer and Ann J. Abadie. Jackson: UP of Mississippi, 1996. 20–47.
———. "Man in the Middle: Faulkner and the Southern White Moderate." *Faulkner and Race: Faulkner and Yoknapatawpha, 1986.* Ed. Doreen Fowler and Ann J. Abadie. Jackson: UP of Mississippi, 1987. 130–51.
———, and Neil McMillen. "Faulkner on Lynching." *The Faulkner Journal* 8.1 (1992): 3–14.
Rafter, Nicole Hahn. *Creating Born Criminals.* Urbana: U of Illinois P, 1997.
———, ed. *White Trash: The Eugenic Family Studies, 1877–1919.* Boston: Northeastern UP, 1988.
Railey, Kevin. *Natural Aristocracy: History, Ideology, and the Production of William Faulkner.* Tuscaloosa: U of Alabama P, 1999.
Ramsey, D. Matthew. "'Lifting the Fog': Faulkner's Reputation and *The Story of Temple Drake.*" *The Faulkner Journal* 16.1–2 (2000/2001): 7–33.
Ray, Robert B. *How a Film Theory Got Lost, and Other Mysteries in Cultural Studies.* Bloomington: Indiana UP, 2001.
Richardson, H. Edward. *William Faulkner: The Journey to Self-Discovery.* Columbia: U of Missouri P, 1969.
Roberts, Diane. *Faulkner and Southern Womanhood.* Athens: U of Georgia P, 1994.
Robinson, Cedric J. *Forgeries of Memory and Meaning: Blacks and the Regimes of Race in American Theater and Film Before World War II.* Chapel Hill: U of North Carolina P, 2007.
Roediger, David R. *The Wages of Whiteness: Race and the Making of the American Working Class.* Rev. ed. New York: Verso, 1999.
Rogin, Michael. *Blackface, White Noise: Jewish Immigrants in the Hollywood Melting Pot.* Berkeley: U of California P, 1996.
———. "'The Sword Became a Flashing Vision': D. W. Griffith's *The Birth of a Nation.*" *The Birth of a Nation.* Ed. Robert Lang. New Brunswick: Rutgers UP, 1994. 250–93.
Romine, Scott. *The Narrative Forms of Southern Community.* Baton Rouge: Louisiana State UP, 1999.
Rosow, Eugene. *Born to Lose: The Gangster Film in America.* New York: Oxford UP, 1978.
Russell, Irwin. *Poems by Irwin Russell.* New York: Century, 1888.
Russell, Jeffrey Burton. *Lucifer: The Devil in the Middle Ages.* Ithaca: Cornell UP, 1984.
Ruzicka, William T. *Faulkner's Fictive Architecture: The Meaning of Place in the Yoknapatawpha Novels.* Ill. R. B. Ferrier. Studies in Modern Literature Ser. No. 67. Ann Arbor: UMI Research P, 1987.
Savoy, Eric. "The Face of the Tenant: A Theory of the American Gothic." Martin and Savoy 3–19.

Saxton, Alexander. *The Rise and Fall of the White Republic: Class Politics and Mass Culture in Nineteenth-Century America*. New York: Verso, 1990.

Scarry, Elaine. *The Body in Pain: The Making and Unmaking of the World*. New York: Oxford UP, 1985.

Schickel, Richard. *D. W. Griffith: An American Life*. New York: Simon and Schuster, 1984.

Schmidt, Peter. "Command Performances: Black Storytellers in Stuart's 'Blink' and Chesnutt's 'The Dumb Witness.'" *Southern Literary Journal* 35.1 (2002): 70–96.

Sedgwick, Eve Kosofsky. *Epistemology of the Closet*. Berkeley: U of California P, 1990.

Seidel, Kathryn Lee. *The Southern Belle in the American Novel*. Tampa: U of South Florida P, 1985.

Sensibar, Judith L. Introduction. *Vision in Spring*. By William Faulkner. Austin: U of Texas P, 1984. ix–xxviii.

———. *The Origins of Faulkner's Art*. Austin: U of Texas P, 1984.

Seshadri-Crooks, Kalpana. *Desiring Whiteness: A Lacanian Reading of Race*. New York: Routledge, 2000.

Shadoian, Jack. *Dreams and Dead Ends: The American Gangster Film*. 2nd ed. Oxford: Oxford UP, 2003.

Sielke, Sabine. *Reading Rape: The Rhetoric of Sexual Violence in American Literature and Culture, 1790–1990*. Princeton: Princeton UP, 2002.

Silva, Fred. *Focus on* The Birth of a Nation. Englewood Cliffs, NJ: Prentice-Hall, 1971.

Skal, David J. *The Monster Show: A Cultural History of Horror*. 1993. New York: Faber, 2001.

Smith, Jon, and Deborah Cohn, eds. *Look Away! The U.S. South in New World Studies*. Durham: Duke UP, 2004.

Smith, Shawn Michelle. *Photography on the Color Line: W. E. B. Du Bois, Race, and Visual Culture*. Durham: Duke UP, 1994.

Somerville, Siobhan. *Queering the Color Line: Race and the Invention of Homosexuality in American Culture*. Durham: Duke UP, 2000.

Spivak, Gayatri Chakravorty. "Can the Subaltern Speak?" *Colonial Discourse and Post-Colonial Theory: A Reader*. Ed. Patrick Williams and Laura Chrisman. New York: Columbia UP, 1994. 66–111.

———. *Death of a Discipline*. New York: Columbia UP, 2003.

St. Clair, William. *Lord Elgin and the Marbles*. London: Oxford UP, 1967.

Stacey, Cpt. Cromwell. *Company Training (Infantry)*. Kansas City, MO: Franklin Hudson, 1916.

Stanfield, Peter. "An Excursion into the Lower Depths: Hollywood, Urban Primitivism, and *St. Louis Blues*, 1929–1937." *Cinema Journal* 41.2 (2002): 84–108.

Stephens, Judith. "Racial Violence and Representation: Performance Strategies in Lynching Dramas of the 1920s." *African American Review* 33.4 (1999): 655–71.

Stokes, Mason. *The Color of Sex: Whiteness, Heterosexuality, and the Fictions of White Supremacy*. Durham: Duke UP, 2001.

Stonum, Gary Lee. *Faulkner's Career: An Internal Literary History*. Ithaca: Cornell UP, 1979.

Strachey, James, ed. and trans. *Standard Edition of the Complete Psychological Works of Sigmund Freud*. 24 vols. London: Hogarth, 1974.
Sugimori, Masami. "Racial Mixture, Racial Passing, and White Subjectivity in *Absalom, Absalom!*" *Faulkner Journal* 23.2 (Spring 2008): 3–22.
———. "Signifying, Ordering, and Containing the Chaos: Whiteness, Ideology, and Language in *Intruder in the Dust*." *Faulkner Journal* 22.1–2 (Fall 2006/Spring 2007): 54–73.
Sullivan, Nell. "Persons in Pieces: Race and Aphanisis in *Light in August*." *Mississippi Quarterly* 49.3 (1996): 497–518.
Tarbell, Ida M. *The History of the Standard Oil Company*. New York: Macmillan, 1925.
Tate, Allen. "The Profession of Letters in the South." 1935. *Essays of Four Decades*. Chicago: Swallow, 1968. 517–34.
Taylor, Clyde. "The Re-Birth of the Aesthetic in Cinema." *The Birth of Whiteness: Race and the Emergence of U.S. Cinema*. Ed. Daniel Bernardi. New Brunswick: Rutgers UP, 1996. 15–37.
Torgovnick, Marianna. *Gone Primitive: Savage Intellects, Modern Lives*. Chicago: U of Chicago P, 1990.
Towner, Theresa M. *Faulkner on the Color Line: The Later Novels*. Jackson: UP of Mississippi, 2000.
Trefzer, Annette, and Ann J. Abadie, eds. *Global Faulkner: Faulkner and Yoknapatawpha, 2006*. Jackson: UP of Mississippi, 2009.
United States. Advisory Commission on Intergovernmental Relations. *The National Guard: Defending the Nation and the States*. Washington: GPO, 1993. 7–12.
United States. Militia Bureau. *Questions for National Guard Officers (Basic)*. Doc. 974. Washington: GPO, 1920.
———. *National Guard Regulations: Under the Constitution and Laws of the U.S., 1919*. Doc. 911. Washington: GPO, 1919.
Vernon, Alex. "Narrative Miscegenation: *Absalom, Absalom!* as Naturalist Novel, Auto/Biography, and African-American Oral Story." *JNT* 31.2 (2001): 155–79.
Vizzard, Jack. *See No Evil: Life Inside a Hollywood Censor*. New York: Simon, 1970.
Vrettos, Theodore. *The Elgin Affair: The Abduction of Antiquity's Greatest Treasures and the Passions It Aroused*. New York: Arcade, 1997.
Wallace, Maurice O. *Constructing the Black Masculine: Identity and Ideality in African American Men's Literature and Culture, 1775–1995*. Durham: Duke UP, 2002.
Wallace, Michele Faith. "The Good Lynching and *The Birth of a Nation*: Discourses and Aesthetics of Jim Crow." *Cinema Journal* 43.1 (2003): 85–104.
Watson, James G. "Carvel Collins's Faulkner: A Newly Opened Archive." *Mississippi Quarterly* 44.3 (1991): 17–35.
———. *William Faulkner: Self-Presentation and Performance*. Austin: U of Texas P, 2000.
Watson, Jay. E-mail to Betina Entzminger. 20 Apr. 2006.
———. *Forensic Fictions: The Lawyer Figure in Faulkner*. Athens: U of Georgia P, 1993.

———. "Overdoing Masculinity in *Light in August*, or, Joe Christmas and the Gender Guard." *The Faulkner Journal* 9.1–2 (1993/1994): 149–77.

———. "Writing Blood: The Art of the Literal in *Light in August*." *Faulkner and the Natural World: Faulkner and Yoknapatawpha, 1996*. Ed. Donald M. Kartiganer and Ann J. Abadie. Jackson: UP of Mississippi, 1999. 66–97.

Watson, Neil. "The Incredibly Loud . . . Miss-Fire: A Sexual Reading of *Go Down, Moses*." *William Faulkner: Six Decades of Criticism*. Ed. Linda Wagner-Martin. East Lansing: Michigan State UP, 2002: 199–210.

Weinstein, Philip M. *Faulkner's Subject: A Cosmos No One Owns*. New York: Cambridge UP, 1992.

———. *What Else But Love? The Ordeal of Race in Faulkner and Morrison*. New York: Columbia UP, 1996.

Wiegman, Robyn. *American Anatomies: Theorizing Race and Gender*. Durham: Duke UP, 1995.

———. "Whiteness Studies and the Paradox of Particularity." *boundary 2* 26.3 (1999): 115–50.

Williams, David. *Faulkner's Women: The Myth and the Muse*. Montreal: McGill-Queen's UP, 1977.

Williamson, J. W. *Hillbillyland: What the Movies Did to the Mountains and What the Mountains Did to the Movies*. Chapel Hill: U of North Carolina P, 1995.

Williamson, Joel. *The Crucible of Race: Black-White Race Relations in the American South Since Emancipation*. New York: Oxford UP, 1984.

———. "How Black Was Rhett Butler?" *The Evolution of Southern Culture*. Ed. Numan Bartley. Athens: U of Georgia P, 1988. 87–107.

———. *New People: Miscegenation and Mulattoes in the United States*. Baton Rouge: Louisiana State UP, 1995.

———. *A Rage for Order: Black-White Relations in the American South Since Emancipation*. New York: Oxford UP, 1986.

———. *William Faulkner and Southern History*. New York: Oxford UP, 1993.

Wilson, Christopher P. "Plotting the Border: John Reed, Pancho Villa, and *Insurgent Mexico*." *Cultures of U.S. Imperialism*. Ed. Amy Kaplan and Donald E. Pease. Durham: Duke UP, 1993. 340–61.

Wolters, Raymond. *Negroes and the Great Depression: The Problem of Economic Recovery*. Westport: Greenwood, 1970.

Woodward, C. Vann. *The Burden of Southern History*. Enlarged ed. Baton Rouge: Louisiana State UP, 1968.

Wray, Matt. *Not Quite White: White Trash and the Boundaries of Whiteness*. Durham: Duke UP, 2006.

Wright, Richard. *Lawd Today!* 1963. Boston: Northeastern UP, 1993.

———. "The Man Who Was Almost a Man." 1940. *Eight Men*. Cleveland: World, 1961. 11–26.

———. *Native Son*. 1940. New York: Perennial, 1998.

Yaeger, Patricia. *Dirt and Desire: Reconstructing Southern Women's Writing, 1930–1990*. Chicago: U of Chicago P, 2000.

Yukins, Elizabeth. "'Feeble-Minded' White Women and the Spectre of Proliferating Perversity in American Eugenics Narratives." *Evolution and Eugenics in American Literature and Culture, 1880–1940: Essays on Ideological Conflict and Complicity*. Ed. Lois A. Cuddy and Claire M. Roche. Lewisburg: Bucknell UP, 2003. 164–86.

Zettsu, Tomoyuki. "Faulkner's Mexican Connections: The Presence of Willa Cather in *Light in August*." *Faulkner Journal of Japan* 2 (2000). William Faulkner Society of Japan. 1 Nov. 2005. http://www.isc.senshu-u.ac.jp/~thb0559/No2/zettsu.htm.

Ziegler, Heide. "The Fragile Pandora's Box of Scrawled Paper: A Different Reading of *Absalom, Absalom!*" *Amerikastudien* 42.4 (1997): 637–48.

NOTES ON CONTRIBUTORS

Aliyyah I. Abdur-Rahman is an assistant professor of English at Brandeis University whose research interests include American and African American literature and culture, gender studies and multiethnic feminisms, and theories of visual, print, and media culture. A two-time winner of the Darwin T. Turner Award for Best Essay of the Year in *African American Review*, Abdur-Rahman's scholarship has also appeared or is forthcoming in *Callaloo*, the *Faulkner Journal*, *Black Camera*, and a number of encyclopedias and edited collections. Her first book, forthcoming from Duke University Press, is *The Erotics of Race: Identity, Political Longing, and Black Figuration*. She has recently begun work on a new book project, tentatively titled *Millennial Style: The Politics of Experiment in Contemporary African American Culture*.

Deborah E. Barker is associate professor of English at the University of Mississippi. She coedited *American Cinema and the Southern Imaginary* (2011) and a special issue on southern film in *Mississippi Quarterly* (forthcoming). She is the author of *Aesthetics and Gender in American Literature: The Portrait of the Woman Artist* (2000). Her recent publications are on postfeminism and the southern chick flick and filmic adaptations of Faulkner's novels, and her current project is a book on racial and sexual violence in southern films.

John N. Duvall is professor of English and editor of *MFS: Modern Fiction Studies* at Purdue University. He is the author of *Faulkner's Marginal Couple* (1990), *The Identifying Fictions of Toni Morrison* (2000), and *Race and White Identity in Southern Fiction* (2008). He has also edited or coedited several volumes, including *Faulkner and Postmodernism* (2002) and *Faulkner and His Critics* (2010).

Betina Entzminger is an associate professor of English at Bloomsburg University. She is the author of *The Belle Gone Bad: White Southern Women Writers and the Dark Seductress* (2002), and she is currently working on a study of contemporary reconfigurations of American literary classics.

Taylor Hagood is assistant professor of American literature at Florida Atlantic University. His publications include *Faulkner's Imperialism: Space, Place, and the Materiality of Myth* (2008); *Secrecy, Magic, and the One-Act Plays of Harlem Renaissance Women Playwrights* (2010); and articles in *European Journal of American Culture*, the *Faulkner Journal*, *Mississippi Quarterly*, and *Southern Literary Journal*.

Chuck Jackson is assistant professor of English and coordinator of the film studies minor at the University of Houston–Downtown. His research has appeared in *African American Review*, *Journal of Popular Film and Television*, *Modern Fiction Studies*, the *Faulkner Journal*, *Camera Obscura*, *Gothic Studies*, and *Pedagogy*. He is at work on a manuscript about fictional and cinematic narratives of race, guardianship, and national emergencies in the U.S. from 1932 to 1976.

Alfred J. López is an associate professor of English and American studies at Purdue University. He is the author of *José Martí and the Future of Cuban Nationalisms* (2006) and *Posts and Pasts: A Theory of Postcolonialism* (2001), and the editor of *Postcolonial Whiteness: A Critical Reader on Race and Empire* (2005). López was also the founding editor in 2007 of *The Global South*, a leading globalization studies journal published by Indiana University Press. His essays have appeared in *American Literature*, *Comparative Literature*, and *Modern Fiction Studies*, among many others, with essays forthcoming in the *Comparatist* and *South Atlantic Quarterly*. López's current work-in-progress is a trade biography of José Martí, due to appear in 2013.

Peter Lurie is the author of *Vision's Immanence: Faulkner, Film, and the Popular Imagination* (2004) and of several articles on Faulkner and related fields. His new book, *American Obscurantism: History and the Visual in American Literature and Film*, is forthcoming from Oxford University

Press. He is currently editing the collection *Faulkner and Film: Faulkner and Yoknapatawpha 2010* with Ann J. Abadie for the University Press of Mississippi. He is associate professor of English and film studies at the University of Richmond.

Jay Watson is Howry Professor of Faulkner Studies and professor of English at the University of Mississippi. He is the author of *Forensic Fictions: The Lawyer Figure in Faulkner* (1993); *Conversations with Larry Brown* (2007); and numerous essays on southern literature, culture, and film. In 2002–2003 he served as Visiting Fulbright Professor of American Studies at the University of Turku and Åbo Akademi University, Turku, Finland.

INDEX

Page numbers in **bold** indicate illustrations.

Abate, Michelle Ann, 78
abjection, 141–42, 143, 174–75, 194, 197
Agee, James, xvii, 55
Allen, Robert C., 152, 153, 154, 155, 157, 159, 161
Allen, Theodore, xvii, xviii, xix, xx
Altman, Dennis, 78
American Breeders Association, 31
American Mercury, 128
Anderson, Sherwood, 8, 19, 26
Atkinson, Ted, 130
Atlanta Constitution, 107, 109

Bacon's Rebellion, xix
Bad Subjects Collective, xv
Baldwin, James, 78, 207n6
Barkan, Elazar, 172
Bederman, Gail, 185
Bentley, Nancy, 5
Bhabha, Homi K., xxviii
Birth of a Nation, The (film), xxv, 109, 110, 113, 115, 116, 118, 125, 127, 133, 138, 139, 144–45, 150, 151, 162, 163, 165, 168
black beast rapist stereotype, 11, 16, 52, 110, 115, 127, 188, 228n18
blackface performance, xv–xvi, xxiv, 92, 104, 105, 156, 173, 214n4
Blackmer, Corinne, 75

bootlegger stereotype, 47, 48, 117, 119, 128, 129, 145
Brickhouse, Anna C., 5
Brown, Charles Brockden, 226n2
Buck, Carrie, 23–24, 25, 37, 39, 40, 54
Buck, Emma, 24, 40
Buck, Vivian, 24, 25, 39
Buck v. Bell, 23–24, 25, 33, 38, 39, 40, 54, 55
"Bungler" family, 43
Bush, Ronald, 172
Butler, Judith, xxii, 91
Byron, George Gordon, Lord, 4

Caldwell, Erskine, xvii, 55
Caldwell, Ira, 43
Capone, Al, 129
Cash, W. J., 88, 109, 111
Chambers, Ross, viii
Chesnutt, Charles, 115
Clansman, The (Dixon), xxv, 109, 110, 111–12, 113, 114, 116, 139, 142
Classical Revival. *See* Greek Revival
Color of Sex, The (Stokes), 77
Company Training (Infantry) (Stacey), 194–95
Cortez, Hernándo, 4
critical whiteness studies, vii–xii, 56–57, 106

Dancer in the Dark (film), 132, 136
Dark Laughter (Anderson), 8
Darwin, Charles, 21
Davenport, Charles, 22, 26, 31

Davidson, Michael, 82
Davis, Angela, 187
Davis, Thadious M., ix, xx–xxi, 8, 90, 174
Deburau, Jean-Gaspard, 95
Degenfelder, Paula, 124, 138
DeJarnette, Joseph, 38
Deleuze, Gilles, 45
Deutsch, Nathaniel, 23, 33, 34
Dick Act, 192
Dixon, Thomas, xxv, 109, 111, 112, 114, 115, 117, 124, 125, 126, 129, 139, 145
Doane, Mary Ann, 163
Donaldson, Susan V., 158
Doubling and Incest/Repetition and Revenge (Irwin), 179
Douglass, Frederick, 83
Doyle, Laura, 197
Dr. Jekyll and Mr. Hyde (film), 131–32, 133, 135
Dracula (film), 135
Dreiser, Theodore, 19
Du Bois, W. E. B., 166, 167, 169, 175, 207n6
Dugdale, Richard, 21, 22, 23, 39
Duvall, John N., xvi, 78
Dyer, Richard, vii, viii, xi–xii, xiii, xiv, xxix, 56, 57, 75, 77, 85, 112, 124, 150, 162, 165

East, Edward M., 24–25, 38
Edison, Thomas, 152
Egerton, John, 99
Elementary Structures of Kinship, The (Lévi-Strauss), 80
Elgin, Lord, 4
Ellis, Havelock, 78, 96
Ellison, Ralph, 102
English, Daylanne, 20, 22, 55
Epistemology of the Closet (Sedgwick), 79
Estabrook, Arthur H., 23–24, 26, 33, 34, 40
eugenic sterilization, 22, 23–25, 35, 36, 37, 38, 39, 40, 41, 45, 48, 209n5; and lynching, 210n12

Eugenical Sterilization in the United States (Laughlin), 23
eugenics movement, xxii, 20; bad mother theme in, 39–40; euthanasia, views on, 53; family studies methodology in, xvi, xxi–xxii, 21–23, 24, 33–34, 44, 54; gendered criteria of deviance in, 36–37, 42–43, 48–49; genealogical strategies of, 20, 21–25; history of, 21–24, 25, 33–34, 55; modernity of, 20; politics of, 21–22, 45
Eugenics Record Office (ERO), 22, 23, 26, 29, 31
Evans, Walker, xvii, 55

Falkner, W. C., 117
Fanon, Frantz, 207n6
Faulkner, William: genealogical imagination of, xxi–xxii, 19–21, 26–55 passim, 171; homosexual culture, knowledge of, 78; marble faun figure in, xxi, 3–18; performances of whiteness, xxix; as poet, 3; and U.S. racial regimes, x–xi; as visual artist, 95
Works: *Absalom, Absalom!*, xviii–xx, xxi, xxiii–xxiv, xxv, 16, 17, 75–91, 99–101, 171; *As I Lay Dying*, ix, xxi, xxvi, 13, 39, 42–47, 50, 53, 55, 147–49, 151–52, 159; "Barn Burning," xxv, 101–5; "The Bear," 78, 82; "Black Music," xxi, 8–12; "Delta Autumn," xx; "Dry September," xxvi, 149, 152, 153–59, 161–68 passim; *A Fable*, xxi, 16; *Father Abraham*, xxii, 13–14, 26–28, 29, 38; *Flags in the Dust*, 28–34, 38, 53; *Go Down, Moses*, xviii, xx–xxi, 78, 81, 92, 171; "Hair," xvi; *The Hamlet*, ix, xxi, 14–15, 26; *Light in August*, xxi, xxii–xxiii, xxvi–xxviii, 15, 56–74, 78, 149, 152, 153, 155, 159–62, 163–68 passim, 170–88, 189–205; *The Mansion*, ix; *The Marble Faun*, 3;

The Marionettes, xxv, 95; *Mayday*, 14; *Mosquitoes*, xxi, xxv, xxix, 12–13, 21, 78, 94–96, 97; *Pylon*, xvi; *Requiem for a Nun*, xviii; *Sanctuary*, xxii, xxv, 47–53, 96, 107, 110, 117, 119, 125, 126–27, 128, 129, 131, 136, 137, 139, 140–43, 145; *Soldiers' Pay*, xxi, 12; *The Sound and the Fury*, x, 17, 25, 34–42, 44, 53, 54, 55, 78, 81, 85, 89, 96–97; "Spotted Horses," 26; "There Was a Queen," 142; *The Town*, ix
Faulkner and Southern Womanhood (Roberts), 69
Faulkner on the Color Line (Towner), xiv
Faulkner's Marginal Couple (Duvall), xvi
Faulkner's Negro (Davis), 174
feeblemindedness, 22, 24, 25, 32, 34, 35, 39, 48, 51, 55; gendered definitions of, 23; sexualization of, 35, 36
Felman, Shoshana, 86
Felton, Rebecca Latimer, 115
First One, The (Hurston), 5
flapper figure, 119
Foucault, Michel, 49
Fowler, Doreen, 176
Freedmen's Bureau, 198
Freud, Sigmund, xiii, 61, 63, 64, 71
Friday, Krister, 171, 175

Galton, Francis, 21, 54
Games of Property (Davis), xx
gangster film, 130–31, 136
gangster stereotype, 48, 117, 119, 129, 137
Garbo, Greta, 136
Gibbon, Edward, 12
Gilbert, John, 136
Gilroy, Paul, 98
Gish, Lillian, 136, 144
Glissant, Edouard, xxix
Goddard, Henry, 22, 24, 27, 38, 40
Godden, Richard, 78, 102, 103
Goddu, Teresa, 191

Gone with the Wind (Mitchell), 127
Gothic genre, 131, 189, 190, 191–92, 194, 197, 200, 203, 204; and whiteness, 190–91
Grapes of Wrath, The (Steinbeck), xvii, 55
Great Migration, 97, 98
Greek Revival, 6
Griffith, D. W., xxv, 109, 110, 111, 113, 114, 115, 117, 126, 129, 133, 135, 138, 144, 150–51, 162, 163, 165, 168, 169
Guattari, Felix, 45
Gubar, Susan, 93, 94

Hale, Grace Elizabeth, xi, 157, 164, 172
Hamlin, Talbot, 6
Handley, George, 20
Haney Lopez, Ian, xx
Harris, Cheryl I., xvii, xx, 154–55
Harris, Joel Chandler, 7
Harris, Trudier, 186, 187
Hawthorne, Nathaniel, 5, 6, 226n2
Hay, James, 162
Hayes Office, 107
Hedges, Warren, 77
Hemingway, Ernest, 19
Heredity in Human Affairs (East), 24
Hill, Mike, xi
hillbilly stereotype, 48, 117, 128, 219n22
Holmes, Oliver Wendell, Jr., 24
homoeroticism. *See* same-sex desire
Homosexual: Oppression and Liberation (Altman), 78
homosexual panic, 76, 78, 83–84, 87, 91, 187, 225n9
homosexuality. *See* same-sex desire
honor, xvi, 105, 112, 138, 140, 142, 143, 178
hooks, bell, xii, xiii
Hopkins, Miriam, **108**, **121**, 123, 131–32, 133, **134**, 135, 136, 219n20
horror film, 130–31, 132, 135, 145, 220n31
Hose, Sam. *See* Wilkes, Samuel
"How Black Was Rhett Butler?" (Williamson), 127

INDEX

Hurston, Zora Neale, 5
hybridity, xxi, 3–18 passim, 31–33, 98

imperialism, 4–7, 10, 11, 12, 16
Intruder in the Dust (film), 129
inversion. *See* same-sex desire
Irwin, John T., 179
"Ishmael, Tribe of," 23

Jackson, Andrew, 13
Jackson, Chuck, 161
Jacobs, Harriet, 124
Jacobson, Matthew Frye, x
James, C. L. R., 207n6
James, Henry, xiv
Jazz Age, 119, 130
Jefferson, Thomas, 6
Johnson, E. Patrick, 93–94
Johnson, James Weldon, 207n6
Johnson-Reed Act, x
Jones, Anne Goodwyn, 90
Jones, Ralph, 109
Jordan, Winthrop, 187
Jukes: A Study of Crime, Pauperism, Disease, and Heredity, The (Dugdale), 21
"Jukes" family, 21, 22, 23, 24, 39–40
Jumanji (film), 62

"Kallikak" family, 22, 24, 27, 40
Keats, John, xxi, 4, 7, 11
Kevles, Daniel, 55
King, Richard H., 19
Kite, Elizabeth, 22
Kristeva, Julia, 141, 142, 174
Ku Klux Klan, 77, 114, 115, 116, 117, 129, 138, 144, 162, 163, 169

Lancaster, Ashley, 25
Lane, Christopher, 58
Larsen, Nella, 75

LaRue, Jack, **134**, 136
Laughlin, Harry, 23, 38
Lawd Today! (Wright), 227n8
Leopard's Spots, The (Dixon), 113, 115
Lessig, Matthew, 102
Let Us Now Praise Famous Men (Agee and Evans), xvii, 55
Lévi-Strauss, Claude, 5, 80, 82
Lipsitz, George, xviii
Literary Speech Act, The (Felman), 86
Little Brick Church, The (Falkner), 117
Lloyd, David, xii
Lombardo, Paul, 23, 54
Long, Robert Cary, 6
Long, Robert Cary, Jr., 6
Long Hot Summer, The, 129
López, Alfred J., xxviii
Lord of the Rings (Tolkien), 62
Lott, Eric, 104, 173
Lumpkin, Grace, 55
Lurie, Peter, 46
lynching, xxvi, xxviii, 35, 50–51, 60, 74, 97, 107, 110, 114, 115, 117, 128, 129, 139, 142, 143, 145, 149, 154, 157, 158, 164, 165, 168, 174, 183, 185–88 passim, 193, 200; and eugenic sterilization, 210n12; photographs of, 157–58, **158**, 172–73; postcards of, 157, 165, 170; as rape, 186

Macbeth (Shakespeare), 35
MacKethan, Lucinda, 8
Mamoulian, Rouben, 135
"Man Who Was Almost a Man, The" (Wright), 101–2
Manliness and Civilization (Bederman), 185
Manly, Alexander, 115
Marble Faun, The (Hawthorne), 5
Marrow of Tradition, The (Chesnutt), 115
Marx, Karl, 22
May, Lary, 150
McCann, Irving Goff, 196–97, 204
McCulloch, Oscar, 23, 34

McDougle, Ivan E., 23, 26, 33, 34
McDowell, Deborah, 75, 76
McKee, Patricia, xiii–xiv, xxix
McMillan, Mattie, 128
Melville, Herman, 17, 226n2
Memphis *Commercial Appeal*, 106
Mendel, Gregor, 24
Michaels, Walter Benn, x, 145
Mind of the South, The (Cash), 88
minstrelsy. *See* blackface performance
Minter, David, 86, 178
Mississippi School and Colony for the Feebleminded, 36
Moby Dick (Melville), 17
Mongrel Virginians: The Win Tribe (Estabrook and McDougle), 23, 26, 33, 34, 55
Morrison, Toni, viii, xii, xiii, xiv, 8, 93, 94
Murnau, F. W., 135
Murray, Albert, xxix

Narrative of Arthur Gordon Pym (Poe), 17
Narrative of the Life of Frederick Douglass, An American Slave (Douglass), 83
National Association for the Advancement of Colored People (NAACP), 168, 217n4
National Board of Review, 150, 168
National Defense Act, 192, 202
national emergency narrative, xxviii, 161–62, 163, 165, 191, 194, 198, 200, 224n21; defined, 193
National Guard, xxvii–xxviii, 161–62, 166, 189–205; history of, 192–93; and hygiene, 195–96; and lynching, 193; and whiteness, 192, 226n7
Native Son (Wright), 227n8
Natural Aristocracy (Railey), xviii
New Woman, 119, 138, 144
Newitz, Annalee, viii, xv, xxii, 57
Noll, Steven, 25
nomadism, 22, 26, 36, 43, 51, 52

North, Michael, 173
Nosferatu (film), 133, 135

O'Connor, Flannery, 99
"Ode on a Grecian Urn" (Keats), 4, 5
O'Donnell, Patrick, 44–45, 46, 47, 152
Omi, Michael, x, 46, 126
"On First Looking into Chapman's Homer" (Keats), 4
"On Seeing the Elgin Marbles" (Keats), 4
Our America (Michaels), x

Page, Thomas Nelson, 7
Passing (Larsen), 75, 76
pastoral, 8
Patton, Nelse, 128, 129
Payne, Frank, 125, 126
Pickford, Mary, 136
Pierrot figure, 95
Playing in the Dark (Morrison), viii, xiii
Plessy v. Ferguson, 152, 183
Poe, Edgar Allan, 17, 226n2
Polk, Noel, xxix, 41, 78, 89
poor whites, xxviii, 94, 97–105, 118, 119–20, 128, 129, 145, 146, 151, 160
postcolonial studies, xxviii–xxix, 98
Postcolonial Whiteness (López), xviii
Powers of Horror (Kristeva), 174
Prehistories of the Future (Barkan and Bush), 172
Priddy, A. S., 40
Production Code, 107, 132, 217n1
Progressive era, 31, 44–46
Prohibition, 110, 117, 130, 140
Pumphrey, Popeye, 128

race, social construction of, 126
race traitor, 88, 106
racechange, 93, 98, 101, 105
Raft, George, 132, 136
Rafter, Nicole Hahn, xvi, 21, 22, 24, 39, 41, 44, 54

Railey, Kevin, xviii–xx
Reconstruction period, xxvi–xxvii, 109, 116, 163, 171, 172, 174, 176, 177, 179, 181, 186, 187, 198, 218n8
"Representations of Whiteness in the Black Imagination" (hooks), xii
Richardson, H. Edward, 3
Riefenstahl, Leni, 223n15
Roberts, Diane, 69
Roberts, Stephen, 107
Robinson, Cedric J., 152–53
Rockefeller, John J., 8
Rogin, Michael, 113, 151
Russell, Irwin, 7
Russell, Jeffrey Burton, 5
Ruzicka, William T., 6

same-sex desire, xxii–xxiv, xxvii, 56–74 passim, 75–91 passim, 171, 172, 179, 180, 182, 186, 187, 188
Saussure, Ferdinand de, 176
Savoy, Eric, 191
Scarry, Elaine, 229n23
Scopes trial, 26
Scribner's Magazine, 153, 156
Sedgwick, Eve Kosofsky, xxii, 79, 83
Seidel, Kathryn Lee, 111, 117, 139
Sensibar, Judith L., 3, 4
Seshadri-Crooks, Kalpana, 82
Sexual Inversion (Ellis), 78
sharecropping. *See* tenant farming
Shipp, Thomas, 157–58, **158**
Sins of the Father: A Romance of the South, The (Dixon), 124
Skal, David, 130, 132, 135
slavery, 82, 174, 176, 187–88, 215n7
Smith, Abram, 157–58, **158**
Smith, Shawn Michelle, 157, 165
Somerville, Siobhan, 181–82
"Souls of White Folk, The," 166
southern belle stereotype, 107, 109, 110–15, 117–23 passim, 137, 138, 140, 142, 143, 144, 145, 146

southern gentleman stereotype, 110, 126, 138, 140, 143
southern lady stereotype, 113
southern rape narrative, xxv–xxvi, 107–46 passim
Spivak, Gayatri, 58
"St. Louis Blues," 132
Stacey, Cromwell, 194–95, 197, 204
Stanfield, Peter, 132
Steinbeck, John, xvi, 55
Stephens, Judith, 187
sterilization. *See* eugenic sterilization
stigmatype, 41, 48
Stokes, Mason, 77, 80
Stone, Phil, 26
Stonum, Gary Lee, 3, 4
Story of Temple Drake, The (film), xxv, 107, **108**, 110, 118, 119, **121**, 122–24, 125–26, 129, 130–31, 132–39, **134**, 143–44, 145–46
Struss, Karl, 135
subject without properties, xii
Sullivan, Nell, 170
Sullivan, William, 129
Sweet, Blanche, 144

Tate, Allen, xi
tenant farming, 99, 152
To Make My Bread (Lumpkin), 55
Tobacco Road (Caldwell), xvii, 55
Torgovnick, Marianna, 172
Towner, Theresa M., xiv
Triumph of the Will (film), 223n15

Vernon, Alex, 76, 86
Villa, Pancho, 196
Virginia Colony for Epileptics and Feebleminded, 23
Virginia Racial Integrity Law, 33
Vizzard, Jack, 120

Wallace, Maurice, 83
Watson, James G., xxix

Watson, Jay, 160, 180
Watson, Neil, 78, 81
Weinstein, Philip M., xiii, xv
Wells, Ida B., 207n6
What Else But Love? (Weinstein), xiii
white trash, xv, xxvi, xxix, 15, 26, 31, 34, 41, 48, 52, 98, 101, 138, 141; racialization of, 46–47, 50–51
White Trash: Race and Class in America (Newitz and Wray), xv
whiteface performance, xxiv, 92, 95, 96, 97, 105, 106, 156
whiteness: as abstraction, 153, 161, 162, 226n5; and cinemagoing, 150–51, 154, 155, 160–61; and film medium, 218n17, 224n21; and heteronormativity, 57, 73, 78, 88, 95, 179, 188; history of in U.S., x–xi; as ideology, xvii–xviii; invisibility of, 4, 56–57, 77, 165; marked forms of, 56, 57, 58–59, 73, 101, 105, 178; and national identity, 46, 149, 153, 163; as norm, viii, xxii–xxiv, 57, 207n2; as performance, xiv–xvi, 92–106 passim; phantasmatic nature of, 163–64; as property, xvii, xviii, xx, 154–55; as spiritual quality, xii, 112, 162; and subject formation, xi–xiii; as unmarked racial identity, vii–viii, 100, 178; and visuality, xiv, 165
white-skin privileges, xvii–xviii, xix, 174, 216n7
Wiegman, Robyn, vii, 176, 186
Wilkes, Samuel (Sam Hose), 223n14
Williamson, J. W., 128
Williamson, Joel, xxix, 127, 128
Wilmington Daily Record, 115
Wilson, Woodrow, 116, 196
Winant, Howard, x, 46, 126
With the National Guard on the Border: Our National Military Problem (McCann), 196–97
Without Sanctuary: Lynching Photograph in America (Allen), 157

"Wolfman" case (Freud), 61, 63, 213n9
Woodward, C. Vann, 19
World War One, 116, 143
Wray, Matt, viii, xv, xxii, 33, 41, 42, 44, 47, 57
Wright, Richard, 101, 105, 227n9

Ziegler, Heidi, 76

www.ingramcontent.com/pod-product-compliance
Lightning Source LLC
Chambersburg PA
CBHW030612230426
43661CB00053B/1946